Race, Sexuality and Identity in Britain and Jamaica

Race, Sexuality and Identity in Britain and Jamaica

The Biography of Patrick Nelson, 1916–1963

Gemma Romain

Bloomsbury Academic
An imprint of Bloomsbury Publishing Plc

BLOOMSBURY
LONDON · OXFORD · NEW YORK · NEW DELHI · SYDNEY

Bloomsbury Academic

An imprint of Bloomsbury Publishing Plc

50 Bedford Square
London
WC1B 3DP
UK

1385 Broadway
New York
NY 10018
USA

www.bloomsbury.com

BLOOMSBURY and the Diana logo are trademarks of Bloomsbury Publishing Plc

First published 2017

British Library Cataloguing-in-Publication Data
A catalogue record for this book is available from the British Library.

ISBN: HB: 978-1-4725-8864-7
ePDF: 978-1-4725-8865-4
eBook: 978-1-4725-8866-1

Library of Congress Cataloging-in-Publication Data
A catalog record for this book is available from the Library of Congress.

Cover image: Portrait of Pat Nelson © Estate of Duncan Grant. All rights reserved, DACS 2015. Photo © Christie's Images/Bridgeman Images

Typeset by Deanta Global Publishing Services, Chennai, India
Printed and bound in Great Britain

To find out more about our authors and books visit www.bloomsbury.com. Here you will find extracts, author interviews, details of forthcoming events and the option to sign up for our newsletters.

For Patrick

Contents

List of Figures

Acknowledgements

Many friends, colleagues and family members have assisted and supported me in writing this book. I commenced my research on the life experiences of Patrick Nelson as part of a wider AHRC-funded project *Drawing Over the Colour Line: Geographies of art and cosmopolitan politics in London 1919–1939* (AH/I027371/1) working with Caroline Bressey at the UCL Equiano Centre in the Department of Geography on black history in relation to the interwar artworld. I am thankful to Caroline for her immense support, advice and friendship. I am especially appreciative of her reading through the draft chapters of the book. My dear friend Ego Ahaiwe Sowinski's support and encouragement has been invaluable to me. I especially thank her for reading through the draft chapters of the book. I am immensely grateful to Tony Kushner, Debbie Challis and Kristy Warren for reading and commenting on the draft chapters of the book. I am particularly appreciative of the support of my mother Jean Romain who read through the manuscript several times.

I have conducted research at a number of archives and collections within Britain and Jamaica in order to undertake this study. I thank current and former staff members of Tate Archive and Library, in particular Adrian Glew and Maxine Miller and Tate curators Emma Chambers and Inga Fraser. I am grateful for the assistance of archivists and librarians at Bangor University Archives, Anglesey Archives, the National Portrait Gallery and The National Archives. I also thank the staff at the Library of the Institute of Jamaica and the Jamaican National Archives, Spanish Town. The research conducted in Jamaica was made possible by the Paul Mellon Foundation who awarded me a Research Support Grant in 2014, for which I am especially grateful. While in Jamaica various individuals provided research advice, information and company and I particularly thank James Robertson, Katie Donnington, Annie Paul, Emma Ranston-Young, Tracy Robinson, Dane Lewis and Amitabh Sharma for their support.

I would like to thank Norman Brown, controller, Royal Pioneer Corps Association for help with my research about Patrick's time serving in the Auxiliary Military Pioneer Corps. I also thank individuals who provided help with research queries, including Carla Stanley, Frances Spalding, Richard Shone,

Darren Clarke and the staff at the Historical Records Disclosure, Army Personnel Centre, Ministry of Defence. In addition, I am grateful to the *Holyhead and Anglesey Mail* and the *Gleaner* for printing letters to the editor about my research and to Holyhead Library for advertising about my research. I would also like to express my thanks to Johanna Lewin and Diana Stewart for contacting me and offering assistance in response to my advertisement in the *Gleaner*.

I presented my research about Patrick Nelson at various venues and I am appreciative of the encouragement I have received, in particular at the annual conference of the Society for Caribbean Studies (UK) in 2013 and 2016 and at the Equiano Centre, UCL Department of Geography *Queer Black Spaces* event series. I have been particularly inspired by the research and archiving of queer black histories carried out by Nadia Ellis and Ajamu and I thank them for their friendship and support.

Many individuals and organizations have helped with my locating and tracking down information about various images of photographs and paintings and I thank Sotheby's, Bridgeman Images, Tate Images, DACS, Mark Wheeler and David Bindman. I would also like to thank the organizations and individuals who have provided images for the book, including Anglesey Archives, the Estate of Duncan Grant, Sotheby's, Houghton Library, Harvard University, the Imperial War Museum, Bridgeman Images and the Tate. I am especially appreciative of my brother Gary Romain's support for the book, including his financial assistance towards the costs of reproducing images.

In addition to those family and friends already mentioned, I particularly thank Carl Romain, Daniel Romain, Phyllis Allen, Ain Bailey, Dominique Barron, Rudy Loewe, Thomas Glave, Kiera Adegbite, Kelly Foster and Diana Paton. I would like to thank all of my friends in the Brixton Housing Co-operative, the anonymous reviewers of the book proposal and manuscript and the editors at Bloomsbury Academic – Emma Goode, Beatriz Lopez, Emily Drewe, Frances Arnold and Jyoti Basuita. I would also like to thank Grishma Fredric and the copy editing team at Deanta and Giles Herman and the Bloomsbury Production team.

Introduction:
Archival Discoveries and Life Histories

In December 1945 Patrick Nelson wrote from Jamaica to his former lover and lifelong friend, the Bloomsbury Group artist Duncan Grant that one day he would be sure to write his life story.[1] To my knowledge this life story was never penned and both this sentiment and the material absence bring to the fore the loss to historical memory arising from the many lives that have never been or never will be documented in historical accounts, memoirs or autobiographies. Patrick's compelling and fascinating life story is more accessible than most as his many personal letters have been preserved within archival holdings. This book represents an attempt to bring to life his story through an examination of these archives in addition to a number of other sources. It examines his life in various ways, by exploring Patrick as a queer black Jamaican man, a queer black migrant in interwar London, a serviceman in the Second World War, a prisoner of war (POW) and a witness to Jamaican histories of colonialism and decolonization. His story truly exemplifies how important it is to remember diverse histories and lives within mainstream historical and public memory relating to modern British history.

Leopold St Patrick Nelson was one of many Caribbean people who migrated to Britain in the early twentieth century. Born in Jamaica in March 1916, he grew up in a working-class black family and as a young man worked in Jamaica's growing tourism industry as a valet at the Manor House Hotel in Kingston.[2] He first travelled to Britain in April 1937 to work as a valet for Lyulph Stanley (the younger brother of Lord Stanley of Alderley) in rural North Wales. Returning to Jamaica for a brief period later that year he remigrated to Britain in March 1938 and went on to serve in the British Army in the Second World War. Captured during May 1940, he was made a POW, imprisoned in various camps including Stalag 8b/344 for over four years. He met the Bloomsbury group artist Duncan Grant at some point during the late 1930s; the pair became lovers and Patrick also modelled for him during this time. They then maintained a long-distance friendship for almost twenty-five years through correspondence which took place in the late 1930s, throughout Patrick's POW captivity and post-war life in Jamaica. Remigrating to London in the early 1960s, Patrick died in 1963.

This biography explores Patrick's life by utilizing letters, paintings and drawings, along with newspaper articles. In particular, the breadth and detail of his personal letters allow the biography to document significant and unexplored insights into wider histories relating to Britain's empire, sexuality and race. The biography posits Patrick's life within histories of Jamaican migration to early-twentieth-century Britain and examines themes and topics including the interwar Bloomsbury group; sexuality, love, class and race; the diverse and complex black presence in interwar Britain; the prisoner of war experience, black POWs and the effects of captivity on post-war life; and empire and colonialism in post-war Jamaica.

Finding Patrick Nelson in the Archives

In 2012 Caroline Bressey and I embarked on a research project entitled *Drawing over the Colour Line: Geographies of art and cosmopolitan politics in London, 1919–1939* based at UCL and funded by the Arts and Humanities Research Council (AHRC), which sought to uncover the life experiences of artists and artist models of African and Asian heritage in interwar London.[3] Within a British context, research on the interwar black presence within art history writing and histories of modernism has been neglected. There have, however, been notable exceptions such as Mary Lou Emery's 2007 *Modernism, the Visual, and Caribbean Literature* which explored the 1930s art of Jamaican sculptor Ronald Moody.[4] Similarly, as regards black British history writing, important works have been published focusing on interwar black London in regard to literature and politics, but there is limited research on the experiences and presence of black people in London's interwar artworld in relation to the broader black presence.[5] *Drawing over the Colour Line*'s main focus was an exploration of the history of black artists and artist models, examining their experiences in posing for portraits and also positioning these narratives within a wider political and social historical context of the black British presence.

First coming across the name Patrick Nelson in a paragraph of Frances Spalding's 1997 biography of Duncan Grant, which mentioned they had been lovers, I sought to research Patrick's personal letters mentioned in this work and find out about his experiences of living and working in interwar London. By the time of our project's commencing, these letters were held in the collections of the Tate Archive.[6] The Tate Archive is one of the key repositories of a number of artists' personal papers, including those who were part of the Bloomsbury Group. Tate Archive's Charleston Trust collection consists of personal papers relating to artists and writers including Vanessa Bell, Roger Fry, Clive Bell and Duncan Grant.[7] The collection is named after the Sussex-located house and garden Charleston, which became one of the key geographical and social spaces of the Bloomsbury group and home to Vanessa Bell and Duncan Grant for decades. Frances Spalding described Charleston as a remote house which was a 'substantial, rather austere two-storeyed building with an attic floor, dating back in part to the seventeenth century ... situated at the foot of Firle Beacon, the highest in a run of downs from Newhaven to Cuckmere'.[8]

The papers relating to Charleston were collected by Vanessa Bell's son Quentin Bell, and in 1965 were deposited for safekeeping by Quentin Bell and Angelica Garnett with King's College, Cambridge University Library where photocopies were then made of the letters. Thereafter between 1965 and 1979 there were sales of some of the letters and the King's College Archive Centre kept a number of boxes of original correspondence, but the majority of the original papers were sold by Sotheby's in July 1980.[9] In total there were 130 lots with provenance from a number of sources including King's College and these items were put on sale to support The Charleston Trust, the charity established to safeguard the property.[10] The lots included letters to and from, for example, Clive Bell, Vanessa Bell, Virginia Woolf, John Maynard Keynes, Jean Cocteau, Roger Fry, Lytton Strachey, Leonard Woolf, Bertrand Russell, Vita Sackville-West and Duncan Grant. Various lots were purchased by the Tate, including, it appears, the letters sent by Patrick Nelson to Duncan Grant (though these letters are not specifically mentioned in the auction catalogue). Duncan Grant's archive at the Tate includes letters sent by Patrick during the 1930s, from wartime France and captivity in Germany as well as from post-war London and Jamaica. In the files of Patrick's correspondence there are also letters about him sent by the Jamaica Central War Assistance Committee; War Organisation of the British Red Cross Society and Order of St John of Jerusalem; the War Office; and from Patrick's parents Gertrude Nelson and Leopold Nelson.

Tate Archive's holdings are of key importance in exploring the lives and artistic representations of other black artists and models, including black queer artist models who we have been particularly keen to research in order to contribute to broadening history writing on both black and queer history.

For example, the Tate Archive collection of artist Barbara Ker-Seymer's papers includes a number of photographic portraits and snapshots of African American Harlem Renaissance performer Jimmie Daniels, who lived in London for a few years during the 1930s with his boyfriend filmmaker and film critic Kenneth Macpherson. In this way the Tate Archive collections on interwar artists have become a crucial archive in revealing the diversity of the black presence in London's interwar artworld. Chapters 4 and 9 provide an examination of queer black life in interwar and post-war Britain, respectively, focusing on geographical spaces, family and romantic connections, and migratory lives including artistic lives.

Along with the Tate Archive, a number of personal records relating to Patrick Nelson are preserved within the Ministry of Defence Personnel archives. Documents held by the Ministry of Defence include records of deceased service personnel, and under their publication scheme records of service can, where allowed, be opened and made available to the general public. Patrick's records include those for his service in the Auxiliary Military Pioneer Corps within the British Expeditionary Force, to his period as a POW and his brief service in Britain after his repatriation from Germany in late 1944. Important personal information is also contained in these files including Patrick's date of birth, the date he joined the AMPC, information on his education in Jamaica, as well as a number of letters from Duncan Grant and Patrick's parents, who were in correspondence with military authorities.

The Jamaican Archives and Records Department in Spanish Town holds a number of important records for understanding and contextualizing Patrick's life. Archive holdings at this repository include correspondence on Jamaican POWs, including a note mentioning Patrick's father Leopold; information on Jamaica's tourist industry such as records on a 1939 strike of employees at the Constant Spring Hotel (nearby the Manor House Hotel where Patrick worked); and maps and photographs of Kingston in the twentieth century.[11] The holdings of the Institute of Jamaica in Kingston not only reveal important information about Jamaica's history, but the Institute is also a space where Patrick's life can be re-remembered and reflected upon. Post-war, Patrick spent much time in the Library of the Institute of Jamaica researching and writing. Letters in the Tate Archive reflect the importance of the Institute's library as a home for Patrick after his experiences of captivity during the war. Digitized genealogical records have revealed much information about Patrick's geographical and migratory life. Passenger lists and census records provide crucial information not only on

Patrick's travels to and from Jamaica and London but also on others he travelled with and those with whom he shared accommodation in Britain.[12]

In regard to Patrick's experiences in Wales as a domestic servant, no personal information about him, to my knowledge, exists in Welsh archives. However, much information on the Penrhos estate where he worked, as well as the Stanley family, can be gleaned from census records, archival records and newspaper articles both online and in Welsh archives including Bangor University Archives and Special Collections. The main family archive was deposited at Bangor by various family members including Lyulph Stanley.[13] These records provide much information on the size of the Penrhos estate house, where the servants lived and the geography and size of the estate grounds and land: all this information is of use in understanding how Patrick might have felt living there and some of the possible duties of his job. Patrick's life and possible experiences in North Wales are explored in Chapter 3, focusing on the history of Penrhos and the Stanley family, domestic service in early to mid-twentieth-century Britain and Patrick's life as a queer black migrant and domestic servant.

Archives, letters and subaltern voices

Despite having access to these records, reconstructing Patrick Nelson's life and background has been and continues to be a complex and difficult endeavour, as is writing the life of anyone who is not famous or an elite or whose life was not the subject of much public attention during their lifetime. However, reading along and against the grain of archival sources can uncover stories and experiences which help to construct life histories. In using the term 'reading against the grain' I refer here to historians and archivists who read and use archives keeping in mind the reasons for the collection's creation and the methodology used by the creator of the collection, but also read the archive in a different way to that intended by the creator of the document or archive. This reading is undertaken in order to uncover 'marginal' or 'hidden histories' such as those found within archives organized by colonial elites, which shed light often unintentionally on the lives of colonial subjects. The archival practice and theory relating to 'reading along' and 'reading against the grain' of the archive has recently been explored by Ann Laura Stoler. Stoler has explored colonial archives by understanding that scholars need to explore the reasons for their construction (by reading along the grain of the archive) and then explore how these reasons serve to shape the contents of the archive. Stoler argues that 'scholars need to move from archive-as-source to archive-as-subject' and 'that scholars should view archives not as sites of knowledge retrieval, but of knowledge production, as monuments of states as well as sites of state ethnography'.[14]

The historical records of the Ministry of Defence and repositories such as The National Archives represent elite government organizations which are not at first glance archives of 'ordinary' people, but these archives can be used for finding out about 'subaltern' voices. Most prominently, Patrick's voice appears in the state archive because of his serving in the military. His personnel files can be read both along and against the grain. In relation to 'along the grain', the letters, reports and files produced, saved and preserved were for the purposes of dealing with Patrick as a military recruit and as a POW. For example, as Chapter 6 of the book highlights, the information that Patrick provides the military shows the manner in which he carefully negotiates his next-of-kin relationship with Duncan Grant through the military apparatus and tells us important things about being a queer man in the military as a result.

It is the aim of this book that Patrick's life experiences be examined from (where possible) his own perspective and not primarily through the lens of elite friends or lovers such as Duncan Grant, though these connections are explored extensively as they were an important constituent of his identity and life story. Patrick's letters provide an immediate and intimate way in which to explore his identity and experiences. Letters preserved in archives are a key source of information for historians and are utilized by scholars of language, sociology and biography. Liz Stanley has found that 'letters disturb binary distinctions: between speaking and writing and private and public, as well as between here and there, now and then, and presence and absence'.[15]

However, letters written by African and Asian people in Britain are often not reflected on or included as sources in constructing histories of modern Britain. Santanu Das has investigated some of the thousands of letters Indian troops wrote from France during the First World War by exploring extracts of the letters now preserved in the British Library, and Das' investigation is of particular resonance for this book. Between March and April 1915, Das states, about 10,000 letters a week were written by Indian soldiers in France and, though the original letters are not preserved in the archive, extracts of the letters were translated by colonial censors and these extracts are now preserved in the India Office Library.[16] Das argues, 'More has been written about the four major English war poets than the four million non-white colonial men who served'.[17]

This biography also focuses on Patrick's emotion and affect; how through his letter writing he comprehends and makes sense of not only significant political and military histories but also his personal role in these histories. He also documents and explores his personal life and experiences including his queer identity, his sexuality and experiences of love and affection. Patrick utilized letter writing for various reasons – to keep in touch with lovers and friends such as Duncan, to help with loneliness, and to share news and ideas. In the Tate Archive, we only have Patrick's letters sent to Duncan so we cannot understand Patrick's experiences of letter writing in relation to keeping in touch with family members and other friends besides Duncan. However, in these letters to Duncan, he expresses a range of viewpoints, reactions and thoughts on political events, religious identity and queer identity. Many of his letters were written during his confinement as a POW in the Second World War. Here we have a crucial narrative formed by a black colonial POW expressing detailed, day-to-day wartime experiences. These are letters composed according to the conventions and censor restrictions imposed on POWs. They nevertheless convey much about Patrick's personality, experiences and emotions from his own point of view.

Narratives such as Patrick's need to be contextualized within mainstream writing on the history of the Second World War. Examining letter writing in times of war is increasingly being carried out by those seeking to understand wartime not only from a non-elite perspective but also to explore a range of other topics that individuals such as POWs would write about in their correspondence. The letters Das has explored from Indian troops in France during the First World War highlight the emotional experiences in times of war and the importance of letters for understanding personal experiences, feelings and thoughts. Das states,

> In recent years, the letters have been used to illuminate the social world of these sepoys in Europe. But they are also some of the earliest testimonies to a subaltern history of feeling: one can imagine the range of emotions – thrill, wonder, excitement, fear, terror, horror, homesickness, grief, envy, religious doubts – that the sepoy must have gone through, as he encountered new lands, people, cultures as well as separation, segregation, loneliness, and industrial warfare. What forms did they take? Extracted, quoted, and summarized, these letters are usually squeezed for information but seldom read in the sense that their narrative structures, the web of associations and assumptions, or the socio-cultural codes and nuances of the 'felt' community within which they have their

resonance are rarely investigated. To read the letters properly, we need to evolve careful strategies that address not only what they say but how they say, to whom they say and what they do not say.[18]

This book often shows the methodology and workings of how and where documents, stories and histories are found, what they reveal and what they do not reveal. The practice of showing the book's methodology is intended as a means to share information on how the biography was constructed and in the process highlight not only that any life history is an incomplete picture of a life but also that this 'incompleteness' is fascinating to document and explore. Further research may come out in light of this book being published. History writing and writing on a life is a complex process and this book being in the public domain will, I hope, lead to more information arising on Patrick's life which can then be shared to a wider audience.

Jamaican Beginnings: Class, Race and Identity in Colonial Jamaica

The preeminent Jamaican newspaper the *Gleaner* published an article on 9 April 1937 entitled 'A Lucky Young Man', picturing a black Jamaican man called Leo Patrick Nelson.[1] It is striking and unusual for the *Gleaner* at this time to feature so prominently the individual migration of a black Jamaican who was not well known. A Jamaican man such as Patrick migrating to Britain for employment was not uncommon. Many Jamaicans had historically made the exact same journey from the Caribbean to Britain, in order to secure employment, to study and to join friends and family. His father Leopold Nelson had once been a well-known wicket player and his father's previous career might have played some part in the reason a newspaper article would be dedicated to his migration.

However, the main focus and probable reason to publish the article (and what was perceived as 'lucky') was that Patrick was leaving Jamaica to live in Britain specifically to be a valet to a titled gentleman. The *Gleaner* reported that Patrick had been the beneficiary of Sir Archibald Hunter, for whom Patrick had worked as a valet at Manor House Hotel. Captain Rutty, the manager and owner of the hotel, had trained Patrick and he valeted for Hunter for five years of his annual visits to Jamaica up to Hunter's death. The journalist went on to state that 'so faithful and well did he serve that Sir Archibald, pleased with his thoroughness and integrity, decided to bestow on him his patronage for life, and dying, willed that his near relative, Lord Stanley, should continue to mete out to young Nelson the same practical good-will'.[2] The author of the article, thus, revered the imperial 'ties' between Britain and Jamaica and proclaimed Patrick as having the 'Jamaican trait of gratitude in response to the privilege of living in an ampler sphere of life with all its opportunities for advancement' and revered the British aristocracy in particular stating 'he has found favour with Lord Stanley also and leaves Jamaica to enjoy the patronage thus transmitted to him and so characteristic of British aristocracy – the recognition of character'.[3] This short

Gleaner article brings to the fore many of the themes of this and the subsequent chapter, exploring Patrick's early life in relation to his family background and the area of Kingston where they lived, specifically class, British imperialism, colonialism and race in interwar Jamaica.

The *Gleaner* newspaper was established in 1834 by Jacob and Joshua DeCordova and, as stated by Roxanne S. Watson who explored the press during the 1938 Labour uprisings, the newspaper 'was considered "respectable" because of age, tradition, and management' and 'the majority of its shareholders were drawn from the moneyed and planter classes'.[4] In their one-hundred-year anniversary special edition published in September 1934, the *Gleaner* recorded the history of the newspaper including its incorporation in 1897 as the Gleaner Company, when a board of directors was established.[5] For many decades, including the 1930s, the newspaper was edited by the conservative novelist and writer Herbert DeLisser (1878–1944).[6] Watson describes DeLisser as being a representative of 'the sugar manufacturing class'.[7] Thus, its championing and romanticization of the British aristocratic tradition in the article about Patrick is not surprising.

Kingston, Jamaica

Patrick was born, according to most sources, in 1916 in Kingston, into an urban working-class black Jamaican family. Kingston would serve as an important geographical space for Patrick in both childhood and adulthood – in the case of the latter, Kingston was central to his 1930s experiences of working in the hotel industry of northern Kingston and also his post-war experiences, when he spent much time in the downtown area of the city carrying out research at the Institute of Jamaica. Kingston was founded during the late seventeenth century, during a period when Spanish Town served as the capital of Jamaica. After England captured Jamaica from Spain in 1655, Spanish Town remained Jamaica's capital town, but the new English colonists started a process of 'anglicization'.[8] James Robertson, the foremost authority on the history of Spanish Town, states, 'Jamaica's Spanish Town became the first place where English administrators and householders took over a foreign townscape and then tried to fit it to their presuppositions'.[9] Spanish Town remained the capital until the 1870s. After the destruction of Port Royal in the earthquake of 1692 King's Town was founded in 1693.[10] It was designed as a grid of roads by John Goffe, to be built on 200 acres of land purchased by the Council.[11] Very soon after its development, Kingston's population and its role as a harbour and centre of trade grew substantially. From its beginning, the wealth and prosperity of Kingston was the result of the profits of the brutal transatlantic slave trade and enslavement of Africans. David Howard comments in his 2005 published survey of the city that 'within fifty years of its original foundation, the local inhabitants numbered five thousand citizens, five thousand slaves and a further one thousand slaves who had been granted their freedom'.[12]

The population continued to grow as Kingston became central to the infrastructure of Jamaica's plantation economy. During the early nineteenth century the majority of its population were enslaved persons of African heritage, though Kingston also had a large free African population and mixed-'race' population as well as a sizeable white population. David Howard states that, at the beginning of the nineteenth century out of a population of 33,000 inhabitants, there were 18,000 enslaved people, 5,000 free 'coloured' and black people and 10,000 white people.[13] Enslaved Africans in urban areas such as Kingston included labourers and domestic servants. The white population included merchants, colonial officials and politicians, managers and attorneys of slave plantations and visitors from Britain (including 'absentee owners' visiting plantations), and the militia. Before emancipation, downtown Kingston was home to a free black population. As David Howard states, 'The freed slaves lived in yards on Duke, Barry, East and Rosemary Streets. Despite their freedom from slavery, lives were harsh and remote from the hierarchical status of upper-class whites'.[14] After slavery, these divisions still remained and were found within divisions of space, place, economic, political, social and employment opportunities. Colin Clarke and David Howard have carried out research on the racialized geography of colonial Kingston, stating that 'spatial patterns became a faithful expression of the social structure once slavery ended and the colour-class hierarchy was fine-tuned by the suburbanisation of the white, and later the coloured, population'.[15]

In 1872 Kingston became Jamaica's capital.[16] This change in the capital city was carried out during the governorship of Sir John Peter Grant, Duncan Grant's grandfather and someone who would be referred to in Patrick Nelson's letters and researched by Patrick in the years to come. In the nineteenth and early twentieth centuries, downtown Kingston became the home of the professions.[17] With the location of businesses as well as cultural institutions such as the Institute of Jamaica (founded in 1879 and located in East Street) and various religious buildings (churches of various denominations and a United congregation synagogue on Duke Street), the downtown area was the centre of Kingston's cultural and institutional life. Brian L. Moore and Michele A. Johnson state:

> The town's importance as a commercial centre was marked by the activities of building societies, fire insurance companies, life assurance companies, marine insurance companies and an ice company. The offices of various arms of colonial government were also to be found in the town and it boasted a theatre, Race Course, Town Hall, the Mico Institution and the Jamaica Institute; it also had within its borders a lunatic asylum, a public hospital and the General Penitentiary.[18]

By the early twentieth century Kingston's economic division between uptown and downtown was becoming more pronounced. Before and during the time of Patrick's birth and childhood, the north of Kingston was increasingly home to wealthy elites as the wealthy were moving northwards to settle in larger homes.[19] The time of Patrick's birth was witness to a great change in Kingston. After the earthquake of 1907 the city was rebuilt. In 1915 Frank Cundall reported on the earthquake that 'the loss of life was variously estimated as between 1000 and 1500. The value of property destroyed amounted to between £1,000,000 and £1,500,000.'[20] After the earthquake not only were repairs carried out but new buildings were also erected.[21] The earthquake directly affected the life of another queer black Jamaican man who also lived for a time in interwar London. Before deciding to establish a career as a poet, Jamaican Harlem Renaissance writer and activist Claude McKay had a trade scholarship in Kingston. When the trade school was destroyed in the earthquake he moved to Brown's Town for an apprenticeship in a trade shop, a shop where he met Walter Jekyll, who assisted in the publication of McKay's poetry book *Songs of Jamaica*.[22]

The twentieth-century harbour continued in the exportation of plantation goods produced within the countryside, a trade increasingly controlled by large companies such as the United Fruit Company. Geographically, Kingston expanded greatly during the late nineteenth and twentieth centuries, with population and business growth north of the downtown area. The introduction of the tram in 1876 impacted growth and change in the economy, with regard to the harbour trade and to tourism.[23] The growth of Kingston also included cultural forms of entertainment such as the cinema and theatre. Cinema arrived in Jamaica in 1906 with the Ireland brothers showing moving pictures twice a week at Rockford Gardens and by 1914 Kingston was home to four large cinemas.[24] Cinema attending was an important and loved activity by Patrick in adulthood, and perhaps he developed his love of attending cinemas in his teenage and early adult years due to the variety of cinemas operating in Kingston. In April 1938, just after Patrick left Jamaica, the Carib Theatre opened. Here is the *Gleaner's* description of the theatre: 'Ultra-modern with its air-conditioning, sound equipment, and spectacular stage and screen background the Carib offers comfort de luxe and pictures released under the banner of Metro-Goldwyn-Mayer generally accepted as Hollywood's stellar producing company.' [25]

In the early twentieth century Kingston was a bustling town, attracting new industries, but along with these new industries came new versions of pre-existing exploitation and inequality. As explored in the following chapter, Kingston was the site of various labour uprisings by black Jamaicans, in order to achieve economic and social equality and political rights. The poverty and exploitation experienced by Kingston's population during the late nineteenth and early twentieth centuries was documented in contemporary surveys and has been explored in recent books such as *'Squalid Kingston'*, published in 2000, which focuses on the period from 1890 to 1920.[26] *'Squalid Kingston'* reproduced a number of contemporary newspaper articles on housing, health and work hardships facing the poor in Kingston mainly sourced from the *Gleaner* but also from the *Jamaica Times*. Editors Moore and Johnson state of these articles, 'Together they paint a grim portrait of poverty and hardship for ordinary people in the city – conditions that remained unchanged in 1938 when widespread riots erupted, and are still to a large extent extant today.'[27]

Kingston's population was growing and diversifying in the early twentieth century and included the professional middle class, colonial elites, traders, business owners and working-class populations working and living in the downtown area and near the harbour. In 1921 the population of Kingston was 62,700 people and by 1943 it was 188,764.[28] Much of the increase was due to people migrating from rural areas to Kingston in search of work.[29] Kingston was also ethnically diverse. This diversity was formed due to the histories of slavery, colonialism and indenture as well as immigration in the late nineteenth and early twentieth centuries. Clarke and Howard analysed the 1943 census for Jamaica. Their findings highlight that the largest percentage of the population was black (60 per cent of Kingston's population), 30.74 per cent of the population was labelled as 'coloured' and there were other smaller populations categorized (in order of size and highlighting the census' racialized terminology) as white, Chinese, Chinese coloured, East Indian, East Indian coloured, Jewish,

Portuguese, Spanish, Syrian and Syrian coloured.[30] There were also Cuban immigrants settling in Kingston during the nineteenth and twentieth centuries. Howard Johnson states that 'crowded into the tenements of central Kingston, male working-class Cubans found waged work primarily in tobacco-related enterprises as cigar makers'.[31] Contemporary writer Kenneth Pringle described the ethnic diversity of the downtown area in the 1930s, stating, 'The centre of Lower Kingston is King Street, with its Government Buildings of a cellular, efficient, uninteresting design in white concrete, and its big stores owned largely by Syrians (the dry goods stores) and the Chinese (who specialise in groceries) …. West of King Street lies China-town with its peaka-peow gambling dens and its rum-shops.'[32]

Leopold Nelson and Jamaican cricket

One of the key characteristics of British colonial life in the Caribbean was the establishment of the game of cricket. Kingston was home to colonial Jamaican cricket, which in its official organization sought to uphold the game as an imperial and 'gentlemanly' sport of the elites. From the late nineteenth century the racialized elitism of the organized game was being challenged by black cricket players and fans. Although not a sporting figure who features in today's Jamaican public memory, in the early twentieth century black Jamaican man Leopold Nelson, Patrick's father, was a famous and celebrated wicket keeper for the Kingston-based team the Lucas Cricket Club, who also played for the Jamaican national team.[33] Leopold Nelson was from, it appears, a Kingston working-class background and represents someone who was a key player in the early transformation of the game of cricket due to his involvement in the early years of Lucas Cricket Club. Lucas was the first organized cricket club in Jamaica to challenge the dominance in the sport of colonial white elites by providing a space for black working-class cricketers to play. Though Leopold's family background is unknown at present, based on research in the records available to me, we know something of his life through his involvement in cricket, including that he had a brother who was also a cricket player. In the 16 September 1899 edition of the *Gleaner* it was reported that 'the Gleaner C.C. scored a victory over the Asylum C.C. on the Asylum grounds on Thursday afternoon' and in the match 'Leo. Nelson joined his brother, and both played the bowling with confidence'. His brother was named in the article as Lionel Nelson and they both played for the Gleaner C.C.[34] Leopold's 1945 death certificate gave his age at his last birthday as seventy-two years old, meaning he was born in about 1873.[35]

In 1922 the *Gleaner* published a letter composed by the trade union leader T. A. Aikman entitled '*The Brilliant Record of a Jamaica Cricketer – Mr Leopold Nelson's Career with the Lucas Club*'.[36] Written with the intention that Leopold's career be remembered and documented, it perhaps signals that some of these early cricketing histories, particularly black Jamaican cricketers such as Leopold Nelson, were being forgotten in 'official' public memory. Aikman's letter provides some clues as to Leopold's background, and also highlights the key role cricketers such as Leopold Nelson played in establishing cricket as a sport for the mass population of Jamaica. Aikman stated that Leopold 'earned in the world of cricket an enviable reputation'.[37]

In its organized form, Jamaican cricket was played through cricket clubs, which were also expensive subscription-based social member clubs run by and for colonial and business elites.[38] As Julian Cresser describes, elite cricket clubs in Jamaica were often at a 'poor level of play', evident in their losing games during the first inter-colonial tournament in 1896, which took place in British Guiana. In 1897 in light of their experiences in British Guiana, players decided to organize the Jamaica Cricket Challenge Club, which became known as the Senior Cup, in order to improve the game. However, the competition was played among the elite white clubs such as Kingston Cricket Club.[39]

During the latter half of the nineteenth century cricket was played by many black Jamaicans, who as Cresser has pointed out 'adopted and adapted the game to their particular material and cultural circumstances'.[40] Cricket became popular among the majority of the population through the development of district teams, workers' teams, but also most significantly the teaching and playing of cricket at schools with black working-class pupils. Thomas Burchell Stephenson developed the latter in his role as a prominent teacher (he was one of the founders of the Jamaica Union of Teachers) and also his role as the headmaster of Calabar School in Kingston. Stephenson organized a cricket club for pupils of the elementary school and this school was to train many cricketers for the newly formed Lucas Cricket Club, including Patrick's father Leopold, who attended Calabar school as a boy.[41]

Lucas Cricket Club was formed in 1895 by David Ellington, who worked as a busman. It was originally called the Jamaica Cricket Club but its name was changed in 1898 to honour one of its initial supporters, the English cricketer R. Slade Lucas. It was a Kingston-based club which was designed to open its doors to black working-class cricketers excluded from the traditional elite cricket clubs.[42] According to T. A. Aikman, Leopold Nelson's career started while he was at Calabar School, 'where the game was fostered as well as it could be among school boys by the late Mr T. B. Stephenson' and Nelson owed 'his entrance into first class cricket to Mr D. Ellington the founder of the Lucas C.C'.[43] Joining either during or just after his school days, Nelson was among the first cricketers to play with Ellington's precursor team to Lucas. David Ellington's obituary published in The *Gleaner* on 22 July 1933 stated that 'in the year 1889 Mr Ellington started a cricket team of schoolboys and played on the team as a lob bowler. They played at the Kingston Race Course and on the Waggonette grounds for some years and he financed the team out of his own pocket. There is at the present time one living member of that early schoolboy team – Mr Leo. Nelson – who attended Mr Ellington's sick bed up to the last.'[44]

Lucas C.C. rose to prominence fairly quickly, through the skills of its players during games played when it was categorized as a second-class club. Eventually – with evidence of the club's successes – those in charge of the Senior Cup had no choice but to move the club into the first-class category, where they were able to compete in the Senior Cup of 1902.[45] Cresser stated that Lucas' entrance into the Senior Cup 'was a very significant step in the democratisation of the game: it represented the participation of lower class blacks for the first time at the highest level'.[46] After its entrance into the Senior Cup, Lucas rose to prominence winning the title of the cup in 1904, 1905, 1906 and again in 1911, 1913, 1914 and 1915.[47] Leopold Nelson was central to the performance of the club and in 1904 (the first year of Lucas' success in the Senior Cup) he was awarded the Lucas C.C. Wisden's prize bat for the best wicket keeping in the Senior Competition.[48] The individual who decided upon the prize, referred to as 'Umpire' of the *Daily Telegraph*, wrote to W. H. Johnson:

> After, reviewing the last season's play I have no hesitation in advising you to present the bat offered to the best wicket-keeping in Senior Club Cricket, to Nelson, the keeper of the Lucas C.C. I cannot say that this task (which you did me the honour to entrust to my care) was either an arduous or a difficult one, for the reason that with one exception, the men who did duty constantly for the other clubs in the capacity of stumper, showed form much below the standard required, for any kind of reward. I decided that Nelson should have the prize owing to the fact that he was, generally safe, and sometimes exceptionally clever, especially on the leg side. Then he had a greater number and variety of bowlers to take – from Moiston's slows to Snow and Fyff's expresses.[49]

Parallel to and spurred on by Lucas' rise to prominence, cricket developed a mass following of working-class African-heritage Jamaicans, who turned in greater numbers to both playing the game and attending matches. Despite being a Kingston-based team, Lucas Cricket Club became popular all over the island. This popularity was also important for black pride, a sport to support, to champion and in which to be proud. Cresser argues, 'The fact that there was such an increase in popular interest and attendance at cricket matches illustrates the impact of Lucas's success on the self-esteem of Jamaican blacks in the early twentieth century. Winning, and winning against white and coloured teams, must obviously have been very important to them, and provided telling blows against the notions of inferiority that they were labelled with.'[50]

Lucas cricket players also played for Jamaica against other teams within the Caribbean and further afield. Cresser states that 'by the end of the first decade of the twentieth century, working-class black cricketers from Lucas had become a fixture in the Jamaica team.'[51] One of these fixtures was Leopold Nelson. For example, in 1905 Leopold Nelson was among the five Lucas players chosen to represent the 'All-Jamaica' team against an English team headed by Lord Brackley. Nelson also played for Jamaica in a game against Trinidad in 1905 and against Philadelphia in 1909.[52]

Despite Lucas' popularity, black Jamaicans still had to contend with racism from the colonial cricket establishment who did not like the challenge to their elitist vision of the game. Brian L. Moore and Michele A. Johnson state, 'So successful were they that the elites began to complain about their attitude and that of their supporters.'[53] For example, Lucas players were criticized for challenging unfair decisions of the Umpire. In the 1906 presentation of the Senior Cup to Lucas, Hon. T. L. Roxburgh stated, 'A great deal of feeling had been imported into the game, but that should be entirely eliminated, if they wanted to play cricket as it ought to be played.' As Cresser points out, this 'very loaded statement ... captured the Victorian values associated with cricket, such as obedience and submission to authority.'[54] Nelson was a victim of early prejudice of a different sort, by means of the selection process. T. A. Aikman, the author of the 1922 letter about Nelson, reflected on prejudice within Jamaican cricket in a further 1928 letter and cited the career of Leopold Nelson as a clear example of discrimination in the past and of how the same prejudice was still taking place. He stated,

> Leo. Nelson the first word in Jamaica wicket-keeping had the hardest struggle
> of his life against people who were infinitely inferior to him. Nothing but sheer

overwhelming ability over his puny rivals and their supporters and the fear of public demonstration gained him his place behind the stumps on occasions in living memory, after a memorable play of some six wickets in one innings put down directly to his credit, he let go one batsman to a difficult chance. He was at once superseded by one of those inferior rivals, and Jamaica remembers to her great chagrin the overwhelming disaster that overtook us as the immediate result of this bit of insane folly.[55]

It is difficult to know whether these details of Leopold's cricketing career were known to Patrick. Patrick mentioned his father's career only a few times in his letters and there is no information on whether Leopold shared any of his career struggles and frustrations with his children. However, the sport overall was a central part of the families' cultural and social life and played a role on a day-to-day basis in how Patrick experienced life in his formative years.

After Nelson's time playing for Lucas, he continued to play for a number of different teams and remained involved in the wider game, commenting on cricket through writing letters to the *Gleaner*. In October 1919 he played in a friendly match between St Catherine Prison Club and Mr Smedmore's Eleven, in which the visitors – Mr Smedmore's Eleven – won by a lead of 55 runs and 'Leo. Nelson, who seemed to have been in somewhat of his old Lucas form, played an undoubtedly fine game for 41 runs (not out), which placed him at the top of his side's batting averages for the day'.[56] On 25 March 1922 Leo. Nelson was in the line-up to play for St Catherine and Prison C.C. in a 'First-Class' friendly match at Clovel Park.[57] Leopold Nelson's correspondence to the *Gleaner* included a letter dated April 1925 where he commented on the current Barbadian cricket team and gave various suggestions for the line-up of the Jamaican cricket team.[58] In 1929 Leopold Nelson wrote to the *Gleaner* again and the paper reported:

> Mr Leo. Nelson writing from No. 41 Prince Albert Street, Allman Town, says that he is in accord with Captain F. W. H. Nicholas' opinion expressed in his letter in our issue of the 5th instant, when he states that no one should blame a stumper for giving a chance to a batsman: a stumper, Mr Nelson observes, is the key of the game as he has to compete in the four departments of the game. The difference of wickets has quite a lot to do with the misgathering of balls by a stumper when he has to keep on two grounds. Mr Nelson congratulates Mr Barrow for the two tips and two stumps and the brilliant gathering of the ball that was thrown in by Hylton in running out the batsman. Mr Nelson also congratulates Mr Nunes the Captain on winning the first match.[59]

Again in 1934 Leopold wrote to the *Gleaner* with a suggestion for players for the Jamaican team who were to play against the English team visiting that winter.[60] He also kept his Lucas connections years after retiring from cricket, as one letter he sent to the AMPC record office in September 1940 was written on headed paper with the address of Lucas Cricket Club at Nelson Oval.[61]

Leopold Nelson and the military

Along with playing cricket, Leopold Nelson was at one time a member of the Jamaican military, and the militia was possibly his main career with regard to paid employment. As he explained in his September 1940 letter sent to the AMPC record office, he was a gunner in the First World War and was in the Jamaica Militia Artillery.[62] As he was well known in Jamaica through his profession as a cricket player, he was referenced briefly in one newspaper report in 1916 in relation to him being in the militia artillery. On 8 February 1916 the *Gleaner* reported that they wanted 'the public to know that the Leopold Nelson who was rescued in the harbour a few days ago during a boating accident, is not Gunner Leopold Nelson of the Jamaica Militia Artillery'.[63] In a 1940 article in the *Gleaner* it was reported that Leopold 'was a gunner in the Jamaica Militia Artillery for a period of 22 years and was in active service at Island forts for 3 ½ years'.[64]

Jamaican militias were established in the period of slavery. As Richard Smith states, 'In Jamaica, as in many frontier and settler societies, the right to take up arms was closely linked to the defence of property and racial privilege.'[65] The organization Leopold Nelson was to serve, the Jamaica Militia Artillery, was created at the end of the nineteenth century through legislation entitled the 1879 Militia Law. This law also created the Jamaica Infantry Militia (JIM), which was disbanded in the early twentieth century.[66] White Jamaican elites desired to defend their power by expressing opposition to the arming of the black majority of the population and this continued into the twentieth century. With the start of the First World War, Smith states, 'The ongoing anxieties of the white minority, rather than the minimal threat posed by Germany to British rule in Jamaica, often appeared to be the greater concern.'[67] However, official calls for black Jamaicans to serve were made. In late October 1915 an appeal for troops by George V was read out in Jamaica's churches. Smith has argued that 'the inclusive language of the 'King's Appeal' found an echo among the Jamaican masses' but that 'inclusive language could not erase historical attitudes to the deployment of black soldiers or override anxieties surrounding white masculine performance during the war'.[68] The appeal of the King arose in a context of previous discussions and disputes involving both the War Office and Colonial Office. Stephen Bourne states, 'In 1915 the War Office and the Colonial Office realised that they could not ignore the requests of West Indian men to join up. However, when the Colonial Office proposed a separate West Indian contingent to aid the war effort, the War Office refused. Eventually the Colonial Office, with the intervention and support of King George V in April 1915, were able to raise a West Indian contingent'.[69] However, within this regiment black soldiers were prevented from serving in ranks above Sergeant.[70]

In relation to the racism within British recruiting, Smith states, 'Prevailing racial attitudes, inconsistencies in official policy and the approach of individual recruiting officers interacted to ensure that black and brown Jamaicans met with varying degrees of success in joining regular army units'.[71] Jamaicans and other Caribbean people based in Britain took part in the war effort in various ways, often having to fight for their rights to participate and often experiencing racism when involved in service, particularly when black or brown people held some kind of authority over white recruits. The future Jamaican premier Norman Manley reflected on his experiences of serving in the British army during the First World War. By January 1916 Norman Manley had been promoted to corporal, but due to racism from a sergeant in his unit he transferred out of the unit and returned to the rank of gunner. He reflected on the 'violent colour prejudice' he experienced stating 'the rank and file disliked taking orders from a coloured N.C.O. and their attitude was mild by comparison with that of my fellow N.C.O.s'.[72]

With regard to the Jamaican home forces, during the First World War there was a Volunteer Defence Force established by legislation in 1914 and military forces such as the Jamaica Militia Artillery were mobilized. The Artillery mobilized for wartime was demobilized in 1918. The *Gleaner* reported in December 1918 that 'the Jamaica Militia Artillery, which was mobilized on the outbreak of war, paraded at Headquarters Local Forces yesterday, returning from four years of service at the outforts'.[73] The governor's address thanking the JMA is particularly interesting with regard to the role of family archives and history in sustaining wider historical memories of individuals not usually in the public eye. Within the speech the governor stated,

> Now, before you are disbanded, I, being the representative of His Most Gracious Majesty the King, wish to thank you for the services that you have rendered and

I being the Governor, wish to thank you on behalf of Jamaica also, for those same services; and I would ask you to follow my advice. It is, that you will be careful to keep your papers safely, because those papers which perhaps to-day you look on as having little interest will hereafter be of ever increasing interest, and your grandchildren will be interested and proud when they read the papers and see and appreciate that during the great war you rendered services to the Colony, to the Empire and to His Majesty.[74]

When serving in the artillery, it appears that Nelson also played for the militia's cricket team. On 6 August 1918 the *Gleaner* reported that a cricket match would be played the following day between the Jamaica Militia Artillery Cricket Club and the Port Royal C.C. and those playing for JMA included Gunner Nelson.[75] As explored later in the book, Leopold expressed his pride that Patrick participated in the allied effort in the Second World War and in these letters we can find glimpses of his life story and his feelings on various subjects including the war, conditions in Jamaica and family life, including the love for his son Patrick.

Leopold Nelson died in 1945, just a few months before Patrick returned to Jamaica after his POW repatriation to Britain. The *Gleaner* reported on 2 March 1945 that 'Leopold Constantine ("Poley")' Nelson had died the previous day at the Kingston Public Hospital after a brief illness'.[76] Although they were never reunited, Leopold died having known his son Patrick had been released from the captivity of the Germany POW camps.

Gertrude Nelson and genealogical reconstructions

The life experiences and biography of Patrick's mother Gertrude Nelson is more difficult to reconstruct than Leopold's. As explored in the introduction to this book, archival absences often appear when researching individuals not in the public eye, and we have to often read against the grain to find out experiences of individuals whose lives do not at first glance appear to touch official archival sources. This 'absence' has particularly raced, gendered and class dimensions, where lives marginalized or ignored in public discourse, including working-class women and men's lives, often need to be explored through records such as genealogical records (birth, marriages and death), migration records and records relating to their interaction with official institutions such as poor law workhouses, asylums and prisons. However, those exploring these histories have utilized a number of alternative sources, often by reading against the grain, in order to reconstruct life stories and experiences.

Additionally, these sources, along with oral histories, letters, photographs, personal ephemera, and other forms of life history such as life writing and autobiography, are explored by historians and activists working in the 'history from below' tradition. In follow-up work to this book, by exploring institutional records and recollections I have not so far had access to, I hope to find out more about Gertrude's life and experiences in early-twentieth-century Jamaica. Unlike Leopold, Gertrude does not appear in newspapers such as the *Gleaner*. However, Gertrude wrote to Duncan Grant and to the War Office several times during the time Patrick was a prisoner, seeking to find out information on Patrick's whereabouts, along with passing on information to the War Office and to Duncan. These letters, explored later on in the book, contain snippets of information on her life and experiences. Additionally, there is some information about Gertrude included in Patrick's letters. Gertrude appears in genealogical records, showing that she died fifteen years after her son Patrick. Jamaican death records confirm that Gertrude Nelson, widow of Leopold Nelson, died on 23 July 1978.[77]

In addition to Patrick, Gertrude and Leopold Nelson had several other children. The 1945 *Gleaner* announcement of the death and funeral of Leopold Nelson stated that he left a 'wife and seven children to mourn their loss'.[78] In various letters from Patrick, Leopold and Gertrude to Duncan Grant there is mention of various brothers and at least one sister of Patrick's. For example, his brother Cecil was mentioned by Leopold Nelson, who wrote to Duncan in 1942 that 'Patrick's younger brother Cecil will be leaving Jamaica shortly to work in munition factory in England'.[79] By 1944 one of Patrick's brothers was promoted to a corporal in the Jamaican Home Guards and another was due to join the RAF.[80]

During Patrick's adulthood he was a practicing Catholic. His full middle name was St Patrick, a name given to him probably from birth (and definitely a name he used as a child). It appears likely that his family were Roman Catholic and he was brought up Catholic. Catholicism was one of the main religions in Jamaica.[81] In Jamaica it was historically practised in a syncretic way by the majority African-heritage population, with religious beliefs taking shape and developing in the context of enslavement and colonial exploitation, which led to a fusing 'between largely European and African practices and belief systems'.[82]

There were a number of Catholic churches in Kingston. A *Gleaner* article published in January 1937 described the various events which took place for the Centenary celebrations of the Viciate Apostolic of the Catholic Church in Jamaica, which included a number of visitors from abroad. The article noted, 'Catholic Leaders in Education in America, Writers, Rectors and Masters of Novices and Novitate and noted preachers in the Land of Liberty, all unite in speaking in glowing terms of Jamaica's response to the call of the Church, their culture and hospitality which is unsurpassed.'[83] Patrick's Catholicism was central to his identity and sense of self. He attended and became involved in a variety of Jamaican Catholic churches, which provided him with emotional and other types of support, particularly in the post-war period after his release from captivity as a POW.

Exploring genealogical records such as birth, marriage and death records provides probable information about Patrick's family, including important information about Gertrude Nelson's working life. One likely family that is probably Patrick's is a family recorded as living in the Kingston area of Allman Town (the area where Patrick Nelson and his family certainly lived during the 1920s and 1930s), with a father called Leopold Nelson and a mother called Gertrude Nelson. This family had several children. Charles Alexander Nelson was born in 1906 to Gertrude Coles, who was listed as being employed as a higgler. Another child was born in 1908 to Gertrude Coles, who described herself as a washerwoman. Another child, Florence Una Coles was born to Gertrude Coles in 1908. In 1914 a child called Cecil Theodore Coles was born to Gertrude Coles, who was listed in this record as a domestic servant. Henrietta Winifred Coles was born in March 1916 to Gertrude Coles. All of these children were born at 21 Stephen Street, Allman Town and the informant for all of these births was Leopold Nelson, who also lived at 21 Stephen Street. Doris Muriel Coles was born in 1918 also at 21 Stephen Street to Gertrude Coles, and in this record Gertrude is described as a washerwoman. The birth record was signed by Charles Nelson (perhaps her oldest child). A set of twins was born in October 1921, and by this time the father's name which had been blank in all the previous entries was given as Leopold Nelson, 12 Wild Street, Allman Town. In this document, Gertrude is now described as 'Gertrude Nelson, formerly Coles'. Leopold Nelson is described as a shoemaker.[84] A marriage certificate for Gertrude Coles and Leopold Nelson dated 22 June 1921 gives the address of their civil marriage as Duke Street in Kingston.[85]

Gertrude's employment as a domestic, a higgler and washerwoman is important to explore in the context of the history of experiences of Caribbean women during the early twentieth century. Winnifred R. Brown-Glaude states: '"Higgler" is a term commonly used by Jamaicans to identify a particular kind of street vendor – a so-called lower-class black woman who sells a range of items on the streets or in government-appointed market areas and arcades (covered passageways with stalls on either side where vendors display their wares)' (Figure 1.1).[86] Higgling is traditionally an important type of work carried out by women of African heritage in the Caribbean from the period of enslavement onwards, where enslaved women sold produce and products at markets. Higglers in the early twentieth century appear in the pages of the *Gleaner*, often in reports of trials of themselves or others – we can, however, read against the grain of these reports by exploring how women sought to make an income and piece together snapshots of biographies of women's lives through the information presented in these articles. Trials concerning people using counterfeit coins often included higglers as witnesses. As witnesses the reports highlight the names and often addresses of higglers, as well as the type of goods they sold and produced and the markets or stalls or shops where they worked. For example, in 1908 Dorcas Allen was charged with breaking into Ann Wood's higgler's shop. In the shop the items sold included coal.[87] A higgler's shop was mentioned in another 1908 case of receiving goods under false pretences. Arianna Warren's shop, based in Passmore Town, sold among its items wood bundles, bread, bun, escallion and pears.[88] Higglers also worked

Figure 1.1 A busy morning in the Jubilee Market, Kingston, Jamaica, 27 April c1923, Library of Congress.

at Jubilee Market in downtown Kingston. In a 1911 case of counterfeit coining, two higglers from Jubilee Market were witnesses, Emily Jonah a higgler in Jubilee Market sold items including yams and Sarah Ann Parkinson, another higgler in the Jubilee Market also sold yams.[89]

By the time of Patrick's birth, Gertrude (if indeed this is Patrick's family) was employed as a washerwoman, another type of employment carried out by mainly black working-class women in Jamaica. Images of washerwomen were often used in colonial tourist propaganda imagery through a process which Krista A. Thompson has termed tropicalization.[90] Michele A. Johnson has carried out research on domestic service in Jamaica from 1920 to 1970 (work Gertrude Nelson carried out). Johnson documents that

> Jamaican domestic service grew out of a heritage of slavery. Abhorred by some as one of the lingering symbols of bondage, relegated by many because of its demeaned status as 'women's work', domestic service provided one of the few opportunities for many poor black women to find employment. In Jamaica's modern history, because of a growing demand for servants by the emerging bourgeoisie, pressure on exhausted land in the rural areas, and a trend of urbanisation without commensurate economic development, domestic service was the chief sector into which many women could go.[91]

Letters written to the *Gleaner* by Leopold Nelson show that Patrick's family did live in the Allman Town area. For example, a letter written to the *Gleaner* in 1925 by Leopold Nelson was signed with the address of 3 Hannah Street, Allman Town. In 1929 the address he gave within a further letter was No. 41 Prince Albert Street, Allman Town and in 1934 the address given was 4 ½ Prince Albert Street, Allman Town. The Nelson family might have bought or rented the Hannah Street house or a part of the house and perhaps moved in after seeing the building advertised by W. Leslie Logan, a real estate and commercial agent, in a 1923 edition of the *Gleaner*, which stated for sale '3 Hannah Street, Allman Town, consisting of 6 tenement rooms, large oven and necessary outbuildings'.[92] Additionally, as Patrick did have brothers called Cecil and Charles, there is a strong likelihood that the family found in these genealogical records is Patrick's family. However, no likely birth record can be found at the time of writing this book in the digitized sources which correlates to Patrick's birth. Another factor which goes against this family being Patrick's is the father's profession, a shoemaker. However, it is likely that Leopold would have needed an extra profession in addition to being in the military, so perhaps shoemaking was at this time a source of income.

Allman Town in the early twentieth century

Allman Town was a suburb of Kingston. In 1915 Frank Cundall wrote 'Allman Town, which came into existence soon after Emancipation, was, so Mr G. F. Judah stated, named after George Allman, who was either an officer in the army or the son of one.'[93] In the early twentieth century, Allman Town was described in the fictional story *Jane: A Story of Jamaica* by Herbert George de Lisser as being an area which was home to the 'lower middle classes' and 'servants'. Jane, the central character in De Lisser's novel, worked as a domestic servant when she first moved to Kingston.[94] Exploring references to Allman Town in the *Gleaner* newspaper, addresses located in the suburb often appear in advertisements placed by domestic servants. For example, in the *Gleaner* for 27 April 1935 there were several domestic workers looking for work who lived in Allman Town, including a 'young woman' called Mary who sought a position as a 'butleress, laundress' who could also 'do gentlemen's suits', 'plain cooking', and had experience working in a lady's home and as a nurse. Her address was given as 25 Steven Street, Allman Town. A woman called Ettie, who described herself as a 'decent black girl', advertised for a position as a 'washer, or cleaner' who would 'make herself generally useful in a home or country' gave an address of 10 Great George Street, Allman Town.[95] In the 22 April 1939 edition of the *Gleaner*, a 'competent chauffeur' called Sydney who lived at 35 Prince Albert Street in Allman Town advertised for work and a nineteen-year-old 'decent lad' called F. Bailey who lived in Allman Town advertised seeking employment as a 'waiter, cook, valet, children caretaker, one who can do his work; can also drive and care motor cars; can iron and press government suits; make any kind of desserts, will also do a little garden work, with over three years of experience of Hotels and private houses'.[96]

Significantly, Allman Town was the political home during the same time to Marcus Mosiah Garvey. Born on the north coast of Jamaica in 1887, Garvey founded the United Negro Improvement Association (UNIA) and after being deported from the United States in 1927 he returned to Jamaica. He continued his political activism in Jamaica, forming the anti-imperialist People's Political Party in 1929.[97] At their first meeting in September 1929 Garvey spoke of the injustices and abuses in the colonial Jamaican legal system and thereafter he was sentenced to three months in jail for contempt. As Watson explores, during his imprisonment he was elected to serve in local government for the Kingston and St Andrew Corporation's Allman Town No. 3 Urban Ward.[98] Watson states,

> Under the Kingston & St. Andrew Corporation Act, seats that were vacant for three consecutive months without leave were declared vacant. Realizing that

he would not be able to attend meetings, he wrote a letter from his jail cell, requesting leave from the KSAC, as required by statute. The leave was denied, and he was not allowed to take the oath for office.[99]

After being released from jail, although Garvey took the oath, his seat was declared vacant and, as Watson states, 'A large crowd, dissatisfied that the Council was discussing vacating his seat and demanding legal representation in the meeting, gathered in the gallery during the January 13 meeting, but the mayor refused to allow an attorney to speak on No. 3 Ward's behalf.'[100] After this meeting the UNIA's newspaper *The Blackman* published an editorial by literary editor Theophilus Aikman entitled 'The Vagabonds Again' which referred to the criminality of the council and thereafter Garvey, Aikman and John Coleman Beecher were charged with sedition.[101] What impact would this have had on the Nelson family, including a young Patrick, living in this area? Aikman knew of Patrick's father Leopold; as already mentioned Aikman had written about Leopold Nelson's career in a letter to the *Gleaner* in 1922 and perhaps they knew one another. Exploring Patrick's life, his politics as a young child and adult during the 1920s and 1930s were likely far removed from the radical politics of Garveyism. In the post-war period when Patrick became more critical of British rule in Jamaica perhaps he might have reflected on the thoughts of figures such as Garvey when he witnessed and wrote about the injustices in Jamaican colonial society.

This chapter has aimed to document some of the historical context of Patrick's life, including his parent's experiences of work and aspects of the social, economic and political world of interwar Kingston. In the subsequent chapter I examine the construction and features of Jamaican-class identities which surrounded Patrick and his family, those propagated in the Jamaican Scout movement, which served to shape Patrick's identity and outlook during his formative years. I explore themes such as the growing exclusive tourist industry in Jamaica and how Patrick's experience of this industry – hinted at in the *Gleaner* interview – influenced his identity as a colonial subject. I also posit and contextualize Patrick's life within the wider Jamaican political and socio-economic environ of the 1930s, in particular in relation to anti-imperialism, racism, struggles against unemployment and poverty, the growing labour and trade union movement and mass working-class protests for social, economic and political rights – themes which Patrick would later reflect upon in his letters to Duncan Grant following his return to Jamaica in 1945.

Patrick in 1920s and 1930s Jamaica: Cultural, Political, Social and Sexual Identities and Histories

Patrick's childhood and young adulthood were shaped by multiple experiences of geography, class and colonialism which exhibited themselves in a variety of ways. One influence was his being involved in organized imperial and colonial childhood activities. In addition to elite cricket explored in the previous chapter, other ways in which English-influenced colonial and imperial identity permeated Jamaican society can be located in specific forms of social recreation, member clubs and societies. These were clubs founded to create and forge community, albeit with specific rules and philosophies which served to promote and solidify imperial ties between Britain and its empire. One of these organizations was the Jamaican Scouts. Scouting was a major influence over Patrick Nelson's life. He was a Scout when young and his being a Scout was cited in the 1937 *Gleaner* article as a particular attribute which exemplified his good qualities. The article stated that he was 'a handsome youth of fine physique and good address, a product of Scoutcraft'.[1] This chapter explores some of these organizations and activities, focusing on Scoutcraft, and concludes with an exploration of Patrick's adult life before his migrating to Britain, looking at his experiences within a wider context of political and social movements of the 1930s, the tourism industry and histories of sexuality.

Scoutcraft in Jamaica

The Scout movement was established in 1908 by Lieutenant-General Robert Baden-Powell in order to counteract what Baden-Powell viewed as the negative effects of modern civilization. Robert H. MacDonald states of Baden-Powell's philosophy,

> He hoped that Scouting would make things right. He would teach the soldiers and sailors of the coming war – the present boys of Britain – to be real men; becoming healthy and strong, and understanding their duties as citizens and patriots, they would be the saving of the country. For the movement's hero he offered himself, not as a soldier, but in the character of that up-to-date invention, a scout of the Empire.[2]

Along with its stereotyped views of masculinity and desire for fostering patriotism for the Empire, the Scouting movement also utilized imperial myths of the 'other' both to enable Boy Scouts to follow the rules of duty and to experience a corresponding adventure and exploration inspired by the 'exotic' warrior. From its beginning, scouting grew quickly. In Britain by 1909 there were 60,000 Boy Scouts and by 1913 there were 152,000.[3] Scouting, in combination with other youth activities, was embraced by many across the world and, to some extent, provided a space where boys of different social, class and racial backgrounds socialized and befriended one another. However, as in the case of cricket, scouting had a financial cost (expenses included uniforms, equipment and activities). In Britain, this expense was one reason why Scouts was not as popular in poorer communities, and troops recruited their members from 'lower-middle-class' and 'upper-working-class' families.[4]

Scouting found particular resonance in Britain's colonies and Dominions.[5] The imperial element of scouting was further cemented through Scouting rallies, which soon became known as international jamborees. The third international Scouting rally which took place in Birmingham in 1913 included 5,000 Scouts camping for a week, and Scouts from across the Empire participated.[6] The Scouts were an organization that colonial administrators and elites found of immense value; the organization sought to instil doctrines of obedience, loyalty, duty and also patriotism towards Britain and Empire into the minds of young people within Britain's colonies, and in turn it aimed to help foster the type of colonial subject the authorities desired. For example, the 1912 Empire Day message to the Boy Scouts of the Empire from Lieut. General E. R. Ellis was printed in the *Gleaner*. It stated,

> On this day set apart for Imperial rejoicing it is particularly appropriate that Scouts throughout the Empire should especially consider the meaning of that portion of the three old promise which deals with loyalty to the King. It is loyalty

which to a large extent is responsible for the consolidation of the British Empire in one great confederation, and on that one foundation rest the present bond of sympathy and brotherhood between the Dominions and the Mother country.[7]

Scouting in Jamaica had been established by at least the year 1911. Boy Scouts outside of Jamaica were referenced in the *Gleaner* from 1909. In a picture article in the 13 November 1909 edition of the *Gleaner* entitled 'Spread of the British Scout Movement' photographs were published of Naval Scouts; a Boy Scout's Bible; a group of Sea Scouts; a 'Scout at Work'; a group of Scouts in the Transval; a Boy Scout carrying baggage; and Boy Scouts in China.[8] Instead of reporting on Scouts in other parts of the world, by 1911 the *Gleaner* reported on the existence of both Girl Scout and Boy Scout troops within Jamaica. The former, a girl Scout group linked to the Wolmer School, was short-lived and was replaced by an organization which promoted more stereotypical 'female' activities. The *Gleaner* of 14 July 1911 reported that

> the girl scouts have changed into girl guides. They still maintain their interest in all the out-door work of the scouts but they are encouraged by the head of the Association – Miss Baden-Powell to devote more attention to work which is particularly woman's work. I hope that during the holiday's some of the guides will win badges for sewing, cooking and dress-making.[9]

In October 1911 Mr Harry Miles of the Jamaica Railway presented a talk to the 'Church of England: Men's Society' arguing for the benefits of the Scouting movement, which had 'adopted the law of the ancient knights, who were renowned for their strength of character, chivalry and patriotism'. Miles added that 'if it is thought that this movement would benefit the boys of Kingston I shall be glad, as a Scoutmaster, to help others to start a troop and will gladly furnish further information on the subject'.[10]

Scouting in the Empire was directly fostered and encouraged by Baden-Powell and his staff who visited Britain's colonies, including Jamaica, for recruitment and propaganda. During January 1912 Baden-Powell arrived in Jamaica as part of an eight-month world tour. The *Gleaner* reported that 'the visit of the hero of Mafeking was looked forward to with much interest and the Parish Church and Wolmer's troop of Boy Scouts, numbering 20 under the command of Mr. Duncan McCorkell, Scout Master, went down to the wharf to meet the General'.[11] In an interview with the *Gleaner*, Baden-Powell reported that Major Fetherstone Haugh planned to visit the West Indies to organize and assist the Scouting movement. By 1914 there were well-established groups in both

Kingston and Spanish Town, and in March 1915 a 'corp' of Boy Scouts organized by the Wesleyan Church was established in Port Antonio.[12] Along with church groups such as the Wesleyan group of Port Antonio, other groups were set up which reflected the island's religious diversity. By 1915 there was a Jewish Lads Troop of Baden-Powell's Boy Scouts whose patron was Mr Altamont DaCosta and Jamaica's Scouts also included Catholic troops.[13]

It appears that the Scouting movement became less popular during the war years as by August 1917 there were attempts at its 'revival'. Steps taken to revive Scoutcraft included a conference where various military activities were planned such as the establishment of combined instruction parades, a class for 'physical culture', a musketry course, the formation of 'shooting patrols' in the troops, and lecture to be given by Lieut. Brandon of the Jamaica Reserve Regiment.[14] This military aspect of scouting was perhaps an influence for Patrick and this training in addition to the example of his father's long career in the Jamaican military undoubtedly influenced Patrick when serving in the war. Additionally, the importance of the Scouts for Patrick could be seen in his decision to continue his association with Scouting after the Second World War.

By the 1920s Jamaica's Scouting tradition was fully established, to the point where they sent a contingent over to the Imperial Jamboree held in England in connection with the British Empire exhibition taking place in Wembley during 1924–5.[15] The Imperial Jamboree attracted twelve thousand Scouts from across the Empire.[16] The Jamaican contingent led by Assistant Scout Commissioner Noel Crosswell travelled to Britain on the *Oriana*, arriving in Liverpool on 25 July 1924.[17] Again the romanticization of the Empire is exemplified in a speech the Prince of Wales gave to the Scouts assembled at Wembley, where he proclaimed his pride in the occasion and that 'this Exhibition gives you some idea of the boundless possibilities of the British Empire', and told them that they were the Empire's future and that 'the Empire is like a bundle of sticks, any one of which may be broken, but which when they are tied together cannot be broken. The bond which binds the Empire together is the splendid spirit of loyalty to the King and to one another.' [18] This romanticization of the Empire would undoubtedly have influenced Patrick's formation of his identity and his early view of Britain and Empire. Patrick was of scouting age in 1924, though by looking through the list in the *Gleaner* as well as the shipping passenger returns we see that he was not one of the Jamaican Scouts who took part in this trip.[19]

Patrick took scouting seriously and it was factored into his philosophy of life. He joined the Scouts, it appears, in 1924, the year of the Empire exhibition. He continued his involvement in the Scouts during his time in Jamaica post-war. In 1954 he wrote that 'I am still a[n] active member of Saint Alloysious Boy Scout Troop and have up to over 30 years, service in the movement of which I am a Master'.[20] By the age of sixteen Patrick had become a Scout pack leader of the St Aloysius Troop of Boy Scouts.[21] In September 1932, when aged sixteen, Patrick took part in an event as a Scout pack leader performing a 'well-acted' 'short dialogue' in a scout concert at Brown's Town. The *Gleaner* reported that the concert included songs, folk dances and plays, including a 'cannibal play', a 'Red Indian play' and an 'African play' which included 'a medicine man with his weird incentations [*sic*], and wild dances'.[22] These types of plays – focusing on racialized stereotypes of the lives of imperial 'others' such as 'medicine men' and 'cannibals' – highlight how imperial stereotypes were transmitted within colonial societies through organizational activities and events, including theatre and performance. These types of plays were common activities for Scouts and had particular resonance when performed in the Empire by colonized people. Performances such as these transmitted imperialist stereotypes about so-called 'primitive' cultures, including cultures of colonized peoples such as the performing of 'African' plays.

As Jialin Christina Wu has explored in the context of British Malaya, Boy Scouts 'playing Indian' was a tradition of British Scouting from its earliest days, in, for example, Baden-Powell's 1908 Scouts play 'Pocahontas; or the Capture of John Smith'.[23] Wu explored two Scout plays which highlighted that 'Malayan forms of play-acting could incorporate other "natives" even local indigenous peoples of Malaya such as the Sakai' and that these plays featured a 'common narrative' of a

> Scout-hero who encounters a native counterpart or leader in the midst of Scout activity. Consequently, the encounter leads to dramatic tension which is resolved when the Scout imparts Scout values to his fellow native partner, who will have been converted as a 'brother' Scout by the end of the play.[24]

These Jamaican plays also took place within a context of the colonial criminali-zation of Jamaicans who practised African-derived creolized religious, spiritual and healing practices such as Obeah. In the 2015 *The Cultural politics of Obeah*, Diana Paton has noted that 'the lack of attention to religion in the Moyne Commission's analysis was particularly noteworthy because the period leading up to the rebellions was one of religious ferment'. As Paton stated, during this period 'concern about Obeah was a widespread element of public discourse' which 'worked on multiple levels'.[25]

School and education

Patrick's school life was partly documented in official British records relating to his later military service. In his official Army Personnel Records, it was documented that he matriculated school in Jamaica, taking the subjects English, French, geography and science.[26] He did not attend higher education in Jamaica and before going to France during the Second World War he had been a private student in London preparing to go to university.[27] The army records do not document when he left school in Jamaica and what school he attended, but perhaps he went to Calabar, the school his father attended.

In addition to Scouting and schooling, the *Gleaner* also includes an intriguing reference to Patrick in relation to education, namely his involvement in or support for elocution competitions. In December 1935 the *Gleaner* reported the elocution championships taking place in St James parish, which were open to children and adults. It was reported that those in attendance included Mr Leo P. Nelson.[28] In a later interview with Patrick after he returned to Jamaica from his war experiences, the journalist described him as having a 'natural Oxford accent'.[29] Elocution was an essential part of European education in the eighteenth, nineteenth and twentieth centuries. Joy Damousi has explored the history and use of elocution teaching and elocution manual writing in relation to Britain and the British Empire.[30]

As the British Empire expanded, language was also a key tool of colonialism. As Damousi states, 'Although not everyone practised elocution, its existence enshrined a particular exemplary type of, and approach to, the delivery of the language – the correct use of English.'[31] Elocution lessons and competitions were often mentioned in the *Gleaner* and in an imperial context elocution was part of an overall movement cementing imperial educational ideals. In the late nineteenth century The Collegiate School in Kingston ran various competitions including an elocution competition with the medal given by Dr Bowerbank.[32] A private academy run by Reverend H. Peckover at the Kingston North Street Congregational Parsonage advertised tuition of subjects described as being in the 'Ordinary Branches of an English Education' which included various subjects such as reading, etymology, elocution and grammar.[33] Annual prizes and competitions were also run by the Montego Bay Secondary School including, as reported in the 1899 *Gleaner*, a competition for elocution.[34] Elocutionist lecturers from England visited and gave lectures in Jamaica; for example, in 1887 it was reported that Mr A. Huntley, described in the *Gleaner* as 'the eminent elocutionist', would give a recitation at the Town Hall.[35]

In addition to elocution being practised as part of a wider system of organized education, elocution was also a skill practised among Caribbean activists and artists involved in public oratory. For example, Marcus Garvey was also involved in elocution. The *Gleaner* wrote on 28 May 1913 that '"Fairplay" writes congratulating Mr Marcus Garvey on getting up the island elocution contests, and expressing dissatisfaction at the awards made at the recent Port Antonio contest'.[36] In 1931 the *Gleaner* reported on the All-Island Elocution Contest at Edelweiss Park. At the contest Marcus Garvey, who the *Gleaner* stated 'on behalf of the Edelweiss Amusement Co. really got up the contest', made a speech stating, 'This is the first of the annual contests in elocution that we shall be holding in Jamaica and I believe, at Edelweiss Park.' The joint first- and second-place prize winners were Una Marson and E. M Cupidon.[37] In announcing the 1932 contest the *Gleaner* reported that Garvey was the All-Island Elocution Contest Committee chairman.[38] In 1940 the *Gleaner* reported that the All-Jamaica Elocution Contest Committee of the Poetry League and the Jamaica Arts Society had announced that the fifth annual all-Schools Elocution Contest would take place on 24 May and the all-Island Open Championship would take place on 29 May.[39] Patrick's interest in elocution was probably partially fostered due to his role as a valet, first in the Jamaican tourist industry serving Europeans and then in valet service for British aristocrats.

Tourism in Jamaica

By young adulthood Patrick had started a career in the booming, but exploitative, Jamaican tourist industry. By the 1930s Jamaica was fully immersed in developing its tourist economy and this economy was to shape various aspects of Patrick's economic and social life, as well as provide a reason for his migrating to Britain. The 1937 *Gleaner* article – referred to in Chapter 1 – reported on the reason for Patrick leaving Jamaica, that of continuing his career as a valet within Britain.[40]

Between 1891 and 1925 tourism in Jamaica was worth at least £3.5 million.[41] Tourism's development was fostered by a mixture of official policy by Caribbean governments, individuals, and companies, including large overseas companies with bases in the Caribbean as an alternative or additional economy to the declining plantation economy. The agricultural economy of the late nineteenth century involved a number of large overseas companies and these US- and British-owned fruit companies were involved in running hotels and transport to hotels. As Catherine Cocks states 'United Fruit, which invested the most in Caribbean leisure travel, built what was for a time Jamaica's most successful resort hotel, the Titchfield, in Port Antonio in the mid-1890s.'[42] The *Illustrated London News*' West Indies special supplement of 1936 highlights the link between the fruit companies and tourism. In the section on how to travel to the West Indies, the Bahamas and Bermuda, lines which were mentioned included the Fyffes Line sailing direct from Avonmouth to Kingston, Jamaica and the weekly Jamaica Banana Producers' Line, which sailed into Kingston.[43] In 1922 the Tourist Trade Development Board was established which continued to run until 1956.[44] Tourism expanded greatly during this time. Frank F. Taylor states, 'At the beginning of the interwar period the Jamaican tourist trade was still in its infancy, yet it held fourth place among the island's industries in 1924, contributing some £15,000 to general revenue and £158, 540 to domestic income as a whole.'[45]

Those involved in the industry also sought to promote the region as a health destination. In a 1924 edition of the *Lancet*, Joseph Geoghegan, a medical doctor based in Kingston, Jamaica, published an article on 'Jamaica as a Health-Resort', where he wrote about the benefits to health emanating from Jamaica's climate and the mineral springs, but ended the article with a plea for increased tourism using imperial-based arguments, stating 'Our insular attachment to certain foreign climes might with wisdom be subordinated to the welfare of the undeveloped resources of the Empire. It is hoped, therefore, that patriotism will stimulate, as self-interest would urge, the greater exploitation of the charms of the Queen of the Antilles.'[46] This article was not the first piece in the *Lancet* to explore Jamaica as a health destination. In 1905 Thomas W. Thursfield, a medical doctor from Warneford Hospital, Leamington, wrote about his visit to Jamaica during March and April 1905. This trip was organized by the managing director of Elder, Dempster and Co. who arranged to take a group of medical doctors to Jamaica on the New Imperial Direct Mail Steam Line. Thursfield reported that 'the general impression made on me by the voyage was that the endeavour to make Jamaica a resort for tourists and certain classes of invalids ought to be a very great success and I believe it will.'[47] As can be seen in this 1905 article, the health promotion of Jamaica was intrinsically tied to commercial interests, with commercial organizations involved in promoting Jamaica directly to medical professionals. Additionally, newspaper adverts in British periodicals promoting tourism in Jamaica advertised it as a destination beneficial to health. However, health was just one factor among many including scenery, geography, flora and fauna, animal life and recreation such as golfing.

In 1910 the Handbook of Jamaica listed for the Kingston area alone twenty-two lodging houses, hotels and taverns.[48] The Manor House Hotel was one of these establishments and was to become one of Jamaica's small luxury tourist destinations popular with Europeans and Americans during the early to mid-twentieth century. The building was originally used as a hotel from 1905. In 1906 it was listed in the Handbook of Jamaica as a lodging in Constant Spring run by Mrs Kemp. By 1908 it was described as the 'Constant Spring Manor House'. Up to 1919 the Constant Spring Manor House was still run by Mrs Kemp. The hotel was properly established as a tourist destination during the ownership of Captain Rutty, who ran it with his wife from 1926, where it was described as the Manor House Hotel.[49]

In 1960 the *Gleaner* published an article by Inez K. Sibley focusing on the history of the Manor House Hotel, in turn documenting its links to plantation slavery through documentary evidence and oral testimony. Sibley reflected on the Manor House of 1960 by stating that 'Manor House on the Constant Spring road, in a tropical garden of great beauty, and with its atmosphere of Old World graciousness, has a history – as most places of this kind usually do'.[50] After Cromwell's occupation of Jamaica the majority of the Liguanea Plains was under the control of Lieutenant Colonel Henry Archbould and the Archbould family established Constant Spring as, according to Sibley, 'one of the largest sugar estates in the island'. In 1765 the family sold the estate to Daniel Moore who was then joined by Jasper Farmer. After the death of Moore, in 1785, Sibley stated that 'Constant Spring and Snow Hill with its slaves were sold under a decree' in Kingston for £33,000. Thereafter it was owned by George Cuthbert, the administrator of Jamaica, who mortgaged the estate to 'Alexander Lindo, a merchant, and the latter sold the mortgage debt in 1810 to his son, Abraham Alezandre Lindo, the proprietor of Kingston Pen'. During 1832, Sibley states, 'old timers remember that Constant Spring became the property of Mrs Jasper Cargill (nee Marston)' and that it was sold to Cargill by George Atkinson and Hozier who had owned the estate from 1826 to 1830. Though not mentioned as an owner by Sibley, exploring the Legacies of British Slave-ownership database, during the compensation process £5,489 5S 7D was awarded on 9 March 1836 for 293 enslaved people on the Constant Spring estate to Simon Taylor, a Kingston merchant.[51] Thereafter, according to Sibley, the next owners of the estate were the merchants 'Chrystie and Porteous and the name of the latter is still remembered in a part of the estate which was named "Porteous Pen"'. Sibley then states that it was a sugar estate in the post-emancipation period up to 1888 when it was owned by a member of the assembly Hon J. Swayers, who then sold it on to Arthur Farquharson and J. C. Farquharson. Arthur Farquharson then sold thirty-two acres of the estate, along with the manager's house, to Mr and Mrs Kemp who renamed the Manager's House as Manor House and opened it as a guest house.[52] Thus within the space of less than a century we can see the direct route of the estate buildings and land use moving from plantation slavery to tourism. The stark changing of plantations into tourist sites can be seen in the Southern states of the United States, whereby sites of horror were turned into sites of luxury, in a form of 'Great House' plantation tourism.[53]

Captain Rutty was also to play a role in Patrick's life up to the 1950s, as an employer and also as a friend. Captain Rutty, or Ronald Coy Swire Rutty, was from a colonial white elite family originally from London who settled in Jamaica during the apprenticeship period (1834–8); his family tree also exemplifies a specific genealogy of Jamaica's imperial economy moving from plantation slavery and 'apprenticeship' to post-emancipation mass agriculture to tourism within the biography of one colonial family. The history of the Rutty family was researched by Frank Rutty, the brother of Captain Rutty. This research, as far as I am aware, has not been published and was deposited as an article at the Spanish Town Jamaica Archives.[54] In addition Sibley explored the Rutty family in their 1960 *Gleaner* article.

According to Frank Rutty, from approximately 1836 to 1837 their grandparents Thomas and Elizabeth Rutty travelled to Jamaica with their four children to purchase the estate Siloa from an owner who wanted to sell and return to Britain. Siloa was in the parish of St Elizabeth. Captain Rutty's father, Joseph Waterhouse Rutty, was twelve when the family migrated and he also went into work on the sugar estates, travelling to Trelawny and working as a bookkeeper. Ronald Coy Swire Rutty was born in 1883 in Trelawny and he also 'entered the Planting line'.[55] He worked in the fruit industry as an agent for the Lanasa & Goffe S.S.Co. at Oracabessa and then Frankfort. Later on he lived in Ocho Rios and in 1914 he volunteered for the war and was sent to Egypt as lieutenant in the Second Battalion of the British West Indies Regiment. After the war he continued working in agriculture as the manager of Hopewell Estate, which was owned by the Atlantic Fruit Company. He eventually started working for the Jamaica Producers Association and when Manor House was put on sale he and his wife Hilda Franklin bought the property and opened Manor House as Manor

House Hotel.[56] Rutty's entrance into the world of tourism was thus linked to his involvement in working within the fruit trade. Additionally, Rutty continued this involvement in the fruit trade during the time he ran Manor House, working in the mango trade by growing and exporting to Britain 'Bombay mangoes'.[57] Sibley interviewed Rutty for the 1960 Gleaner article. Rutty renovated the main house and opened it as a hotel in January 1928 and 'Manor House has had under its roof many famous persons amongst them Lord Allensbury of the 1st World War, and General Sir Archibald Hunter'.[58] Sibley further reflected, 'Captain Rutty has been married twice, his second wife, in particular, was known to many of us and we realize that it was along with her, and their children that Captain Rutty has been successful in making Manor House (a part of that historic estate Constant Spring) one of the most delightful places to stay at – when in Jamaica, and for locals, a pleasurable spot for dinners, lunches, or teas, served in the best Manor House style.'[59]

During the interwar period the Manor House Hotel was advertised in various tourism brochures and newspapers, including British newspapers which advertised Jamaica's luxury tourist industry. In *The Illustrated London News'* West Indies tourism special supplement of 1936 the Manor House Hotel took out a pictorial advertisement, appearing on the same page as an advertisement for Constant Spring Hotel. Manor House was described as 'charmingly set in beautiful grounds six-hundred feet above sea-level'. Located six miles from Kingston, the hotel charged 'moderate' rates at £1 per day.[60] It was also advertised in the *Gleaner*. In one 1929 advertisement for special summer rates, the Manor House Hotel was advertised as having excellent cuisine, the majority of rooms with private baths, having its own beautiful grounds and 'adjoining Constant Spring Golf Links'.[61] Guests staying at the Manor House Hotel in the 1930s included William Lyon Mackenzie, the prime minister of Canada.[62] The Manor House Hotel also produced a number of postcards highlighting the hotel's amenities (Figures 2.1 and 2.2). These were coloured postcards printed by the Curt Teich company, described by the Lake County Discovery Museum that holds its archive as operating 'from 1898 to 1978 as the world's largest printer of view and advertising postcards'.[63] Krista A. Thompson has explored tourism in the Caribbean in relation to photography and other visual cultures, exploring the way in which the picturesque was used for propaganda. Thompson has argued that

> through the exhibition of photographs internationally, the presentation of images and people at colonial expositions, the distribution of photography books, the creation of postcard and stereo-view series, and the delivery of lantern lamp

lectures (a precursor to slide lectures) across the United States, Canada, and Britain, tourism promoters literally used photographs to project a new vision of the islands before the eyes of North American and British traveling publics.[64]

The Manor House Hotel also held functions and catered for various events and meetings, including a number for local organizations. For example, in May 1928 the hotel hosted the Empire Day Dinner for the fellows of Jamaica of the Royal Colonial Institute. The *Gleaner* reported that 'the room in which the banquet was held was very appropriately decorated for the occasion with Union Jacks and a charming red, white and blue floral effect in front of where the Governor sat'.[65] The hotel also held a number of dances and evening events. In 1926 the *Gleaner* published an article by 'Dardenella' on a dance at the Manor House Hotel. The journalist reported that 'although not as well attended as on some previous occasions, [it] was yet a very enjoyable affair' and described the pleasure in listening to the 'Pep' orchestra and the women who were present such as Mrs Rutty.[66] In December 1933, the Manor House Hotel advertised its seasonal programming which consisted of a supper dance on the evening of Saturday 30 December, costing 10s. 6d. and then two dances per month were planned for January, February and March and one dance for April 1934. The entertainment for the dances was provided by the Thunderstorm Orchestra, and evening dress was required.[67] The Thunderstorm Orchestra played in various hotels and

MANOR HOUSE HOTEL, CONSTANT SPRING, JAMAICA, B.W.I.

Figure 2.1 Postcard of Manor House Hotel by J. Arthur Dixon.

MANOR HOUSE HOTEL — CONSTANT SPRING, JAMAICA, B. W. I.

Figure 2.2 Postcard of Manor House Hotel, Constant Spring, Jamaica. C.T. Photo-Varicolor, Curt Teich & Co, Chicago, USA.

venues over Jamaica during the 1920s and 1930s. In 1923 the 'Thunderstorm Novelty Orchestra' played in the Myrtle Bank Hotel.[68] In December 1936 the Thunderstorm Orchestra, under the direction of Sidney Gruchy, played at a dance organized by the Parish Church taking place at the Royal Jamaica Yacht Club, where they played 'rumbas and native "shay-shay" numbers.'[69] The Thunderstorm Orchestra had previously played at Manor House. In 1926 they held an anniversary dance at Manor House Hotel for the Orchestra and on 24 October 1931 the *Gleaner* reported that 'the Thunderstorm Anniversary Dance at Manor House next Saturday night promises to be a very enjoyable and well patronised affair.'[70]

The story of the interwar luxury tourist industry in Kingston can only be partially recreated through newspapers and adverts, which, on the surface at least, provides an elite reading of the hotels. So what was the industry like for Jamaicans who worked within it and lived their lives in its presence, specifically Jamaicans of African heritage such as Patrick? What experiences did Jamaicans have of working at the functions and dances just described or of serving the various European guests who stayed at the hotel? Sources such as Patrick's letters documenting his hotel work in the 1950s, as explored in later chapters of this book, are of great importance in understanding the experiences of working-class Jamaican life and Jamaican tourism.

Tourism and protest in 1930s Kingston

The late 1930s strikes and protests in Jamaica took place in industries including tourism. For example, a small strike by hotel staff at the Constant Spring Hotel, the hotel next to Manor House Hotel took place on 31 December 1938.[71] The mid-to-late 1930s strikes throughout the Caribbean were carried out to protest the economic, social and political abuses which restricted the lives of the population. The economic, social and educational situation in Jamaica was highly skewed against the lives of black Jamaicans. Working-class Jamaicans did not have an electoral say in local or national politics. Since 1866, in the aftermath of the Morant Bay Rebellion of 1865, Jamaica had Crown Colony rule whereby political power was given back to the governor. As Colin A. Palmer has explored, the 1866 Order in Council 'created a single-chamber Legislative Council consisting of six official members and an equal number of unofficial ones, all appointed by the governor.'[72] A further order in council in 1884 allowed for nine members of the Council to be elected and the 1895 Constitution stated that the Council should be controlled by the governor and include 'five ex officio members, no more than ten members appointed by the governor, and fourteen elected members.'[73] The majority of the population could not vote. As Roxanne S. Watson states, 'In 1935, only 66,000 people (approximately 7 per cent of the voter-age population) met the £40-per-year income or 10d.-per-annum tax franchise threshold.'[74]

In 1938 Jamaicans, including agricultural workers, dockworkers and street cleaners, carried out strikes and protests demanding better pay and conditions. These strikes and collective organizing by working-class Jamaicans influenced and occurred during the establishment of the organized trade union movement in Jamaica.[75] As a result of these actions, the pre-existing political activism in Jamaica culminated in, for example, the development of political parties led by Norman Manley and Alexander Bustamante. These strikes were part of a larger Caribbean-wide movement of social and political protest. During the 1930s, in light of these various protests and strikes, along with the establishment of the trade union movement, there was some official examination of social and economic conditions of Jamaicans, for example, in the form of social surveys, trade union investigations, reports and the official enquiry known as the Moyne Commission inquiry.[76] Two surveys undertaken on the conditions of the urban and rural poor in Jamaica in 1938 were led by members of Jamaica Welfare Ltd. In the introduction to the 1990 publication of the surveys by the Social History

Project, Claus F. Stolberg states that 'the detailed sociological fieldwork for the surveys was carried out immediately after the severe social unrest in May and June 1938' and that both surveys were filed as 'appendices of a Memorandum of Evidence on behalf of Jamaica Welfare Ltd. for the sittings of the West India Royal Commission in Jamaica which were held publicly during November and early December 1938 at the Constant Spring Hotel "near Kingston".[77] The social surveys were conducted by teams of, Stolberg states, 'investigators, volunteers, who were not specifically trained for their task but, who were apparently quite familiar with the economic and social plight of the urban and rural poor in Jamaica.[78] Were hotel workers such as Patrick mentioned in these reports or interviewed in the process of the research collecting? And if so, what according to these surveys were the conditions and experiences of the hotel workers during this time? The tourist trade is briefly mentioned in the Moyne Commission report, mainly in chapters 2 and 13. The former chapter describes the growth of the trade in Jamaica, Barbados and Trinidad stating that 'it affords in various ways a considerable amount of employment, though this is mainly, like the traffic itself, of a highly seasonal character.[79] The specific experiences and working conditions of those employed in the hotel trade was not, however, focused on in Moyne's report, even though their headquarters, when carrying out the commission, was the Constant Spring Hotel, the site of the hotel labour strike which took place on 31 December 1938, during the time the commission was meeting.

Those working in the tourism industry would have worked, like Patrick, not only as valets but also in a wide range of other jobs within the industry. In Patrick's case he acted as personal valet to annual hotel guests such as Archibald Hunter. The history and experiences of these types of valets in Britain are explored in the next chapter. Within early-twentieth-century Jamaica personal valets worked not only within the newly formed tourist industry but also within rich, elite Jamaican's homes. Several advertisements for valets or gentlemen's valets appear in the *Gleaner* during the 1930s – perhaps one of them was Patrick's during the period of time he briefly returned to Jamaica in 1937–8. For example, adverts placed in the 'Domestic – (Male)' section of the 'Position Wanted' column in the *Gleaner* during January and February 1938 included various advertisements for those seeking valet positions. One man placed an advertisement stating a 'young man requires position as a gentleman's valet; has had years of experience and is also willing to travel.[80] Another man, George Kirvin, placed an advertisement seeking a position as a waiter, a 'gentleman's valet' or a wine steward, either in a private home or hotel.[81] Another man, advertising himself as a young, intelligent man with good testimonials, sought a position with a lady or a gentleman as a waiter, valet, storeman or shopkeeper.[82] Another man, describing himself as a decent young fellow from the country, sought a position as a gentlemen's valet or as a gardener who could 'make himself generally useful in a home'.[83]

Like in agriculture, tourism's profits were not shared equally among the majority of Jamaicans and tourism relied on the continuation of pre-existing forms of racism and exploitative labour. Tourism during the interwar period also suffered from Jamaica's imperial economic racism whereby black Jamaicans were most likely to work in service jobs within the industry and not management and ownership. Polly Pattullo has explored the continued economic racially based exploitation in modern-day tourism, with roots in enslavement stating 'indeed, tourism in its early days rekindled memories of slavery. For a start, the best jobs in Jamaican hotels were reserved for white Americans, while black Jamaicans were left with the most menial tasks.'[84] Pattullo also focuses on the service aspects of the tourist industry, including the racism experienced by serving staff, the white tourist privilege and the subservient way in which hotel staff were viewed and treated. Hilary Beckles explored this history in Barbados looking at the racism inherent in the tourist industry and described it as the 'new plantocracy'.[85]

Frank F. Taylor states, 'The color question had always hung over Jamaica, but with the growth of tourism it festered further, for the industry revitalized distinctions of color that had faded with the widespread planter destitution since Emancipation.'[86] Both black travellers and workers in Jamaica's hotel industry experienced racism. Taylor states that before the First World War there was not too much difficulty for black Jamaicans to travel from New York to Jamaica.

> In the post–World War I years, however, the situation had changed dramatically, in that the United Fruit Company came to exercise a virtual monopoly over the passenger service between the city of New York and Jamaican ports. With the growth in popularity of the Caribbean cruise trip among Americans, it became exceedingly difficult for black Jamaicans to secure reasonably humane treatment on ships belonging to the company.[87]

The case study of the Myrtle Bank Hotel provides one example of this racism at play, whereby white American tourists would influence the exporting of US-style racism, contributing to Jamaica's pre-existing racial divisions to promote an unofficial colour bar within elite hotels. Krista Thompson has explored the importance of Myrtle Bank Hotel within the development of Jamaica's elite tourism. The hotel was built in 1870 when James Gall bought a property on the Kingston waterfront where he constructed a sanatorium for 'invalids' and tourists, calling it Myrtle Bank after the name of family property in Edinburgh.[88] As David Howard states, 'During much of the nineteenth and twentieth centuries, the Myrtle Bank Hotel on East Street, and to a lesser extent, the South Camp Road Hotel, were the mainstays of colonial and commercial gentility.'[89] Myrtle Bank developed into an elite, racialized hotel catering for white tourists. In the newspaper *Public Opinion*, black Jamaican feminist, writer and social worker Amy Bailey protested the racism permeating Jamaican society. Krista Thompson states, 'Spaces of tourist occupation, the very visible centers of social distinction for tourists and white elites, and especially the Myrtle Bank Hotel provided places where the issues of race, skin colour, and class discrimination could be articulated and, ultimately, ... contested.'[90]

Apart from the Constant Spring Hotel strike, what was the nature of hotel workers' protest and trade union activity? Trade Union activity and protest campaigning reveals a lot about the conditions of hotels, the experiences of hotel staff and their work in trying to improve their situation. In 1937 the Jamaica Hotel Employees' Association was established. The Association met in downtown Kingston and, in June 1938, during the period of strikes and protests, members of the Association held a meeting where they expressed their grievances and shared their experiences. The *Gleaner* reported that those at the meeting spoke about the low wages and long hours with little or no overtime pay. They also spoke against the discrimination they experienced with regard to pay, that 'cooks were often imported from abroad and placed over the heads of natives who knew their jobs much better, these importees being paid sometimes £14 14 – against £3 3 – paid to natives'. Those attending the meeting also included 'waiters, bar-tenders, pantrymen, bell boys, bus boys, porters, laundry maids, housemen, doormen, checkers and others' who 'all aired their grievances'. Some hotels paid just 18s. a week with no payment for overtime work and some speakers mentioned that there were hotels paying just 8/- a week to waiters. At another hotel the waiters worked fifteen hours a day and often worked until 3 am and had to find their own transportation home. The *Gleaner* further reported that 'in addition to their regular duties, maids at one hotel had to scrub the floor and were paid only 8 – and 10 – a week, one speaker declared, and waiters there worked until 2 am and got no overtime pay'. Those at the meeting organized a deputation of five members to bring their grievances to the Conciliation Board, with recommendations for increases in pay and overtime pay.[91]

Patrick and the hotel industry

Did Patrick take part in any strike or protest action or would he have been sympathetic? There is no evidence that he took part in industrial disputes and by March 1938 he had left Jamaica, but at a later time in his life, he certainly expressed opposition to colonial exploitation of resources after he returned to Jamaica in 1945. Again we only hear of his hotel working life during the 1930s through the *Gleaner* article, which was a newspaper led by Jamaican elites. Although Patrick did not directly critique the industry, his experiences in hotel work in the 1950s, described in his letters to Duncan, attest to the harsh nature of the industry with short-term, unreliable and seasonal work. More research, particularly by carrying out oral histories, will uncover the many experiences of people who worked in the hotel industry of the mid-twentieth century.

Many questions arise when exploring Patrick's hotel experiences. What were Patrick's experiences of the industry in the 1930s in relation to emotional connections, friendships, sex, romance and relationships? Did Patrick enjoy aspects of his experiences working in hotels? How did Patrick relate to other valets and domestic workers and did he make friends within the industry? How did Patrick meet Captain Rutty and become employed at Manor House Hotel? Perhaps he replied to an advertisement. Alternatively, perhaps Patrick's father knew Captain Rutty because of their military careers. Though it was not a career Patrick wanted to carry out long term, he seemed to have made lifelong friends with Captain Rutty. Again these are questions to which the answers are currently not known, but I hope to be able to answer.

Patrick's valet work included valeting for special guests of Rutty's such as Sir Archibald Hunter. Hunter represents one type of tourist coming to Jamaica during this time, elite British aristocrats and British elites with imperialist backgrounds. Hunter's presence in Jamaica was often mentioned in the press. For example, in October 1935 the *Gleaner* reported 'Back with us for a vacation of several months are General Sir Archibald Hunter, G.C.B., G.C.V.O., D.S.O., and Mrs Sinclair Westcott, who will be staying at the Manor House Hotel.'[92] In a June 1936 edition of the *Gleaner* they reported the death of Hunter at age 79, stating 'General Sir Archibald Hunter left Jamaica an ailing man in the spring of this year; most of his friends in this island felt that they would never see him here again.' His health improved and he visited Jamaica again but then fell ill and 'they dug his grave at Up Park Camp so that everything should be prepared and in good order'. But, as the *Gleaner* described 'the hour of the old warrior was not yet come' and it was 'not until Saturday, at the age of seventy-nine, did he pass away at last'.[93]

Friendship, sexuality and queer interwar Jamaica

Who did Patrick socialize with at work and what friendships and relationships were formed at this time in his life? It is difficult to know about the intimate and personal history relating to Patrick when aged twenty-one before he migrated to Wales in 1937. Patrick did not mention friends and family or events relating to this period of life in later letters to Duncan Grant. Did he have sexual relationships, form romances or forge friendships with other valets, hotel workers or guests? Did he explore his queer sexuality while in Jamaica before his travels abroad? In relation to queer identity and the tourist industry, working in industries such as tourism could enable people to socialize and form romantic and sexual relationships away from the enclosed space of living in small communities. Similar to Matt Houlbrook's investigation of London's queer spaces in the early twentieth century, in the Caribbean domestic arrangements in spaces such as hotels undoubtedly provided opportunities for queer romance and sex. Newspaper reports occasionally give information on staff living arrangements in hotels, including the Manor House Hotel. In 1934 a court case was heard relating to a woman, Christa Love, staying at Manor House Hotel without authorization. The judge, according to the *Gleaner*, 'did not feel he could convict Love for vagrancy and dismissed her'. In the course of the testimony, two men who were gardeners at the hotel, Amos Martin and Arnold Wilmot, provided a different testimony on who invited the woman to stay in the hotel. The living arrangements and information on some of the staff members was also given in the report, including that both men, Martin and Wilmot, occupied the same room.[94] Did most of the staff at Manor House share rooms? Perhaps Patrick had relationships while working at Manor House. Perhaps he formed homosocial bonds with other male workers.

In recent years, there have been a small number of significant publications on the personal life stories and identities of queer peoples of various identities in the Caribbean. Makeda Silvera's 1991 essay on Jamaican queer women in *Piece of My Heart: A Lesbian of Colour Anthology* is a poignant and powerful essay on Silvera's experiences and identity as a lesbian Jamaican, exploring family histories, homophobia, silences and previously untold stories of queer Jamaican women's lives from the 1920s onwards.[95] In 1997 Rosamund Elwin edited *Tongues on Fire: Caribbean Lesbian Lives and Stories*, a work which shared various stories from Caribbean queer women.[96] In 2004 Kamala Kempadoo published a work exploring sexuality in the Caribbean, including lesbian and gay sexuality.[97] More recently, in 2014 Kofi Omoniyi Sylvanus Campbell published *The Queer Caribbean Speaks: Interviews with Writers, Artists, and Activists*, a work 'born out of', Campbell states, 'the near-silence surrounding the lives of queer Caribbean citizens'.[98] There have additionally been works exploring queerness in Caribbean literature and publishing new works on queer Caribbean prose, poetry and history. Thomas Glave's significant works include the 2008 edited collection 'Our Caribbean: A Gathering of Lesbian and Gay Writing from the Antilles'. This work is particularly important in its documenting and publishing of a wide range of articulations of Caribbean queer identity and experience, including poetry, memoirs, fiction and non-fiction from across the Caribbean.[99] The significant and insightful work of Nadia Ellis who has explored various literary, historical and artistic articulations and manifestations of the Queer Black diaspora is of great relevance to Patrick's life.[100]

Grass-roots activists in Jamaica and the diaspora have been at the forefront of excavating and documenting experiences of queer people in Jamaican and wider Caribbean life, including archiving the campaigning work of human rights LGBT organizations in the Caribbean. The archive of materials created as part of the group Gay Freedom Movement in Jamaica (GFM), established in 1974, preserved by Larry Chang and the Jamaica Forum for Lesbians, All-sexuals and Gays (JFLAG) has recently been digitized and made available through the Digital Library of the Caribbean.[101]

However, in terms of historical examinations of the queer Caribbean there has not been (as far as my research has uncovered) a detailed focus on the experiences of everyday queer Caribbean people of the 1930s and 1940s. In relation to early-twentieth-century history and historiography there is much more to explore and document, particularly in relation to everyday histories and memories. Exploring life histories such as Patrick's, as well as sources such as newspaper articles, can allow us to understand how queer life in the Caribbean was lived including how colonial Jamaican authorities viewed and criminalized queer people. It also serves to highlight the neglected history of Caribbean queer people of African heritage.

Details on Patrick's life as a queer man in post-war Jamaica can be found later on in the book. Along with official documents, newspaper accounts are important for exploring queer histories, by, for example, reading against the grain of reports of criminal cases to bring to the fore experiences of queer lives and reading along the grain for exploring the ways in which queer people were criminalized. As Alison Oram's research has shown, interwar British tabloids such as *The News of the World* and *The People* reported salaciously on British trials or stories involving queer women.[102] In a Jamaican context, the *Gleaner* occasionally reported on or alluded to criminal convictions and trials involving queer Jamaicans and stories relating to queer people living in or visiting Jamaica. One case in the 1930s highlights the difficulty in exploring newspaper reports on queer lives. The preliminary examination trial and court trial during 1933 of two men, Frederick and Joseph, who were found guilty of committing an 'unnatural offence', was reported in the *Gleaner*, but the case was discussed without going into any details or referencing any of the defendants' testimony (something not done with other court cases referred to in this newspaper at the time, where testimony relating to, for example larceny, would often be explored and quoted at length).[103]

Other cases involving 'unnatural offences' were reported but it is difficult to know if these 'offences' relate to men having sex with one another. However, it is possible to find cases reported which definitely relate to queer peoples being prosecuted. One 1938 case, in which slightly more information is given in the newspaper, was also reported as an 'unnatural offence'. Gerald, described in the *Gleaner* as 'formerly an efficient newspaper reporter with a real sense of public duty', was convicted in the St James Circuit Court in the tourist area of Montego Bay to twelve months' hard labour. The article went on to state that 'the facts of the case were extremely objectionable' and involved the defendant and another man 'committing of an unnatural offence at a hotel in the town', with the police 'who got information as to what was happening' setting 'a trap'. Gerald's defence lawyer Dickson said that he served in the 'Great War' attached to the Medical Department of the United States Army but was disabled in the line of duty, was possibly shell-shocked, suffered from apoplexy, described as a 'slight form of insanity', was in poor health and was drunk on the evening. Dickson also stated that he was married and asked the judge to take these facts into consideration and 'pass as lenient a sentence as possible, consistent with His Honour's duty to the community'. Inspector Harvey described the defendant as hard-working but neurotic and the newspaper reported (I believe summarizing Harvey's comments) that 'it was uncertain where [he] had contracted the habit which was prevalent among the better classes here. [He] was a British subject and his character otherwise was excellent.' When passing the sentence, the judge reported on Gerald's character and service, that he hoped to see the prisoner reform and that he required physical and mental medical aid, which he would be able to receive in prison.[104]

This case highlights several important themes, including how hotels could potentially be not only a space of freedom for queer peoples but also a space subject to surveillance by the police and by authorities and a space used for entrapment. It also highlights how same-sex attraction was characterized by the paper as an upper-class phenomenon, despite the instances of non-elites being tried for 'unnatural offences' as described in the *Gleaner*. Additionally, it highlights how medical health was utilized as a legal defence. Despite giving more information on this case than other reports found during this period, the 'unnatural offence' is always alluded to. Through newspaper accounts it is sometimes difficult to explore fully these cases, and even more difficult to find evidence on the lives and experiences of interwar gay, bisexual and queer people of African Jamaican heritage from their own perspective.

Significantly, memoirs and letters are important for showing the every-day lived experiences of queer Caribbean peoples. Again these letters and other writings are explored in more depth in later chapters of this book. As mentioned in Chapter 1, Claude McKay was a queer Jamaican man in the early twentieth century. McKay was a poet, writer and activist, who, before migrating and living in the United States, Europe and North Africa, published significant books of poetry in Jamaica. Some of these poems record and testify to his queer bisexual sexuality and identity and his feelings of love and romance for a possible colleague of his when serving in the police force in Kingston.[105] Richie Riley was a queer black Jamaican man who was friends with Patrick towards the end of his life. Richie Riley and Patrick Nelson knew each other for some time and perhaps met in Jamaica in the 1930s. Riley was living in Jamaica in the 1930s where he performed ballet in a company with another queer black Jamaican man Berto Pasuka. Riley's post-war London experiences, including their 1946 co-founding of *Les Ballets Nègres*, are explored later in the book. Writing on the background of this ballet company, Keith Watson explores the first collaboration between Riley and Pasuka in Jamaica before they both migrated, stating that 'the history of *Les Ballets Nègres* actually dates back to 1931, when the young Riley and another young Jamaican, Berto Pasuka, got caught up in the excitement generated by Marcus Garvey's plans for a spectacular show to celebrate the opening of an amusement park in Kingston. The show was short-lived, but Riley and Pasuka had caught the dance bug (italics added)'.[106] In an oral history interview with the Black Cultural Archives, Riley reflected on his growing up and history within performance.[107] Riley was born in Kingston, Jamaica. He lived with his parents in Cuba for a while when he was a child and returned from Cuba to go to school in Jamaica. His father worked at a sugar mill in Florida, Cuba. He recalled that he always had an interest in theatre and when Marcus Garvey decided to create the Eloise Park amusement centre and advertised for young people to join his dance company, Riley went along with a friend of his (probably Pasuka). Though the company folded, they then went on to form their own company. Riley recalled 'We toured the island, and we had shows at Ward Theatre in Kingston, and shows everywhere.'[108]

References to queer life in 1930s Jamaica appear in an article in a 1938 edition of *Public Opinion* on the hotel industry. In the column 'The Philosopher Views the Passing Show' there is a discussion on tourism and 'vice' stating 'homosexuality is not a pretty trait. Montego Bay, which has based its economy largely on the tourist trade, has the tourist traffic to thank for the epidemic of this particular vice.'[109] By reading against the grain of the article's viewing homosexuality as a 'vice' and its linking of same-sex attraction and experiences to white tourists, perhaps the article points towards the existence of queer life in interwar hotel resorts, such as the resort where Patrick lived and worked and the Montego Bay hotel in the case described in the *Gleaner*.

During the late 1920s and 1930s, with knowledge of the work of sexologists and the British publication and suppression of books such as Radclyffe Hall's 1928 *The Well of Loneliness*, public discussion of homosexuality took place in a range of arenas within Britain and also in Jamaica. The British trial for obscenity against Hall's book was reported in the *Gleaner*. On 4 January 1929 the newspaper reported Radclyffe Hall's appeal against the Bow Street magistrate's decision to ban the publication. The article includes a description of the court proceedings with no journalistic viewpoints or opinion given on the book.[110] By August 1929 *The Well of Loneliness* became available for Jamaican audiences to read. On 10 August 1929 'Click' in the 'Snapshots' section of the paper reported that 'at last *The Well of Loneliness* has trickled to Jamaica, and I have been fortunate enough to read a copy of this much talked of book. The one strong feeling this book arouses in us is the conviction that the author herself is an invert. It is perfectly amazing the psychological details into which Radclyffe Hall carries us (italics added)' and concludes by stating 'I have read works far more detrimental to public morals and I quite fail to see

Sir William Joyson Hicks' reason for asking for its withdrawal.'[111] In 1937 E.C. of the *Gleaner* reviewed *The Well of Loneliness* and *Lady Chatterley's Lover*, stating that both 'have outlived their malodorous reputations' and each is 'now available for mass reading in cheap editions'. Of the Well of Loneliness the reviewer stated

> Written obviously with the most sincere intentions, it is an honest study of a girl on the strange borderline of sexual division, its fault being that because of the extremely sympathetic attitude of the author it lapses into a sentimentality that offends far more than its theme. Affronted England promptly forbade the supposedly mature and intelligent people who compose her adult population to read it. At the same time, an extremely clever book by Compton Mackenzie entitled *Extraordinary Women* was published and sold freely. This was a remarkably well-informed and exceedingly cynical novel on precisely the same theme, much more dangerous, in spite of its suave air of ridiculing the whole of the society it mirrored, than the sentimental blatherings of *The Well of Loneliness*, because of the alluring flavour of sophistication it gave to the strange practices of its characters (italics added).[112]

It is not known to the author of this book how many copies of *The Well of Loneliness* and *Extraordinary Women* were sold in Jamaica and if they were available at different areas of the country or just in Kingston.

Public discussion on homosexuality took place in a Jamaican context in late 1937, which was documented in the *Gleaner*. On 8 November 1937 the newspaper advertised a lecture open to the public which was due to take place the day afterwards on the subject of homosexuality given by Dr Royes and hosted by the Readers and Writers Club at 4 Central Avenue, Kingston Gardens.[113] On 2 December 1937 the *Gleaner's* report on the meeting had the headline 'Interesting Lecture by Dr Ken. Royes. Speaks on Homosexuality to Large Gathering at Readers and Writers Club. The Tragedy of It'. Mentioning both *The Well of Loneliness and Extraordinary Women*, the article stated that 'a capacity audience of local literati, desirous of hearing medical explanation of the theme dealt with in the novels', attended the meeting. It then stated that 'abnormal sex was also the central motif of "The Green Bay Tree", a sensational play produced in London.' After exploring homosexuality in history and literature, referencing ancient Greece, Royes went on to give a lecture focusing on an 'explanation of cell growth and division', arguing, according to the article, that the accepted cause of natural homosexual instincts was that in the early stages of life, evidences of the attributes of both sexes were discernible. It was not necessary to deal with the causes of sex determination: much controversy surrounded this and no infallible arguments, supported by proofs, had been brought forward in support of the various theories advanced by scientists. However, it was known, without doubt, that in some very rare instances, attributes of both sexes persisted.[114]

Kenneth Royes was a medical doctor based in Jamaica. Frederick W. Hickling has reflected in a recent publication on the history of psychiatry in Jamaica and his role developing it from a postcolonial perspective. Working at Bellevue Mental Hospital during the time Kenneth Royes was there, Hickling recalled that he challenged their use of unmodified electroconvulsive therapy and when he became the senior medical officer there he banned the use of electroshock treatment. He stated that Ken Royes, who was his mentor during this time, was born in Kingston, studied at the Wolmer's Boys School and then medicine at Oxford as a Rhodes scholar and 'had introduced many revolutionary psychiatric practices during his period as a psychiatrist at the Bellevue Mental Hospital, including occupational therapy and the use of social workers'.[115] This November 1937 event and the *Gleaner* article are important in their revealing of an example of the way in which homosexuality was discussed in public forums in 1930s Jamaica. Patrick was travelling back to Jamaica during Royes' event, having left Wales on 1 November 1937. Could he have read the *Gleaner* article on the event and, if so, how might he have interpreted the discussion? Other questions arise from reading this article. Did more events discussing issues relating to sexuality and gender take place in interwar Jamaica? How did this event influence those attending in their understanding of and experiences of sexuality?

These examples provide snippets of information but much more work needs to be carried out on exploring sexuality in 1930s Jamaica, and the diverse experiences of Jamaican queer men of African heritage such as Patrick. After staying at the Manor House for five years, Patrick travelled to Wales to embark on a new career in Britain, continuing his work in service and his work for the British aristocracy, but working in one of the large British aristocratic estates. The next chapter explores his experiences in Wales working as a 'gentleman's servant', contextualizing his experiences within larger histories concerning domestic service, race, class, employment and sexuality.

Patrick in Interwar Wales:
Race, Sexuality and Employment

Patrick migrated to Britain to work as a domestic member of staff within a private household. Exploring a range of archival sources such as the photographic and paper records of the Penrhos family estate, along with contemporary newspapers and Patrick's letters, this chapter reflects on Patrick's memories and experiences of migrating and living in Britain, his life as a valet in the domain of the British elite, and the life experiences he had or might have had as a queer black domestic servant in rural Wales. It also investigates and documents the life story of perhaps a one-time lover as well as the social politics of domestic service, queer identity, life in interwar Penrhos and the black presence in Wales.

As explored in the introduction to the book, the archival sources relating to Patrick's time in Wales which are available to me at the time of writing this book are sparse, and this chapter explores Patrick's life in context but with much information about his day-to-day experiences currently unknown. This book does not attempt to recreate Patrick's life in its minute and complete detail but instead it focuses on what the archive tells us and what it does not tell us about Patrick's experiences of life in Britain and contextualizes Patrick's life experiences (and possible experiences) within its broader historical context.

Patrick and Penrhos

As the 1937 *Gleaner* article reported, Patrick migrated to Wales to be a valet in the service of the British elite. Though the *Gleaner* journalist stated he was going to work for a 'Lord Stanley', he went to work in the household of Lyulph Victor Henry Owen Stanley (L.V.H.O. Stanley), Lord Stanley of Alderley's younger brother, probably being employed directly by their mother Lady Stanley who also resided at Penrhos.[1] Passenger returns list that Patrick travelled on the

SS *Dalia*, a Fyffe Lines steamship first class from Jamaica to Liverpool, arrived on 13 April 1937. He gave his proposed address in the passenger return as Penrhos, Holyhead, North Wales, and the profession he listed was a valet.[2] Although this work was in a private domestic residence, this type of employment would have been familiar to Patrick because of his work as a hotel valet at the Manor House Hotel.

Penrhos estate in North Wales was one of the main historical residences of the Stanley of Alderley family, and from the early 1930s it became home to Lyulph Victor Henry Owen Stanley, who on his twenty-first birthday in late 1936 inherited it from his father Arthur Lyulph, the fifth Baron Stanley of Alderley (Figure 3.1). This inheritance was put into place with his father's death in 1931, and Lyulph Stanley lived there with his mother and sisters both before and after he inherited it.[3] Lyulph was born in Australia in 1915, while his father was governor general of Victoria.[4] After his father's death, Edward John, Lyulph's older brother, inherited the titles of Baron Stanley and Lord Sheffield and also inherited the main and larger family estate of Alderley Park in Cheshire. When Lyulph's brother Lord Stanley sold the Cheshire estate in the 1930s, the *Manchester Guardian* reported that 'the estate comprises Alderley Hall and park, the home of the Stanleys of Alderley for nearly five centuries; several thousand acres of pasture, arable land, and woods, eighty farmsteads, and the townships of Nether and Over Alderley'.[5] Penrhos estate was built and originally owned by the Welsh Owen family and after Margaret Owen married Sir John Thomas Stanley of Alderley in 1763, the Penrhos estate became part of the Stanley family estate.[6]

In addition to his brother Edward (who in 1931 became the sixth Lord Stanley of Alderley), Lyulph had three sisters: Pamela, Victoria and Adelaide. Lyulph's mother Margaret Stanley and sister Victoria also lived at Penrhos during the time of Patrick's arrival in 1937, and probably as Lyulph was still a young man Margaret continued to run the household instead of Lyulph. In a January 1937 shipping return of a journey from New York to Liverpool, Lyulph, his sister Victoria, his mother Margaret (Lady Stanley) and Winifred Hills, a maid, all listed their residence as Penrhos, Holyhead.[7]

Various members of the wider Stanley family had an involvement with social reform. The previous generation of Stanleys (including Lyulph's paternal grandfather Edward Lyulph Stanley later shortened to E. Lyulph Stanley) comprised family members involved in education, social reform, religion and politics.[8] Alan W. Jones, who explored the life of E. Lyulph, states that the Stanleys, 'though a cadet branch of no great national moment, shared a common ancestor

Figure 3.1 Photograph of Penrhos Holyhead, Anglesey Archives, WSD/541/12.

with the Earls of Derby, and could trace their lineage back to the twelfth century at least. They had farmed their estates at Alderley in Cheshire for centuries, and had acquired a baronetcy at the Restoration, and, a week before Lyulph's birth, the title Baron Stanley of Alderley.'[9] E. Lyulph's father was a Whig politician, working as a secretary for Lord Durham and from 1835 to 1841 worked in Lord Melbourne's government as patronage secretary to the Treasury.[10] E. Lyulph studied at Eton and Balliol College, Oxford, from 1857. At Oxford he was involved in debating. His politics were liberal and by 1859 he was a supporter of universal suffrage.[11] E. Lyulph was elected a fellow at Balliol, trained in law and eventually became a significant figure in educational reform. E. Lyulph's sister Blanche married the Earl of Airlie (descendants of this family include Clementine Churchill and the Mitfords) and E. Lyulph's sister Kate married Lord Amberley and her children included Bertrand Russell. E. Lyulph was therefore uncle to philosopher Bertrand Russell, and Russell stayed in Penrhos on occasions with the family.[12] Maude Stanley, an older sister of E. Lyulph and Kate, was heavily involved in welfare and health and founded girls' clubs.[13] E. Lyulph's wife, and Lyulph's grandmother, Mary Katherine Stanley, formerly Bell, was born in 1848 in Newcastle. Her father was Sir Lothian Bell, a steel magnate and her mother Margaret Pattinson. Mary Katherine was the aunt of Gertrude Bell, imperial archaeologist and administrator in the Middle East. Mary Katherine married E. Lyulph in 1873.[14]

Lyulph's father, Arthur Lyulph, was born in 1875, the eldest child of six. He also went to Oxford and in 1902 entered the Bar at the Inner Temple. He started a career in politics in 1906 before being appointed governor of Victoria, Australia, in 1913. He remained governor until 1921 and then returned to Britain. He was a member of the Manchester Reform Club, president of the Knutsford Liberal Association and president of the North-Western Free Trade Union.[15] Lyulph's mother Margaret Evelyn Stanley was born Margaret Evelyn Evans Gordon in approximately 1876. Her father was Henry Evans Gordon and mother was May Sartoris. Margaret Stanley's paternal uncle was the well-known right-wing politician, William Evans Gordon, who was instrumental in fostering anti-alien bigotry and legislation targeting Jewish migrants in the early twentieth century.[16]

In January 1937 the *Holyhead and Anglesey Mail* reported on Lyulph's twenty-first birthday celebrations which occurred during autumn 1936, stating 'The Hon. Lyulph Stanley, son of Margaret Lady Stanley and of the late Lord Stanley of Alderley, came of age during the autumn, the celebrations being largely attended at Penrhos, when presentations were made on behalf of the tenantry, etc.'[17] In an airport manifest document of March 1937, Lyulph was described as being five feet eleven inches in height, fair complexion, with light hair and green eyes.[18] Lyulph Stanley was a young man of twenty-one when Patrick went to work on the Penrhos estate in April 1937, as was Patrick. Perhaps his 'coming of age', representing coming into adulthood, was why he employed a gentleman's servant. The similarities between Patrick and Lyulph due to their age and their sexuality provides a comparative, but their class, racialized identity, migration and family backgrounds meant that they were worlds apart in relation to experiences involving economic and social privilege and employment security. Like Patrick, Lyulph Stanley was a queer man. Both Stanley family biographies, published by family members, mention that Lyulph was gay. In the 1998 biography of the wider Stanley family, the author Peter E. Stanley wrote about Lyulph using homophobic language, stating that 'in order to indulge in his bizarre habits, he had to get out of the country' and so sold the Penrhos estate in 1948.[19]

After inheriting the estate from his father, Lyulph took an interest in farm management and studied farming practices in both Canada and in Jamaica, albeit from the elitist perspective of a landowner. When Patrick arrived in Wales, Lyulph was abroad, first in Jamaica and then in the United States. Arriving in Jamaica on the Royal Netherlands Steamship Company's ship *Costa Rica* on 15 March 1937, Lyulph no doubt met Patrick for the first time in Kingston, before Patrick's departure for Penrhos in April 1937.[20] From Jamaica Lyulph flew to Miami, Florida arriving on 25 March 1937 and went on to stay in New York at the Waldorf-Astoria Hotel.[21] He stayed abroad until 20 April that year, when he disembarked at Southampton on the *Queen Mary*, a Cunard White Star liner travelling from New York.[22] The *Gleaner* announced Lyulph's March 1937 arrival in Jamaica stating, 'The Honourable Lyulph Stanley, second son of Lady Stanley and the late Lord Stanley of Alderley, and brother of the present Lord Stanley, is on his first visit to this country. He is intensely interested in farming, and as a matter of fact, has his own farm at Penrhoss [*sic*], Anglesey, where he resides. His purpose in coming to Jamaica is to study the agricultural conditions, because from all sources he has heard the highest recommendation of Jamaica. His aunt, the Honourable Mrs Arthur Henley, who spent some time in the island last year, spoke very highly of Jamaica and the people here and advised him to take the trip. He will stay in Montego Bay.'[23]

Lyulph's relationship with Jamaica would continue post-war. Patrick did not mention Lyulph in his letters sent from Jamaica after the war but evidence from newspaper sources and passenger returns shows that Lyulph visited Jamaica for months at a time and was interviewed in the *Gleaner* on subjects including the debates around West Indian Federation. His knowledge of Jamaican politics and agriculture was nevertheless very much from the perspective of an elite visitor. However, he was to make several anti-racist points on racism in the United States and Jamaica. During a visit in 1948 Stanley expressed pleasure 'to see coloured Jamaicans now frequenting such places as the Myrtle Bank Hotel, where I didn't see them when I was here before' and that it was 'a good thing for the white visitors, not merely because Jamaica belongs to the Jamaicans, but because it is easy to see that they are playing their part creditably in all social aspects of life in the Island, and are often an example in behaviour to many English and American visitors' and that 'I take particular note of this development here, after having lived in America for some while, and observing a colour prejudice which is something without reason'.[24]

Patrick's time at Penrhos was short-lived as he returned briefly to Jamaica in November 1937, and when he returned to Britain in early 1938 he lived in Bristol and London. Whether his stay in Wales was always intended to be short or whether he returned for other reasons is not known, but possibly Patrick's return to Jamaica was for personal reasons. In 1945 after he had been repatriated to Britain from the POW camps, Patrick wrote to Duncan Grant of a falling out he had with Lyulph and it appears that, before his relationship with Duncan, he might have had a brief romance or sexual relationship with Lyulph. Patrick wrote to Duncan that he thought he would be pleased he had made friends with L. O. Stanley after nine years of malice, that he had visited the admiralty, had a long chat with him and would be seeing him that weekend, but that Lady Stanley could not know. He wrote that 'as Sailor, and Soldier we have to be friends the future may bring us closer together' but 'only I have you now and hardly think I will ever find a friend who has been to me in deed and in need like you so I'm afraid I will never give you up and I'm sure you love me too'.[25]

During the Second World War, Lyulph Stanley served in the admiralty, hence Patrick's reference to visiting the admiralty and to sailor and soldier. From Patrick's description of their meeting in this letter, it appears perhaps Lady Stanley found out about the love affair and perhaps he was made to leave his employment (though Patrick and Lady Stanley did continue an occasional friendship after the war). Having a sexual or romantic relationship with an employer (or the son of an employer if Patrick was directly employed by Lady Stanley) with the power dynamics of employer–employee at play meant that Patrick's job and home life would have been extremely insecure. As Matt Cook has found, 'For some queer servants, "living in" provided an opportunity to find sex, relationships, some camaraderie, and a means of living away from possibly restrictive family homes. Living on site, though, often also meant compromised privacy and double insecurity: both job and home could be lost if they were found out.'[26] Additionally, Patrick's experiences of a romantic life in the confines of the country house were shaped by race, by his migrant status, and by the class and socio-economic privilege of Lyulph.

Domestic service

What were Patrick's experiences of life in Penrhos as a black queer domestic servant in the household of the British aristocracy? Little direct evidence exists in Patrick's letters which shed light on his time in Wales. We can, however, explore some of the general experiences and history of domestic service in Britain, and in particular North Wales, during this time which can provide an insight into at least some of Patrick's experiences.

Several significant studies of domestic service in European, and specifically British history, have been published recently. The interwar period and domestic service is, however, underexplored in historiography. As Raffaella Sarti has documented, domestic service was previously considered by theorists to be a carry-over from the past, something anachronistic which would disappear 'thanks to progress and modernisation' and was therefore seen as not worthy of great attention when studying modern society. However, Sarti states, 'between the twentieth and twenty-first centuries the so-called "resurgence in waged domestic labour", *Rückkehr der Dienstmädchen* and *retour de la domesticité* stimulated social researchers to turn back to the subject'.[27] Lucy Delap has recently explored the history and experiences of domestic staff in twentieth-century Britain with the 2011 publication *Knowing Their Place*, which documented the deep-rooted and complicated presence of domestic service in British history, culture, memory and identity.[28] Delap has explored the myriad of cultural ways in which domestic service is central to modern British history in relation to gender, class and emotional histories, arguing that 'domestic service has served as a foundational narrative amongst the stories British people tell about the twentieth century and its changes'.[29]

Lucy Lethbridge points out that 'in 1900 domestic service was the single largest occupation in Edwardian Britain'.[30] In 1881 one-ninth of Bath's workforce worked in service, and for London this figure was one in fifteen.[31] Delap points out that between 1890 and the Second World War 'census records and other evidence reveal that a very wide range of households were employing servants ... though there was a declining role for live-in servants'.[32] During the First World War many domestic servants entered into war work and after the war, Delap states, there was a 'particularly potent period of discontent with domestic service, and of intense middle-class anxiety as to whether women would willingly return to domestic service'.[33] After a post-war dip, numbers employed in domestic service rose in the 1920s.[34] During the 1930s, some women returned to service due to the bad economic situation and, as Delap explains, 'the coercive nature of the unemployment benefits system'.[35]

Exploring the history of domestic service tells us much about the experiences, identities and the lived realities of diverse ethnic communities in twentieth-century Britain that laboured within the profession. Britain's diverse population in the Victorian and Edwardian periods, including African, Asian and Jewish communities and individuals living throughout the country, was certainly involved in carrying out domestic service. During the 1930s European refugees worked in Britain as domestic servants. As documented by Tony Kushner, up to 20,000 Jewish refugees from Nazi Europe came to Britain to work as domestic servants through Ministry-of-Labour work permits or visas for domestic service.[36] Black domestic servants in the nineteenth and twentieth centuries are a relatively underexplored area of research and rarely integrated into larger histories of domestic service. The pioneering research of Caroline Bressey on black Victorian and Edwardian working lives is challenging this absence, explicitly highlighting many Black people with experience working in domestic service who advertised for employment in British newspapers.[37]

Patrick first worked in British service within the remit of a 'great house', a geographical space that we might immediately imagine when thinking of domestic service, but one which, as Delap points out, was not the norm within domestic service work. Up to 1931, 'only 30 per cent' of domestic servants were employed in households 'employing more than one servant.'[38] With regard to men working in domestic service, how common was Patrick's experience and position as an indoor domestic servant in a grand house in Britain? Delap has stated that 'the employment of men in indoor and outdoor domestic service was not large in the early to mid-twentieth century.'[39] Certain financial issues limited or disguised male employment in domestic service. There was a tax on employing male domestic servants (in 1930 the tax was fifteen shillings per annum per male servant).[40] In 1924, 173,363 men were employed in domestic service in the country.[41] Patrick's work as a valet within the house and not in the grounds was a minority male occupation among male servants. Delap found that though the number of men employed as indoor domestic servants rose between 1921 and 1931 in England and Wales, the vast majority worked in institutions such as hotels.[42]

Although women were in the majority in domestic work, there, as Delap states, 'had been discussion amongst policymakers of encouraging more men, particularly ex-servicemen and the disabled, into private domestic service after World War I' and though 'increasing numbers of men did indeed temporarily enter service ... the sector was so firmly feminized that most employers found the prospect of male servants alarming or ridiculous.'[43] There was also a critique of the tax on male servants. For example, in 1934 *The Manchester Guardian* argued that 'if the tax were removed – and at this time of day when retainers no longer threaten the monarchy it is an anachronism, – and if men-servants were obtainable on the same principles as women, it is not only probable that more men would be employed but also that the status of domestic service might go up'.[44] Of those men who entered domestic service post-First World War, a number consisted of ex-soldiers as, Lethbridge argues, 'a training in the armed services equipped one well for many of the duties and disciplines of, say, valeting, cleaning silver or managing menial staff'.[45] Those seeking work publicized this link to a potential employer as a positive attribute; for example, an advertisement in the Situations Wanted section of a 1931 edition of the *Portsmouth Evening News* stated 'Military, conduct exemplary, seeks Employment as gentleman's servant, watchman, caretaker, place of trust'.[46]

The position of the valet

One of the key jobs male domestic servants were employed in was as a valet, a personal domestic servant who carried out the role of servant and personal assistant and often confidant and friend. Newspaper adverts of men seeking work as gentleman's valets and of employers advertising for valets appeared in various regional newspapers in Britain. These give a sense of what roles men expected to undertake and what skills they thought would be of use for an employer in search of a male domestic. In 1937 a twenty-eight-year-old man advertised in the *Surrey Mirror and County Post* as a 'Valet, Gentleman's Servant; excellent knowledge waiting, wines, etc; sleep in'.[47] In 1932 a man advertised in the *Buckingham Advertiser* describing himself as a 'Gentleman's Servant experienced all branches of house work, capable cook, or cleaning, desires daily work or part day. Permanent or temporary'.[48] In April 1934 an advertisement was placed in the *Western Morning News and Daily Gazette* stating 'well-trained gentleman's servant, seeks post, driver-mechanic, any car; valet, wait table; handy-man; interested in his work; abstainer; age 27. Anxious to marry when suited. Ten years present situation'.[49] These adverts highlight the duties valets would carry out from part-time to live-in work, temporary to permanent, or the skills required for a good valet such as having expertise in wines, to carrying out multiple tasks including driving.

The types of jobs a gentlemen's valet undertook were diverse. In Edith Waldemar-Leverton's 1912 *Servants and their Duties*, the instructions for valet's duties were as follows:

> The valet is expected to attend entirely to his master's personal needs. He attends to the wardrobe, sees that the suits are well pressed, and kept in proper order; checks the laundry; attends to his master's bath; packs and takes tickets, orders carriages, &c., when travelling; and generally saves his master any undue exertion or responsibility; in fact, a valet is to a man what a lady's maid is to a woman. Bachelors and elderly gentlemen are the people who usually need a

valet's service, especially when they are in the habit of travelling much, or paying many visits. At shooting parties valets go out with the guns, and act as loaders to their masters. With older men they sometimes need to undertake the duties of a male nurse, and should acquire a knowledge of sock-room nursing, sitting up at night, helping their master up and down stairs, or to take him out walking. Such a valet might also be required to read aloud to his master, and to write letters for him.[50]

These are some of the roles Patrick is likely to have undertaken. Though, because he was a valet on a farming estate his role might have differed or been more varied depending on Lyulph's day-to-day activities. Gentlemen's valets were 'a common feature of the bachelor about town'.[51] In 1930 the LSE's New Survey of London Life and Labour found that posts with the 'man about town' were popular among male servants.[52] The valet (like the lady's maid to the aristocracy or wealthy) also travelled between residences, between country and the town properties, overseas and on holidays and visits to friends, wherever required. As Lucy Lethbridge states, 'Valets were ... a necessity for the single man with a private income who aspired to the life of a gentleman. Away from home they were also an indispensable guide to the intricate workings of the sporting house party.'[53] Stanley Ager, who was a valet during the interwar period, stated that 'any gentleman of any consequence' has a manservant.[54]

Lyulph, like many British elites, had more than one home – a country residence and a city residence; apart from his residence in Penrhos, he had a home in London. This city residence was perhaps not just a home for spending leisure time in the city. In the autumn of 1937, Lyulph enrolled for study at the Royal College of Music while Patrick was still in his employ, and both men probably spent much of their time together in London.[55] How much travelling did Patrick carry out with Lyulph between these residences? Shipping records indicate they did not travel abroad together, but it is likely they would have travelled between residences and to friends of Lyulph's. Did Patrick also work as a chauffeur? Lucy Lethbridge found that 'the chauffeur-valet' was 'an increasingly popular double role'.[56] Patrick could drive; in his military documentation listing his qualifications he states that he was a driver in civilian life but with no licence.[57]

Work colleagues played a key role in the personal life of a domestic servant within a large estate. Other domestic servants Patrick may have known include a woman called Winifred Ellen Hills (previously mentioned) who was employed by the family for decades. Hills worked as a personal companion to Lady Stanley and was a live-in domestic in their residences in both London and Penrhos. Winifred Hills not only accompanied Lady Stanley on visits abroad, she also dealt with employing other domestic servants. During the time of Patrick's employment at Penrhos, in September 1937, Lady Stanley advertised in the domestic-help-wanted section of the *Derby Daily Telegraph* for a 'capable Cook-Housekeeper and Parlourmaid, both with experience in good service' and those seeking this employment were to apply to Miss Hills in Penrhos.[58]

The Penrhos estate was run by the Stanley family for several centuries and the estate was central to the Holyhead landscape, covering large parts of the town and influencing the town in various political, economic and social ways. In the 1960s Geoffrey Butterworth wrote, 'Reminders of the family which for nearly 200 years owned and lived at Penrhos remain in the names of streets in the town, a printing works, the Stanley hospital and memorials in the parish church, and it is only in the church where any public record can be found in Holyhead of the earlier and truly native family, the Owens.'[59]

Penrhos was a large estate comprising farmland, tenant lodges and the Penrhos mansion house. Additionally, the Stanleys were landlords to the various tenants on their estates in both Cheshire and Penrhos and within the town of Holyhead. Information can be gleaned from the 1881 Wales census about the size of the estate and also the number of servants living and working on the Penrhos estate lands. With regard to the Penrhos mansion, in 1881 H. Owen Stanley, the Lord Stanley of Alderley at that time lived in the mansion along with his niece Jane Adeane, who was thirty-eight years old at the time. Also residing at the estate was a substantial presence of domestic service staff consisting of a butler, a footman, under footman, coalman, under coalman, groom, housekeeper, cook, ladies maid, two laundry maids, housemaid, two day maids, under house maid, two kitchen maids and a scullery maid. As well as the live-in servants, there would have been other servants undoubtedly working in the estate house who lived elsewhere. Additionally, there were lodges on the estate where the estate gardener and his family lived. For example, during 1881 the head gardener lived at 50 Penrhos Garden lodge, a property on the estate, with his wife, two sons, and his wife's brother. [60]

In the 1931 inventory of the contents of Penrhos taken for the purposes of estate duty in light of the death of Lord Stanley, information can be gleaned about the size of the estate and the number of rooms within the main Penrhos house. The estate had an attic with four bedrooms and a lobby. On the first floor there were two bathrooms, a dressing room, two WCs, a housemaid's closet and fifteen bedrooms. On the second floor there were eight bedrooms, a turret room, a bathroom and WC. On the ground floor there was a dining room, hall, an inner hall, a small room off the inner hall, a saloon, library, drawing room, WC and boudoir. Domestic rooms included the housekeeper's room, the butler's bedroom, servants' hall, covered yard, store room and cutlery, still room, ironing room, kitchen, larders, scullery, footmen's bedroom, housemaids pantry, housemaids sitting room, butler's pantry, cellar, gardens, gun room, office, chauffeur's room, bedrooms and carpenter's shop.[61] Within the schedule of real and leasehold property for the Penrhos estate, which was calculated when Arthur Lyulph Stanley died in 1931, it was stated that the gross value of the property the family owned was £2313 12 shillings 2 pence for small cottages, £682 for houses and shops at half-yearly tenancies, £363 for the Market Hall, £5757 10s 2d for farms and lands, £130 for Llanfawr lands, £567 for Penrhos Mansion with home farm and cottages and £1788 6s 2d for ground rents for houses in lease.[62] Today the Penrhos estate remnants and land forms a nature reserve called Penrhos Coastal Park and Nature Reserve (Figure 3.2).

Figure 3.2 Photograph of Penrhos Nature Reserve, Holyhead taken by author, May 2015.

1930s Holyhead

Oral history interviews conducted during the 1980s with estate workers and Holyhead residents, including some who were working in the 1930s, shed further light on working as a domestic at Penrhos and life in Holyhead. These interviews document important memories and life experiences of interwar North Wales, including the devastating effects of the 1930s economic crisis on the lives of people who lived in Holyhead. They also reveal information on some of the individuals who were working at Penrhos in the 1930s, a few years before Patrick.[63] Hugh Jones was born in Holyhead in February 1902. Jones' mother was brought up on a farm and his father was a stone mason. He started his working life in December 1915, just two months short of his thirteenth birthday on a farm called Bryniau Geirwon. Though he was supposed to stay at school until age fourteen, a neighbour of the farm he started working on – Sam Williams who used to work for Lord Stanley of Alderley – applied for his release from school.

After working on this farm, Jones went to work with his father as an apprentice stone mason and then moved on to work in the garden for Lord Stanley. By this time, he was twenty-two or twenty-three years old and had been living on the Penrhos estate. A couple of years later he was married and was living at one of the lodges called Lodge-y-Bont. He recalled seeing his employers in the summer for about six weeks and during the Christmas holidays. He remembered information about the estate employees: 'Well I remember thirteen in the garden. I remember seventeen staff in the house and ground about seventeen on the farm. They would never sack anybody, when you got too old for anything else sort of thing they used to put you on the paths.'[64] The working hours were long. He recalled that they did not get holidays: 'No, we used to get Christmas day providing it wasn't on a Sunday. If Christmas day, such as this year, was on a Sunday you wouldn't get it. There was no Boxing day you know, and we used to get Easter Monday and White Monday and that was the four – no holidays at all.'[65] Significantly, Hugh Jones remembers Lyulph Stanley:

> When Lord Stanley died, and that was Lord Arthur, his son Edward became Lord, so they shared – there was two estates, one at Alderley edge and the other Anglesey here, and Master Lyafath [*sic – in transcript*] as we used to know him before he died he was Lord for about three or four months. He wasn't very healthy although he was twice my size. Big hefty gentelman. Alderley Edge was Bigger, the estate was bigger than this, so they divided them like that, because of Death Duties.[66]

Jones also recalled knowing Lyulph personally. When asked by the interviewer if he did any hunting while working there, he stated 'Yes, I used to go off with Master Lyafath [*sic in transcript*], that was the second son and he'd allow me to take my gun with me.'[67] He remembered working there until 1934 (leaving three years before Lyulph officially took over Penrhos and before Patrick arrived at the estate), before moving on to work at the Holyhead Park. He moved from Penrhos because, he recalled, 'Well it was going down fast. They didn't sack me of course but I'm sure they were glad to see me going for the simple reason that things were going down.'[68] Jones' interview suggests Patrick arrived at an estate falling into decline.

Holyhead during this time was a rural area, with industries tied to both the maritime trades and to farming, with town amenities including a town hall and cinemas. Just before Patrick's arrival, in March 1937, there had been a ferocious storm with much destruction. The destruction described in the local newspaper provides detail on some of the architecture, industry and geography of interwar Holyhead. The *Holyhead and Anglesey Mail* recorded on 5 March 1937 'that it was the worst storm within living memory is generally conceded' and that 'roads were blocked by trees which had been uprooted and, to add to the perils of the roads, broken telephone wires were strewn all over the highways'. Property damage was considerable and they reported 'at Holyhead the night was one of terror to many of the inhabitants. Very few houses have escaped suffering some damage ... . In the main street of the town, shop blinds were torn from their moorings.' Businesses were affected with 'several small boats' sunk and a 'failure of the electric light between 2 and 3 a.m.'. As a result of the storm 'heavy goods destined for Ireland' were not loaded. It was also reported that 'both the Empire and Hippodrome Cinemas' were closed.[69] Much of this damage would have been evident when Patrick arrived in Penrhos a month later and would have probably impacted the duties he would have had to perform, perhaps assisting in the clean-up and maintenance of the estate. If Patrick had time away from work he would have no doubt visited one of these cinemas when they reopened after the clean-up as film was a lifetime passion for Patrick.

As well as being the chief landholder and landlord, the Stanleys played other key roles in Holyhead's cultural and political life. The Stanley Hospital in Holyhead held an annual fete at Penrhos, a tradition stretching back to at least the 1860s.[70] The Stanley family also ran a Penrhos Alms House endowment fund.[71] Lady Kathleen Stanley, a relative of the main Stanley family, played a role in local politics in the area. In March 1937 just before Patrick's arrival, Lady

Kathleen Stanley was elected in the Anglesey Council elections in the district of Holyhead North-Western. The *Holyhead and Anglesey Mail* reported, 'As was anticipated she secured election by a handsome majority. The Stanley influence is strong in all parts of the town, and Lady Kathleen has, on numerous occasions and in many spheres demonstrated that she has the interests of the town and its people very much at heart.'[72]

The political, economic and social dominance of the Stanley family would have affected the day-to-day lives of the servants, and must have affected Patrick's economic life and prospects of employment in the area after leaving the Stanley residence. If he had been sacked due to a relationship with Lyulph, it would have possibly been difficult for him to stay in the area or find similar employment elsewhere. Even if Patrick had left the Stanleys amicably, finding employment in 1930s Holyhead would have been difficult. Exploring oral histories and personal reflections of Holyhead residents during the 1930s, the devastation of the unemployment crisis permeated all aspects of Holyhead life. Cyril Parry reflected on his memories of life in Holyhead in the 1920s and 1930s, including his memories of political struggles against unemployment. He first went to work in shipping in 1927 at age fifteen and returned to Holyhead in 1928 but left again for Liverpool, transferring his unemployment benefit there in order to find work in the shipping industry. He thereafter found work on a number of ships as a seaman. Recalling life in Holyhead in the 1930s after returning from maritime employment, he stated:

> Holyhead in the 'thirties is something, you know, that I very often think about. I do sit, sometimes, and think back at those times. It was very, very bad. Holyhead, as I said to you before, was a town of people who were despondent and didn't seem to have much hope for the future. You had young people who had matriculated at school but, having done so, they had little hope of any job that was worthwhile, and most of them trickled away from this town: some, of course, never came back.[73]

He remembered soup kitchens, queues for the labour exchange, dole tribunals, bad health and poverty in the community. He also reflected on class and politics in Holyhead, recalling 'I was a member of the Labour Party and have been since nineteen twenty-nine. I joined the Young Socialists when I was only 17, and I'm so very proud of that and my connections with the socialist movement and the trades union movement.'[74] The interviewer also asked him about his recollections of the Stanley family and what he knew about them, to which he responded, 'Very little I know about them because, truly, I didn't seek to find much about them. They were a people, the people that we were expected, I think, to look up to, but I never looked up towards anybody.'[75]

In February 1937, during the announcement of the election contest, it was reported of Lady Kathleen Stanley that she had 'a long record of useful public service to her credit. She has also taken a very active and sympathetic part in alleviating the lot of the unemployed in the town.'[76] However, as mentioned by Cyril Parry in his oral history interview, there were importantly left-wing political movements in Holyhead which provided a more radical focus on the unemployment crisis than the paternalistic politics of elites such as the Stanleys.[77]

Patrick's experiences of Penrhos life would have been profoundly shaped by his experiences as a black man living in rural Wales as well as a black man working in elite households as a servant. As Alan Llwyd has shown in *Black Wales* there has been a black presence in Wales over many centuries; newspaper adverts, baptism records and other documents in archives and printed sources attest to this diverse black presence. These records highlight the role of slavery in the early modern black Welsh presence. In the baptism records of St John's Church, Cardiff an entry in the parish register on 30 May 1687 recorded, 'A black boy belonging to Sir Rowland Gwin was baptised'.[78] Due to the shipping industry, a multi-ethnic and multinational diverse community in Cardiff developed from the late nineteenth century onwards and this community included many people of African and Caribbean descent working in dockside and shipping employment. Alan Llwyd stated, 'By 1914, the first year of the First World War, an estimated 700 black people lived in Cardiff, but there would also be many hundreds of other black seamen there on a temporary basis between jobs.'[79]

Though Holyhead was not as diverse as Cardiff, its residents included individuals from various ethnic backgrounds. In 1937 the *Holyhead and Anglesey Mail* reported 'Hugh Rowlands (21), 3, Market Street, Holyhead, appeared at the Petty Sessions, on Wednesday, charged with the theft of a silk blouse, value 8s. 11d., the property of Shah Mohammed, a native of India. A charge of receiving the blouse was preferred against Mrs Katherine Williams (40), of 3, Hedsor Street, Holyhead.' It went on to describe the evidence Mohammed gave in court, stating 'Mohammed, who gave his evidence in broken English, said he left his case, containing the blouse, in Chiorsi's shop on Saturday, the 15th of August. Later, he saw Mrs Williams wearing a blouse which he identified as his property. He asked her where she had bought it, and she replied, "The pawnshop". She further declared that she did not want to tell the witness anything. He informed her that the blouse was his property, and she thereupon took off her coat, divested herself of the blouse, and threw it at him.'[80]

Many black people in Britain in the early modern period, both free and enslaved, laboured in domestic service. This domestic service work was highly racialized. In elite households often black servants were seen as exotic status symbols. In eighteenth-century portraiture, black servants were represented in or made to dress in turbans, skullcaps and liveries. Beth Fowkes Tobin has observed 'this conflation of Arabic, African, and Indian origins is typical of many eighteenth-century representations of black servants. What seems to matter is not that these servants are African, Muslim, or Indian, but that they are exotic, that they originate in tropical, fertile, and remote lands.'[81] This exoticized fashion for black servants decreased in the modern period. However, there needs to be more work carried out on the extent and nature of the black presence in domestic service in the modern era, by, for example, looking at the everyday lives of black people who worked in service. Caroline Bressey's work is extremely important in revealing and interrogating the black presence in nineteenth-century domestic service within Britain as a whole, exploring the presence through photography and newspaper adverts.[82] As Bressey's work has shown, the colour of someone's skin would not be systematically recorded in official documentation relating to employment, migration and census records, so the true diversity of the black presence in different sectors of the working-class economy, including domestic service, during the nineteenth and early twentieth centuries has been under-researched and underestimated.

There is little evidence of how Patrick fared in Wales with regard to his emotional and friendship connections, beyond his relationship with Lyulph, or how he may have been treated by other members of the household as a black man. Lucy Lethbridge has argued, similarly, 'for the most part the civilian valet, like the lady's maid, was a casualty of the particular loneliness of the upper-servant: stranded somewhere between the camaraderie of the servants' hall and that of the drawing room.'[83] It is difficult to come to a conclusion on the emotional life of Patrick in relation to the social space of the grand house and whether he felt this disconnect from other servants because of his status as a gentleman's servant as contemporary letters written during his time in Penrhos do not, as far as I am aware, exist.

Matt Cook has recently explored queerness in relation to domesticity and commenting on men who worked in service 'in hotels or the private houses of the wealthy' argued that 'there seems to have been a preponderance of queer men in these roles in the first half of the twentieth century'.[84] Cook additionally found that 'some men used domestic employment as a cover. The collector, Edward Perry Warren's live-in "secretary" in Lewes, East Sussex, for example, was actually his lover and life partner.'[85] As Cook has observed, being a valet and living away from family meant freedom to a certain extent away from the strictures of what was expected but also constraints in living within a household that was not your own and having your home tied to your employment. Many of Patrick's queer experiences took place in households – either households where he worked or households of his lovers, such as Duncan Grant's studio. In relation to Patrick and Lyulph's experiences in London, again it is difficult to know but they probably socialized in queer London spaces together and perhaps this is how Patrick got to know members of the Bloomsbury group such as Duncan Grant. This aspect of Patrick's life is explored in more detail in the next chapter.

Patrick's emotional life would have been shaped by multiple experiences and identities; by his being a young black queer man living in rural Wales, a working-class man in domestic service, and a migrant without a local family network for support. Patrick's time in Wales was short-lived. Considering the fanfare he was given in the *Gleaner* just a few months prior, for a migration that appeared to be intended to be long-lasting, it seems his time in Wales was curtailed. Again, whether this curtailment was due to Lady Stanley finding out about a love affair or sexual relationship is difficult to know and these uncertainties are one of the common issues when recovering autobiographical voices with limited source material. The next chapter will focus on Patrick's experiences in pre-war London, contextualizing these experiences within an examination of race, black history, queer identity and the Bloomsbury group in interwar London.

Queer Black Spaces and Cosmopolitan Interwar London

This chapter explores Patrick's meeting with Duncan Grant and others associated with the artistic and literary network known as 'the Bloomsbury Group'. It reflects on and explores his sexual and romantic life, life as lived in the imperial metropole, in addition to his experiences of posing as an artist's model and his quest for education and learning, particularly in the study of law. The chapter explores these 1930s experiences by exploring his letters composed in the 1930s and 1940s, which document his employment, friendships and relationships, and the social spaces he inhabited. It also positions his experiences in the context of London's queer and black presence, *including* queer black spaces and social groups.

Patrick returned to Jamaica from Penrhos sailing from Swansea in first-class travel on 1 November 1937. Four months later, in March 1938, he travelled back to Britain, again listing his profession as a valet.[1] He later reflected on leaving Wales in a letter sent to Duncan Grant from Jamaica in 1953, where he stated he had just finished reading an article in the *Gleaner* about Queen Elizabeth. This article prompted a recollection: 'I did sail from there in October 1937 – after our beloved late King George's Coronation, direct back to Jamaica on a Banana Boat. I still gaze on the magnificent sight in my memory of that passing Monarch wearing Robes of State.'[2] On his return documentation to Jamaica in November 1937, he listed his future intended permanent residence as Jamaica. On this trip he was aboard the same ship as a man called Henry Walter James, a 52-year-old tobacco advertiser, whose address was 48 Beauley Road, Southville, Bristol.[3] This Bristol address was the same address listed by Patrick Nelson as his 'proposed address in the United Kingdom' when he returned to Britain in March 1938, sailing from Jamaica to Liverpool.[4] Perhaps Patrick and Henry met on the November 1937 ship travelling to Jamaica and it was during this meeting that Patrick told him of his work availability and decided to be his valet. Alternatively, perhaps they met in Britain and Patrick was employed by the tobacco merchant to be his valet during the time Patrick spent at home in Jamaica from late 1937 to March 1938. There is one individual called Henry Walter James who appears in the 1911 census. He was also born in 1885, lived in the same area of Bristol with his wife Ellen James and their three children and worked as a tobacco packer for British American tobacco.[5] How long Patrick stayed in Bristol is unknown. His experiences of valeting or being in domestic service for Henry Walter James and his family would have been markedly different from his previous experiences valeting at a large country estate and Caribbean hotel. Unlike Holyhead, Patrick was now living in a large British city, and would have encountered a more ethnically diverse population.[6] At some point, soon after moving to Bristol, he moved on to reside in London, where, it appears, he first met Duncan Grant. This chapter focuses on these London experiences.

Patrick and black London

Patrick was one of many people of African heritage living in late 1930s London. Interwar London was very much a space of cultural, national and ethnic diversity, with individuals from throughout the African and Asian diasporas travelling, working and living in the imperial metropole. As Maroula Joannou notes, 'Inter-war London acted as a mecca for a varied assortment of radical subaltern networks in which the Indian student might exchange ideas informally with the Jamaican sailor or the Somali visitor converse with the politician from Kenya, or the exile from the Gold Coast.'[7] The most significant black presence that Patrick Nelson would have encountered in London would have been the working-class black presence in the East End of the city, where Africans and Asians worked in the shipping industry. The development in the nineteenth century of steam shipping expanded the British trade port economies. London's docks included the West India Dock which opened in 1802 and was created for the purpose of importing goods made by enslaved people on the Caribbean plantations. Jacqueline Jenkinson states, 'London's complex of docks, eventually stretching for 70 miles, underwent expansion throughout the early twentieth century' and the ports of London and Liverpool accounted 'for 58% of all insured shipping by this time.'[8]

Claude McKay was one black person living, working and socializing in the East End of London between 1919 and 1921. As previously explored, McKay was born in Jamaica and after residing in the United States he moved to London in order to publish a book of poetry. In London he worked as a journalist for the radical communist newspaper the *Workers Dreadnought* edited by Sylvia Pankhurst and based in Bow, where he reported on the lives and struggles of black and white seamen in the docking communities. He visited a number of bohemian, political, literary and radical spaces, where he socialized with radicals, including fellow queer Londoners in clubs such as the International Socialist Club. However, East London was also one of the London areas where he experienced racism on the streets and in clubs including the ISC.[9] During McKay's time in London, Britain experienced racist rioting against African and Asian populations in various port towns, including the dockside East End of London.[10]

There was a diverse black presence in interwar Soho where people of African heritage were involved in operating and performing in the large number of jazz clubs which opened during the period. In 1936, a year before Patrick first came to Britain, the *Melody Maker* published an article by Rudolph Dunbar entitled 'Harlem in London: Year of Advancement for Negroes', which explored black life in 1930s London, focusing on Soho and the West End in relation to the jazz world (Figure 4.1).[11] The pages of the *Melody Maker* in general during this time attest to the number of musicians of African American and Caribbean heritage who were performing and living in interwar London. Dunbar was a clarinettist and writer from British Guiana who moved to London in about 1930. In *Harlem in London* he reported that 'during the last twelve months or so a great deal has happened in the domain of coloured people', and went on to discuss the film *Sanders of the River* featuring Paul Robeson and the hundreds of extras recruited for the filming; black student life in London; sports; and the Italian invasion of Abyssinia, where he believed that 'despite its horror there is no doubt that this war will do much to gain sympathy and understanding for the Negro'.[12] He ended his piece with a focus on the Shim Sham Club, one of the many jazz clubs which opened up in Soho at this time. The Shim Sham was also one of many clubs which acted as private parties or 'Bottle Parties'. These venues, although clubs, worked to circumvent alcohol legislation by acting as private parties instead of public venues.[13] Bottle parties were often the subject of police surveillance and raids. As Walkowitz states, 'In December 1936, twenty-seven West End and Soho bottle parties were raided, including venerable old timers like the 400 and Old Florida. The round-up included many black clubs, such as the Nest, Frisco's, Cuba Club, and the Shim Sham.'[14]

Figure 4.1 'Harlem in London: Year of Advancement for Negroes', *The Melody Maker*, 7 March 1936, p. 2.

Most importantly for Patrick was the significant African, Caribbean and Asian presence in interwar Bloomsbury, which included students, anti-colonial activists, writers, poets, musicians, artists and actors including C.L.R. James, Mulk Raj Anand, Florence Mills and Una Marson. Bloomsbury was a cosmopolitan space, and far more diverse than has been remembered, partly due to the prevailing historical memory which often defines Bloomsbury in relation to the 'Bloomsbury Group'.

Due to the key importance of universities, such as University College, London within the area, Bloomsbury was a space where many people from Africa, the Caribbean and Asia studied. Students attending University College, London, in the 1920s and 1930s included Jamaican sisters Edith, Olive and Joyce Baxter who all won the Jamaica Scholarship to study in London.[15] The handwritten address for Patrick on his application form for the AMPC is difficult to transcribe, but it appears to state 70 Marchmont Street, WC1, highlighting at some point that he lived in the Bloomsbury area.[16] Perhaps he moved to Bloomsbury to be close to his work, or to Duncan, or in anticipation of starting his law degree.

As well as being a place for students, Bloomsbury was a space inhabited by performers, writers and poets. African American Harlem Renaissance entertainer Florence Mills was one of the many performers who lived in Bloomsbury in the 1920s due to its location near the theatres of the West End. From 1926 to 1927 she performed to mass acclaim in the *Blackbirds* revue at the London Pavilion and in 1926 she lived in Mecklenburgh Square, before moving to Gower Street.[17] Other performers lived in Bloomsbury as it was near the jazz clubs of Soho; for example, Trinidadian Augustus Newton played drums in a jazz band which performed at the Shim Sham Club and in 1936 lived in Bloomsbury at 43 Marchmont Street.[18]

The British Museum, as well as its surrounding bookshops and cafes, provided an important social and political space for many people of African and Asian heritage in interwar London including queer black Jamaican poet, writer and activist Claude McKay, who carried out research on Marx in the British Museum Reading Room during his time in London. African American archivist and librarian Ruth Anna Fisher also researched in the British Museum Reading Room in 1920 during her time as a student at the London School of Economics and lived nearby in Tavistock Square in Bloomsbury.[19] Later on in the 1920s and 1930s Fisher was employed by both the Carnegie Institution and the Library of Congress, for whom she carried out important archival research (for the latter institution, she led the London-side of an international photostating project). In 1933 *The Crisis* reported that 'Miss Ruth Anna Fisher, a coloured woman formerly of Lorain, Ohio, has for many years been a resident of London, England. She has qualified as an expert in the British Museum. She has had an office there for five years and is one of the few workers who has her own key.'[20] Mulk Raj Anand, an Indian activist, writer and philosophy student who was based in Bloomsbury in the interwar period, recollected visiting the museum with poet Nikhil Sen to meet with Mr Binyon, the Keeper of Prints, and

explore some of the Indian miniatures on display.[21] Anand's writings also show
the relationships between people of diverse backgrounds within the space of
Bloomsbury, and the interactions between artists, writers and activists. Anand
recollected going to a cafe Whytelady's for crumpets with anti-racist writer
and activist Nancy Cunard and Catherine Carswell, having been introduced
to Cunard by Jacob Schwartz in his bookshop.[22] Their conversations reference
aspects of black cultural life in interwar Bloomsbury. According to Anand, after
Carswell reported that she had heard that Robeson was asked to play Othello,
Cunard told Carswell

> Just you wait. Charles Cochrane has been persuaded to bring Blackbirds to play
> Piccadilly Theatre. And Nigel Playfair wants to produce Eugene O'Neill's *Emperor
> Jones*. And I might get Langston Hughes over, to come and recite his poems in
> Harold Monro's poetry bookshop. I am doing a big book called Negro.[23]

Fitzrovia, nearby Bloomsbury and home to the studios of various artists
including Duncan Grant, also had a small black presence. In her memoir, artist
Kathleen Hale recalled, 'The residents were a cosmopolitan population of all
trades, driven to working hard for their living: the dance bands practising in the
basements, the tired waiters emerging from their seedy lodgings to go on duty.
For me it was the nearest thing to my idea of Paris, the city of artists, where I
had always intended to live.'[24] One notable black resident of interwar Fitzrovia
was racing tipster Prince Monolulu. In 1936 Guyanese writer of the Harlem
Renaissance Eric D. Walrond lived in Fitzrovia at 19 Fitzroy Street.[25] Walrond
documented the experiences of people of the African diaspora living in Britain
in 'The Negro in London', published in 1936 in Marcus Garvey's periodical
The Black Man.[26]

   Various autobiographies and writings reveal that many Africans and Asians
who lived in the Bloomsbury area experienced difficulty in finding accommodation due to racism. Guyanese writer and musician Rudolph Dunbar recalled

> The task of a colored man selecting a lodging room in the West End of London
> is not easy to accomplish. In several houses where there are 'Rooms to Let'
> signs, if a black man should apply for a room, the landlady with discriminating
> nicety would say, 'I am sorry but the room I had vacant has just been let.' Others
> would say, 'I am awfully sorry but I do not rent rooms to colored people.' I have
> discovered that in order to be given consideration in renting a room the colored
> man must put on evening dress and be immaculate in his appearance. This only
> goes to show that the great majority of these people who keep lodging houses are
> wallowing in the unfathomable depths of ignorance.[27]

Claude McKay had a similar experience, reflecting

> I remembered my difficulties, when I was studying at the British Museum, to get lodgings in the quarter. The signs were shouting: 'Rooms for rent', but when I inquired I was invariably informed that all rooms were rented. Yet when I passed that way again the signs were still there. I became suspicious. I asked English friends from the International Club to make inquiries. They found that the rooms were for rent. But when they took me along and declared the rooms were for me, we were told that Negroes were not desired as guests. When I left my London hotel I found rooms with an Italian family, and later, a German. And the nearest I got to living quarters close to the British Museum was when I found lodgings with a French family in Great Portland Street.[28]

In Anand's conversation over tea with Cunard and Carswell, he also reflected on the landladies he had met in Bloomsbury: "'As for the landladies,' I said, unable to control myself, "the less said the better ..." . One look at me and most of them slammed the doors in my face when I went looking for digs on my arrival.'[29]

Challenging racism within housing was one of the key policies of the League of Coloured Peoples (LCP). The LCP was founded in 1931 by Dr Harold Moody, a Jamaican doctor who lived in Peckham and worked as a GP. Moody worked as the president of the LCP until his death in 1947. The organization was established at a meeting at the Central YMCA in Bloomsbury in March 1931. The LCP's quarterly journal the *Keys* highlights some of their campaigns and activities.[30] Also focusing on the colour bar in housing, employment and entertainment venues were intercommunity groups such as the Quaker-led initiative during the period 1929–1931 which led in early 1931 to the formation of the 'Joint Council to promote Understanding between White and Coloured People in Great Britain'. Harold Moody was vice chairman, and the Council was started at Friends' House on Euston Road, on the outskirts of Bloomsbury.[31]

As a result of this racism, various hostels were set up to provide accommodation and a sense of community to the Bloomsbury African and Asian student population. One of the most prominent Bloomsbury hostels was the YMCA's Indian Students Union hostel. Opened in 1920 on Keppel Street, it moved to Gower Street in 1923. A vast number of students and others from India lived or socialized there. For example, their 1935 annual report stated that during that year 'we were able to accommodate 794 students in the hostel. In addition, many were found lodgings or homes in families in different parts of London. During the month of September alone we found accommodation elsewhere for over 100 students newly arrived from India ... . Numbers of non-student visitors and an increasing body of Indian women students were similarly helped.'[32] Along with living in private accommodation, African and Caribbean students in the 1930s also lived in hostels within Bloomsbury and west central London. The West African Students' Union (WASU), led by Ladipo Solanke, opened a hostel at 62 Camden Road which was to be an important centre of black community and political life. Another Bloomsbury-based hostel, Aggrey House, organized by the Colonial Office and the LCP was opened at 47 Doughty Street. The involvement of the Colonial Office in the creation of the hostel meant that it was opposed by many anti-colonial radical activists such as Solanke of the WASU.[33] The warden of Aggrey House was Ivor Cummings, a man of mixed Sierra Leonean and English heritage who later went on to work for the Colonial Office. Cummings was also a queer black man in interwar London who knew musicians in the West End, such as John Payne, and whose life story is yet to be fully explored. Val Wilmer reflected in Cummings' obituary:

> A dedicated bon viveur and night-club habitue, Cummings sought out his constituents wherever they might be. But he saw himself as one of 'the group', an exclusive coterie of black academics and intellectuals with a responsibility to uphold the integrity and good standing of the African. They included entertainers and artists who made their mark in 1930s Britain, such as the American singer John Payne and the British composer Reginald Foresythe, to whose Nigerian family Cummings's father was doctor in Lagos. Like these two and many others in the social and diplomatic circles in which he moved, Cummings was gay at a time when openness about homosexuality was impossible.[34]

Due to his career in post-war Britain, as an official involved in assisting Commonwealth migrants, Ivor Cummings was to greet the *Empire Windrush* at Tilbury in 1948 and also travel to Jamaica as a civil servant.[35] This career intersects with Patrick's life history as they travelled on the same ship to Jamaica in 1947.

Hostels such as Aggrey House and the Indian Students Union Hostel were for male students, so women from the African and Asian diasporas studying in London had fewer options of where to reside. Women found accommodation through friends, family connections, or through assistance from these organizations but there were also some hostels and halls of residence set up for women. Sometimes this accommodation was in the Bloomsbury area such as College Hall, Byng Place, which was established in 1882 to accommodate women studying at University College. Stella Jane Thomas, a Nigerian woman of Sierra Leonean heritage who would become a famous barrister in West Africa lived at 23–25 Upper Bedford Place during 1934.[36] Other women of African diasporic heritage resident in this building were Jamaican students and the sisters Olive Baxter, who lived at 24 Upper Bedford Place in 1930, and Edith Baxter, who lived there two years later.[37] Thus, Bloomsbury was a space where interwar African and Asian students not only studied but also lived, socialized and created community and friendship networks.

As well as campaigning against racism within Britain, students, writers and activists of African, Caribbean and Asian backgrounds formed political and social organizations fighting against British imperialism and colonialism. Marc Matera states, 'Black internationalism first captured the imagination of many West Indians and Africans during their time in London, where they formed new black organizations like the Union of Students of African Descent, African Progress Union, Gold Coast Students Union, Nigerian Progress Union, West African Students Union and the League of Coloured Peoples during the early decades of the twentieth century.'[38] Radical anti-colonial, Pan-African or left-wing political activists such as George Padmore also had a presence in Bloomsbury and various activists lived in the area; for example, Indian independence campaigners Devendra Nath Bannerjea and Hilda Margaret Bannerjea lived at 41 Museum Street in 1922.[39]

A hostel set up by the Student Christian Movement in Russell Square called the Student Movement House also served as an important space for the interwar black Bloomsbury population. The activist and writer C. L. R. James recalled spending time at the house in a 1932 article he wrote for the Trinidadian *Port of Spain Gazette* on the subject of life in Bloomsbury, stating 'We walked over to the Student Movement House, which is a club for London students, white and coloured, but with its chief aim giving coloured students in London an opportunity to meet together and fraternise with English students, and with one another. The atmosphere of the place is decidedly intellectual, in intention at least.'[40] Ladipo Solanke lectured at Student Movement House in 1924 to educate the wider public about West African culture, in order to challenge the racist stereotypes about Africa on display at the Empire exhibition at Wembley in 1924.[41]

Duncan Grant

In 1930s London Patrick met Duncan Grant, an artist at the centre of the elite Bloomsbury group (Figures 4.2 and 4.4). The group was a complex network of friendships, relationships and artistic and cultural collaborations of individuals who had connections with the Bloomsbury area of London. The group mainly established itself through the home of the siblings Vanessa, Virginia and Adrian Stephen. David (Bunny) Garnett, a publisher and writer and a lover of Duncan Grant's, was from a literary background. His great-grandfather, Reverend Richard Garnett, was assistant keeper of printed books at the British Museum and his grandfather, Richard Garnett, followed in the footsteps of his father by becoming keeper of printed books. David Garnett's father, Edward, was a critic and publisher and his mother, Constance, was a book translator.[42] David Garnett was to become a book seller and author, running a business in the Soho area in Gerrard Street across from the 1917 club.[43]

The artist Duncan Grant was part of this elite community of artists and writers and as Duncan played such a significant role in Patrick's life, an in-depth exploration of his life before and during the time he knew Patrick is undertaken over the next few pages, which is based primarily on the work of Frances Spalding, Grant's biographer. Grant was born in 1885 on his family estate, the Rothiemurchus estate, in Scotland.[44] His mother Ethel Grant and father Bartle Grant met and married in India and Grant partially grew up there. As Duncan's biography highlights, Empire and imperialism shaped the Bloomsbury Group in multiple ways. Duncan Grant's grandfather Sir John Peter Grant's period as Jamaican governor was mentioned in letters from Patrick to Duncan (particularly during the 1940s when Patrick conducted research on the life of John Peter Grant). Duncan spent his early childhood in India and at age nine was sent back to England for schooling. After his grandmother died and before his parents had returned to London, he lived with various families, including his relatives the Stracheys.[45] He then attended St Paul's School in West Kensington, before enrolling in Westminster School of Art.[46]

In this world, Duncan socialized and met a number of artistic and cultural figures. He was able to visit various artists with his aunt on 'Picture Sunday' such as Briton Rivière.[47] Duncan's art education also developed during stays in Paris, where he went to live for a time after he turned twenty-one.[48] There he enrolled at the *Académie Julian*, before moving on to *La Palette*.[49]

In 1905 Duncan had a romantic relationship with Lytton Strachey and though short-lived their friendship continued. During this period of his life he also had a romance with Arthur Hobhouse and an intense relationship with Maynard Keynes.[50] Through the Strachey's, Duncan became friends with the Stephen family and thereafter became close to Vanessa Bell, with whom he would eventually share his life.[51] From 1909 Duncan Grant set up his studio at 21 Fitzroy Square, joining the already established Fitzrovian community of artists and becoming neighbours of Virginia and Adrian Stephen.[52] He took part in the Friday Club, which held annual art exhibitions from 1910 to 1918.[53] The Club was founded in 1905 by Vanessa Bell and consisted of various members of the Bloomsbury group. However, as Richard Shone states 'with such members as John Nash, Derwent Lees, Wadsworth and Nevinson on its hanging committee, its scope was wider than has generally been admitted'.[54] Shone has described the Friday Club as 'one of the liveliest exhibiting groups before the first War'.[55] Duncan played a key role in the Omega Workshops established in 1913 by Roger Fry, carrying out painting and design work within the collective. Vanessa and Duncan were also co-directors of the Workshops.[56] Fry's curation of the 1910 groundbreaking exhibition *Manet and the Post-Impressionists* had a great impact upon Duncan's work. Duncan also continued his travels abroad, which allowed

Figure 4.2 Duncan Grant by Duncan Grant, oil on canvas, circa 1909, NPG 5131, © National Portrait Gallery.

him to develop his education of art and resulted in more diverse influences within his work.[57]

With the start of the First World War, a number of Duncan's friends had started to enlist. Spalding states that 'having a father who had been in the army, Duncan was all too aware that his family expected him to fight'.[58] During this period of time, Duncan met David (Bunny) Garnett and they began to socialize at the same parties.[59] Duncan and Bunny became closer to one another during a 1914 group holiday organized by Lytton Strachey, where Duncan fell in love with him.[60] Spalding states that in early 1915 Duncan 'saw his young friend daily, slept with him often and realised he had fallen head over heels in love'.[61]

In relation to wartime, Spalding states of Bunny and Duncan that 'both men objected to war, not on religious but on moral grounds'.[62] After a successful appeal to the initial decision to refuse their conscription exemption, Vanessa found farm work in Sussex for Duncan and Bunny, near the property 'Charleston', which Virginia had previously suggested Vanessa rent, and so she organized the farm work and the rental of Charleston (Figure 4.3).[63] Charleston is now open to the public and administered by The Charleston Trust. Visitors can see the incredible decorating of the house carried out by Duncan and Vanessa. Victoria Rosner states 'Over time almost every surface in every room came to be decorated with bright and colorful patterns, underlining the idea that to be a painter was less a profession than a way of life.'[64]

Figure 4.3 Photograph of Charleston Farmhouse, Firle, Lewes, Sussex taken by author, August 2015.

Although based in Charleston for a great deal of the time, Duncan also continued socializing and working in London. Around 1918 he befriended Edward Wolfe, an Omega group artist who was also to work with Patrick Nelson, creating two portrait paintings of him as well as drawings. Edward Wolfe, a painter influenced by Gaudier-Brzeska, Modigliani and Matisse, was younger than the Bloomsbury group generation of Duncan Grant and others. Born in 1897 in Johannesburg, his father Eli Wolfe was a Jewish migrant from Lithuania and his mother Ruth Elizabeth Wedderburn was a Presbyterian Scottish migrant.[65] Edward enrolled with scholarships for art at the Regent Street Polytechnic and acting at the D'Auban School of Dramatic Art.[66] He soon went on to study at the Slade, socialized with artists including Nina Hamnett, joined Roger Fry's Omega Workshops, developed a career as an artist and became a member of the Bloomsbury Group.[67] John R. Taylor states that Duncan was the owner of Edward's first 'surviving datable painting' *Still Life with Omega Cat*, inscribed on the back with 'my first study/painted in 1918 Edward Wolfe/in Nina Hamnett's studio/Fitzroy Street'.[68] Spalding wrote that Duncan gained access on the lease of Sickert's studio at 21 Fitzroy Street and 'there, with Nina Hamnett and a young South African artist who had recently joined the Omega, Edward Wolfe, made an elaborate nude pastel of Bunny'.[69]

In June 1918 Vanessa found out she was expecting a child with Duncan.[70] Angelica was born on Christmas day 1918. Spalding wrote that Clive Bell 'had shown no resentment at the idea of Vanessa having Duncan's baby. Moreover he took steps to secure for the forthcoming child the same financial advantages that his own two children enjoyed, by keeping its illegitimacy a secret from his wealthy parents'.[71] Duncan's feelings towards Angelica were described by Spalding as 'acute, and if she had a bad night or showed any sign of illness he was upset, surprising himself with instincts that he had not previously known were there'.[72] Around this time his affair with Bunny was, as Spalding states, 'drawing to a close'.[73]

Duncan and Vanessa's relationship continued and developed into a lifetime non-sexual companionship where they shared the home of Charleston. After the end of the war, Duncan spent more time in London, socializing in Bloomsbury, visiting art galleries, creating artworks and exhibiting. In 1919 Duncan began showing his work with the London Group and in February 1920 he held his first solo exhibition at the Paterson-Carfax Gallery which Spalding notes 'marked a turning point in his career'.[74]

From 1920 Duncan had a studio at 8 Fitzroy Street which was the former studio of artists including Sickert and Whistler. Duncan had the studio until

1940, when it was destroyed by fire. The studio had large windows and, Richard Shone states, 'high, misted mirrors, its untouched eighteenth century atmosphere of great fires and candlelight, opened out from a small entrance at the end of a labyrinthine journey from the street'.[75] Duncan's studio was host to various parties and this studio was where Patrick and Duncan used to meet. Vanessa Bell had a studio adjoining Duncan's which was also destroyed in the 1940 fire.

During the 1920s Duncan continued to work in theatrical design, decorative work and paintings. In 1923 Duncan exhibited at the Independent Gallery in Grafton Street. The *Observer* described this exhibition as emphasizing 'the work of a mature artist who has derived enormous benefit from his earlier experiments and from his intimate acquaintance with the art of Cézanne and other modern Frenchmen'.[76]

In 1929 Duncan met George Bergen, who soon became his lover. George Bergen was a Russian Jewish migrant, who when six years old, moved with his family to join his father in the United States. George's art career started with a scholarship to the Yale School of Art and at age eighteen he won the prestigious Prix de Rome. He then moved to London and went on to hold his first solo exhibition in 1929 at the Goupil Gallery.[77] He moved back to the United States just before the Second World War, where he went on to marry Helen Gordon.[78] This new relationship was far more of a day-to-day companionship than the previous relationships Duncan had conducted and, Spalding highlights, it brought Vanessa sadness and insecurity, and Duncan guilt and anxiety. However, at the same time, 'Charleston played no small part in binding Duncan to Vanessa. Visitors to it felt they had entered another world – one complete unto itself, satisfying, apart'.[79]

During the 1930s Duncan continued to travel and work prolifically and exhibit his work in decoration, theatrical design, portrait, landscape and still life painting. Spalding writes of this time, 'given the number of exhibitions and decorative commissions that punctuate the early 1930s, it can be reckoned as one of the most productive periods in Duncan's life'.[80] In 1931 Helen McCloy of the *New York Times* wrote that the 'striking prominence' of London's Spring art season was 'the fact that for the first time in nearly forty years of the Royal Academy's annual exhibition succeeded in illustrating the most recent tendencies in modern British art'. McCloy pointed to the paintings on the walls of Burlington House 'with that close-knit design and free interpretation of natural color which modern British art owes to the influence of the London Group, among whose prominent members are Duncan Grant and Vanessa Bell'.[81]

Figure 4.4 Duncan Grant by Lady Ottoline Morrell, vintage snapshot print, 1930 NPG Ax143165, © National Portrait Gallery.

In 1937 personal tragedy struck Vanessa when her son Julian was killed in Spain where he had gone out to work with the Spanish Medical Aid.[82] Both Julian and Quentin were active anti-fascists and left-wing. Duncan's companionship and support was crucial during this time.[83] In late 1937 she and Duncan were to help with the setting up of the Euston Road School run by Claude Rogers, Victor Pasmore, William Coldstream and Graham Bell.[84]

The Bloomsbury Group's interactions with the ethnically diverse interwar presence in London were subject to and shaped by multiple dynamics and manifestations of race, racism and imperialism. In their publishing, Virginia Woolf and Leonard Woolf interacted and collaborated with some individuals from the interwar anti-colonial black presence, in particular C. L. R. James whose work was published by their Hogarth Press.[85] James' *The Case for West Indian Self-Government* was published in 1933 as part of their political pamphlet series.[86] Mulk Raj Anand provides a fascinating insight into the Bloomsbury group from the point of view of an 'insider' and 'outsider'. His memoir *Conversations in Bloomsbury* recalls his personal experiences and views on life in interwar Bloomsbury, including his interactions with individuals such as Virginia Woolf, Leonard Woolf, E. M. Forster and Clive Bell. Anand was a philosophy student from India and in his spare time he worked for the Woolf's Hogarth Press as a proof corrector.[87] In *Conversations in Bloomsbury: Colonial Writers and the Hogarth Press*, Anna Snaith stated of both Anand and C. L. R James: 'The position of these two colonial intellectuals in London – both polymaths and radicals – emphasises the metropolis' role as a crucible of anti-colonial politics. In particular, the Hogarth Press was a key disseminator of anti-colonial thought in the interwar period, suggesting an alternative take on its role as a facilitator of international modernism.'[88]

However, reminiscing about the gatherings hosted by Virginia Woolf, Anand 'noticed that most of the intellectuals, who gathered there for informal meetings, almost deliberately avoided politics in their talk.'[89] He wrote of the group: 'The writers of the Bloomsbury Group, and their affiliates in the Universities of Oxford and Cambridge were, of course, humane people, but like the exalted Mayfair-Kensington-Bayswater-Wimbledon-Kew Gardens middle sections, they remained enclosed in their precious worlds, without guilt about their status as aristocrats having been achieved by the labour of generations of industrial workers in Midlands and the colonies.' He recalled he was a 'young Indian, who had come through Amritsar in 1919' and had been influenced by Annie Besant to accept 'voluntary exile in UK from jail-going in the non-cooperative movement, to study the philosophies of the West' and though he 'valued the contacts and eminences of the Bloomsbury Group, [he] was nervous and on edge about the undeclared ban on political talk.'[90]

Duncan, Patrick and Queer London

Duncan socialized with many of the queer avant-garde London-based artists and writers in the interwar period, for example, Duncan's private view at Agnew's Gallery in November 1937 was attended by William Plomer, a South African gay friend of Edward Wolfe and writer associated with Bloomsbury, as well as Joe Ackerley and E. M. Forster.[91] It was perhaps in this artistic-queer space that Patrick and Duncan may have met. They knew each other by at least August 1938 and perhaps before. They probably met at some point in early 1938, after Patrick had returned to Britain from Jamaica, the year Duncan completed his first portrait painting of Patrick.

Patrick's life has to this point been referenced in just a few studies and though he lived his life outside of the Bloomsbury group of Virginia Woolf and all, he factored into Duncan's life as a lover and friend for many years. It appears that he was first mentioned in secondary literature in Spalding's biography on Duncan Grant. Spalding wrote that Duncan occasionally heard bits of news about George Bergen and 'he turned to others for distraction and made friends with a young black Jamaican, Patrick Nelson, the son of the famous wicket-keeper Leopold Nelson'. She then posits that 'they may have met through the painter Edward le Bas, who liked to cruise the East End from time to time and who, after Duncan let his studio in Fitzroy Street would put him and Patrick up occasionally'.[92] Others briefly mentioning Patrick's life have posited that they might have met in Soho or the Docklands. Exploring Soho as a space of gay sociability and a space 'that allowed for cross-racial encounters', Simon Faulkner argued that perhaps Soho provided the site where Duncan and Patrick first met.[93]

Soho and the East End were key areas of black settlement and socializing, including queer black socializing. In the case of the East End docklands area, queer life has recently been explored by Houlbrook in the groundbreaking book *Queer London*. Lodging houses and hostels were common in various parts of London, including the East End due to the shipping industry and dock industries, whereby temporary accommodation for dock labourers from around the world could be provided at a cheap cost. As Houlbrook states, using the term 'homosex' to describe sexual practice rather than a defined sexual identity, 'many of the workingmen who looked for homosex in London's public spaces depended upon lodging houses'.[94] These lodging houses and hostels were seen by various observers as 'immoral' and 'criminal', and homophobic viewpoints came into play in their reaction to these spaces. With regard to those living at boarding houses who were arrested by the police, one example Houlbrook found in the archives of the Metropolitan Police was of Gordon W., a ship steward who lived at the Sailor's Home in Wells Street, Stepney.[95] Queer and black life in the dockland area of the East End in the immediate post-war era has importantly been analysed by Nadia Ellis, who has looked at how contemporary ethnographers and sociologists viewed and in part pathologized both queer and black life, but also how in their studies and observations of post-war London identities they did not analyse or acknowledge the possibility of queer black identities intersecting.[96] In relation to queer East End life in the interwar period, as explored earlier in the chapter, Claude McKay's memories of life in London in 1919 to 1921 are fascinating. He recalled socializing at venues including the International Socialist Club, a place 'full of excitement, with its dogmatists and doctrinaires of radical left ideas: Socialists, Communists, anarchists, syndicalists, one-big-unionists and trade unionists, soap-boxers, poetasters, scribblers, editors of little radical sheets which flourish in London'.[97]

In Soho queer and black social spaces were in close proximity to each other and often overlapped. Queer black and white socializing in Soho took place in a range of venues, where artists, musicians, writers and others would mingle. An artistic group with links to social spaces including Soho were the Chelsea-based friendship and artistic network surrounding Barbara Ker-Seymer, Edward Burra and John Banting. Edward Burra and Barbara Ker-Seymer were artists who trained together in Chelsea. They socialized with fellow queer artist and performer friends such as the professional dancer Billy Chappell.[98] Though not as aristocratic, they were also linked in the 1920s to the 'Bright Young People' group who socialized in the clubs of Soho and in West End parties. Barbara Ker-Seymer's girlfriend in the late 1920s was society photographer Olivia Wyndham. They lived together in Chelsea at 19 King's Road and attended parties where they socialized with some queer black artistes in London, such as Leslie Hutchinson, a Grenadian bisexual musician and performer. During this time the group had a love of jazz and in 1926–7 often went to the *Blackbirds* revue, as mentioned previously, a highly successful revue of African American musicians and dancers starring Florence Mills. Mills and other members of the cast were the toast of this upper-class social elite, but this success was fused with the casts' experiences of racism from the press, the theatrical industry and even by fans. They also experienced racism at some of these elite parties where they would be exoticized or dismissed as entertainment.

During the 1930s Barbara Ker-Seymer socialized with artists Elisabeth Welch and Jimmie Daniels, two African American Harlem Renaissance performers living in Britain during the mid-1930s. Welch was a black American woman of African, Native American, Irish and Scottish heritage (Figure 4.5). She performed in musicals, cafes and films alongside actors including Paul Robeson. She was good friends with Leslie Hutchinson, socializing with him, as she recalled, in 'the marvellous late-night dives of Soho which, in those days, attracted all the stars and theatregoers'.[99]

Jimmie Daniels was an African American man born in Texas in 1908 who built up a successful career in New York and across Europe as an entertainer and host of nightclubs. As mentioned in the introduction, Daniels lived in London in the 1930s with his boyfriend Kenneth Macpherson, the Scottish film critic and director of the 1930 feature film *Borderline*, starring Paul Robeson and Eslanda Robeson. Jimmie and Kenneth lived together in Knightsbridge at 4 Kinnerton Street, Wilton Place.[100] Photographs in Barbara's personal archive, now housed at the Tate Archive, show a queer, multi-ethnic friendship network. The archive includes pictures of Elisabeth and Jimmie performing together and various pictures of Jimmie and Kenneth's day-to-day life. Patrick was, at one point in

Figure 4.5 Elisabeth Welch by Humphrey Spender, bromide print on card mount, June 1933, NPG x131702, © National Portrait Gallery.

time, part of this geographical world of Chelsea and Kensington, living in 1938 at 24 Netherton Grove in Chelsea and perhaps, being an artist model, he knew some of the members of this Chelsea-based artistic group.

The Shim Sham Club provides an interesting example of a Soho venue that had racially and sexually diverse patrons. The Shim Sham had opened in 1935 and quickly became popular with black, Jewish, lesbian and gay Londoners, among others. Judith Walkowitz reveals in her research on the club that the patrons socializing at the Shim Sham included Jewish anti-fascists and communists, as well as black pan-Africanists, who, she argues, 'transformed the club informally into a "democratic" and "international" space of the Cultural Front'.[101] The queer black musician Garland Wilson was one of the central figures in the creation of the Shim Sham as a major jazz venue. Garland Wilson was involved with the Shim Sham right from the start. He appeared as the second pianist on the opening night of the club in early 1935, with Happy Blake & His Boys as the main attraction.[102] Howard Rye has documented that Ike Hatch, later that year, 'hosted a party in Garland Wilson's honour at the Shim Sham' where Wilson 'introduced vocalist Ola May Bishop and Ike Hatch, and Larry Adler's brother on harmonica, before joining in'.[103] In summer 1936 Garland Wilson also performed at a venue run by Shim Sham owner Jack Isow called the Barn, which was based in Barnet, north London.[104] In September 1936, after returning from Paris, Wilson worked as 'mine host' at the Shim Sham until May 1937.[105] He performed there at the autumn reopening with the 'Shim Sham Swingers', an eight-piece band led by a drummer called Alfie Craig (a drummer who was interviewed by police in a raid against the club).[106] In autumn 1936 Garland Wilson performed on BBC radio his composition *Shim Sham Drag*, one of four solo recordings he recorded in London for Brunswick on 7 September 1936.[107]

Police surveilled jazz and bottle party clubs not only for evidence of their breaking licensing laws but also, similar to queer clubs, for so-called 'indecency', and the Shim Sham was attacked for alcohol but evidence of its perceived sexual 'indecency' was commented on and cited by the authorities as a further reason for the club's immorality. For example, in April 1935 the Shim Sham attracted the attention of the local Vine Street station 'C' Division which began its surveillance of the club. On 5 July 1935 the Shim Sham was raided by S. D. Inspector Deller with thirty officers, during which hundred people's names and addresses were taken. The case against a number of staff members of the club took place during August and September of that year and those convicted were fined in total £200 with costs of £52.10.0.[108]

As well as jazz clubs providing spaces for sexually diverse patrons, interwar Soho had a number of queer clubs. For example, Billie's Club, like the Shim Sham, was also established in 1935. It was based at 6 Denmark Street in the heart of Soho. Billie's Club was one of the queer clubs explored in Matt Houlbrook's *Queer London*. Houlbrook explored the importance of commercial spaces for 'the formation of queer social networks'.[109] In these spaces, particularly in queer club and pub venues, queer men (Houlbrook focuses on male socializing) could dance freely with other men.[110] As Houlbrook also outlines, public displays of queerness in venues such as these (instead of the ways in which middle- and upper-class men were more able to discreetly socialize in exclusive venues) were the main target of police surveillance in the 1930s.[111]

Billie's was run by a woman called Billie Joyce. It opened in October 1935 to promote, according to court files of the testimony of Sergeant Murray, 'social, sporting and recreative intercourse, without any political object'.[112] Joyce ran the club with the help of various individuals, including those who were eventually prosecuted alongside her, Vic Robbins, Connie Ivy Locke and James Rich. In November 1936, at a similar time to the Shim Sham surveillance, Billie Joyce was charged with having kept a disorderly house, with the charge stating 'wherein they did cause and procure divers immoral lewd and disorderly persons, using obscene language and behaving in a lewd, obscene and disorderly manner to the manifest corruption of the morals of His Majesty's liege subjects' and Joyce's co-workers, Vic Robbins, Connie and Rich were charged with aiding, abetting, counselling and procuring 'the said Billie Joyce to commit the said offence'.[113] At the Central Criminal Court in January 1937 Billie Joyce and a number of other people were brought to trial, and on 26 January 1937 she and fourteen others were sentenced to imprisonment, with sentences ranging from six months to two years.[114] The police started surveillance on the club in May 1936. The surveillance records are somewhat different to those of the Shim Sham as here the main motive of the police was to prosecute the club and its patrons due to perceived immorality, indecency and obscenity, and the focus of its surveillance and reporting was on the sexual activities, including 'indecent' dancing, of those in the club, but also on any significant indication of patrons breaking perceived notions of gender, such as gender queer individuals deemed by the authorities as 'immoral' by wearing make-up or clothes considered not appropriate for their perceived gender.[115]

Many of these queer clubs had a small black presence and even if not as large as the presence in bottle or jazz parties it is important to explore and document black life in these queer interwar venues. For example, Sergeant Murray reported on his 5 November 1936 visit to Billie's the presence of James Rich, 'a tall negro, who appeared to be taking an active part in the management of the Club'.

> At 10 o'clock Rich announced that Fred Barnes would sing some of his songs, which he did, to his own piano accompaniment. All the songs were old favourites with the general public. Rich then sang the song, 'Old Man River'. A half-caste man of about 25, who is a fairly regular frequenter of the Club then sang the song, 'Alone'. He has a very effeminate manner. At the time I was sitting on an arm of a settee, and on the same settee were four males. Two of these had their arms about each other and one of them said, 'Isn't she gorgeous' referring to the half-caste.[116]

Patrick and London's interwar queer avant-garde

It is not known whether Patrick visited Soho clubs such as the Shim Sham but there was a West End venue, the Café Royal, which Patrick did frequent and mention a few times in his letters and perhaps he and Duncan met through Edward Le Bas at this venue. The Royal was certainly a space where Patrick and Duncan socialized. Patrick mentioned this cafe in, for example, August 1945, writing that he 'enjoyed hearing of the Caffe Royal, give my love to Edward, and say I will send him a letter'.[117] A bohemian dining establishment founded in 1865, the cafe was popular with artists, writers and other members of London's avant-garde and during the interwar period artists and artist's models also used the cafe as a meeting place for work. It was also an important space for gay Londoners. Matt Houlbrook in *Queer London* states 'The Cafe Royal – and venues like it – remained an informal "home" for queer men from the theatre, literature, and arts well into the 1940s.'[118]

The West End as well as Soho was a geographical space for gay men to meet, have sex and socialize. Houlbrook has explored the range of ways in which individuals socialized with one another, exploring a number of sources including criminal conviction records for gay men and men of various identities who had sex with other men, and a 'reading against the grain' of these records has created a picture of the multifaceted lives of queer men in this period of time.

Patrick's letters during 1938 and 1939 place him firmly within queer socializing of the avant-garde and within the worlds of Bloomsbury and Chelsea, through work, relationships and home. In August 1938 Patrick was living in Chelsea at 24 Netherton Grove. It appears he was seeking work in domestic service and

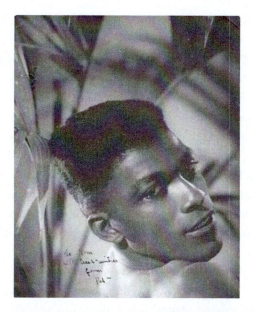

Figure 4.6 Photograph of Patrick Nelson, photographer unknown, 1938.

Figure 4.7 Duncan Grant, Patrick Nelson, 1938 Sotheby Parke Bernet & Co.

also working as an artist model. Work was hard to find and during this time Patrick wrote about the stresses of seeking to find employment.[119] During the time he lived in Chelsea Patrick was friends with Harry Daley, a white queer working-class policeman who had formerly been in a relationship with E. M. Forster. Daley was also friends with Duncan Grant, who painted his portrait in 1930. In a letter to Duncan, Patrick mentioned that after phoning the Vine Street station he was told that Harry had gone away for three days.[120] In a letter sent from Greece, probably in 1939, Patrick wrote 'Give my love Harry and say I would write but I don't know his address.'[121] In his memoir entitled *This Small Cloud*, Harry recalled that he was transferred to Vine Street station in the spring of 1935, so this means he was working there during the period of time when the station was at the centre of surveilling and prosecuting clubs such as the Shim Sham.[122] Harry describes the station as 'a dingy old building' but that he 'was proud to belong there and soon looked on it with affection'.[123] He reflected on the two 'snatchers' who were employed by the S. D. Inspector who he recalled were like 'hired assassins' stating 'when there was nobody to be watched or spied on, no policeman to be put in his place, no flower sellers secretly selling dirty postcards, no tarts congregating in out-of-favour cafés, no club doormen pimping for their girl-friends – they would set about the homosexuals. ... Minor offences in Piccadilly became major disasters when reported in local papers. Decent lonely men must often have looked into these pale pebbles and realised with sinking heart that here could be no softening, no kindness, no forgiveness, no second chances.'[124] Harry also reflects on the homophobia directed at him from Inspector Galloway, someone of higher rank than himself, who 'hated all homosexuals, and disliked me enough to literally snarl and foam at the mouth when discussing me'.[125]

As we can see, archival documents, letters and memoirs on interwar queer London such as Harry Daley's and Patrick's shed light on histories of white and black working-class queer men's lives. However, although queer socializing involving Duncan Grant's network included people of various backgrounds such as Patrick and Harry, there were deep class divisions at work within these wider networks and relationships and exoticized racism within these queer and avant-garde networks.

Patrick was not the only queer black Jamaican to socialize in queer and Bloomsbury circles. As explored in Chapter 2, the ballet dancer Berto Pasuka moved to Britain from Jamaica in 1938/9 and, by 1946, Val Wilmer states, Pasuka 'was part of Bloomsbury intellectual circles and living with a man of Fabian family connections' (Figure 4.8).[126] Similar to Patrick Nelson, Pasuka also posed

Figure 4.8 Berto Pasuka by Angus McBean, vintage bromide print, circa 1946, National Portrait Gallery.

for photographic portraits, working with Angus McBean. McBean was a famous London-based theatrical photographer born in Monmouthshire in 1904.[127] In 1946 when he was twenty-six years old, Berto Pasuka co-founded with fellow Jamaican queer man Richie Riley the all-black ballet company *Les Ballets Nègres*. As documented, Riley and Pasuka had been friends in Jamaica before the war, dancing together within a dance company that Riley had formed. After Pasuka wrote to Riley with news that he was ready to form a dance company in Britain, Riley migrated to London in 1946.[128] During his Black Cultural Archives oral history interview, Riley remembered that Berto Pasuka had decided to move to Britain because they 'discovered that theatrical – black theatrical ventures wasn't very well received in Jamaica by the general public'. After Pasuka wrote to Riley, he 'booked a passage on the very first ship to leave Jamaica after the war and landed in London – 14th January 1946'.[129] Before he left Jamaica Riley registered at a dance school in London and left Jamaica on an educational permit. When arriving in London he found accommodation through the Colonial Office at a student hostel for Caribbean students in Bloomsbury's Tavistock Square. [130]

Wilmer states of the diverse support for and involvement in the *Les Ballets Nègres*:

> George Bernard Shaw was among those who supported *Les Ballets Negres* which were financed in part by Pasuka's lover. Support for their endeavours came from the capital's African diaspora: from London-born dancer John Lagey, who became well-known as wrestler Johnny Kwango, to wardrobe mistress Vi Thompson, the first African girl to attend Roedean and a member of the Yoruba elite. The Ballets's accompanying musicians were all African. Among them was Nigerian bandleader-to-be Bobby Benson and guitarist Ambrose Campbell (italics added).[131]

The ballet company opened its first season of shows in April 1946, which were choreographed by Pasuka, and took place at the Twentieth Century Theatre in Westbourne Grove. The four ballets performed were inspired by African and African Caribbean history and culture; for example one ballet *Market Day* was set in a Caribbean market place.[132] Reviewing the company's 1946 Paris debut for the *Chicago Defender*, Edgar A. Wiggins called *Les Ballets Nègres* 'a unique creation interpreted by rhythmic dancing'.[133] As mentioned earlier in the book and explored in more depth in Chapter 9, Richie Riley was also a queer black Jamaican man and was an important friend to Patrick in the last years of his life.

Patrick and Duncan often wrote to one another during 1938 and 1939 not only to arrange where and when they would meet but also to share news of each other's lives. Patrick shared his artistic expressions and output, enclosing a poem he penned entitled 'The Sun Does Set' within one letter sent during 1938.[134] As well as posing for paintings, Patrick was also a photographic artists' model and his letters document his search for both types of modelling work. In 1938 he wrote about advertising for work as an artist model in *The Daily Telegraph* and received ten replies, with two of interest to him.[135] In September 1938 he sent an artist model-posed photograph of himself from 24 Netherton Grove, signed on the front side 'To Tom with best wishes from Pat'. The same photograph was signed a further, probably later, time on the back 'to Duncan from Tom & Pat with love'. This photograph was found inside a Cecil Beaton catalogue, which was bought at a book fair (Figure 4.6).[136] Patrick may have sent copies to friends and lovers such as Duncan and kept his own copy as a headshot to show prospective employers. The identity of Tom is unknown to the author, as is any information on whether he was a friend or boyfriend. Ephemera and fragmented memorabilia such as these are of significant and symbolic importance, highlighting the role of photographs as friendship gifts and the ways in which photographs were shared between people. They also highlight the difficulty in reconstructing a person's life from archival sources, and that a complete picture can never emerge of someone's life through the archive.

Patrick and Duncan often met in Fitzrovia at Duncan's studio at 8 Fitzroy Street and this became a space for them to socialize and be intimate with one another. As well as writing to one another, the telephone was another important means of communicating for arranging where to meet when Duncan was in London instead of Charleston. At some point, probably in 1939, Patrick moved from Netherton Grove to 9 Devonshire Terrace, Hyde Park. Some of Patrick's house moves may have been related to work, if, for example, he was still employed as a 'gentleman's servant'. Alternatively, perhaps he moved in with a friend or lover. At this time Patrick mentioned in his letters to Duncan a man called Robin.[137]

At some point Patrick embarked on a trip to continental Europe, perhaps because of his employment. He travelled (along with someone else whose identity is not known at present) to Greece, staying at Hotel Falerckon in Athens. For this trip he flew to Holland on 18 May (probably 1939), then travelled on to Germany where they had lunch and then arrived in Rome for dinner. He described the hotel as an old Palace.[138] In this letter he was unable to fully write about his trip. This reticence could have been due to work purposes if he was working for a military official and the visit was confidential or it could be that he did not want to write about any sexual encounters he had on his trip. He wrote, 'You will notice that I am writing from all the things that I have seen could never be written in a letter so the story must stay until I return to England.'[139] In a further letter he wrote when he was back in England, Patrick relayed that he had visited Copenhagen from where he was sent home by the British Council. So perhaps he was working for a British Council official. He reported to Duncan that he could not tell him of the wonderful time he had in Denmark as they had not time for that and also stated that he must join the army and become a decorated soldier, and that he preferred the navy but did not think they would accept him as he was over age.[140] The impending war would profoundly change Patrick's life. As explored in the next chapter he started working for the Royal Air Force in an administrative position based in Uxbridge before enrolling in the Auxiliary Military Pioneer Corps.

During his time working for the RAF, Patrick wrote about having a girlfriend called Olive. In an undated letter he asked for Duncan's opinion on whether he should marry Olive now that he was paying health and unemployment fees.[141] Robin, a boyfriend or friend of Patrick's, was in favour of it, and gave Patrick the furniture that they had used at Devonshire Terrace.[142] In a subsequent letter, also undated, he wrote about not seeing Olive anymore and that he had decided to take his furniture away from her (the pieces Robin gave him as well as the radio Duncan gave him which he wanted to keep at Duncan's studio if the studio tenant agreed).[143] The furniture he mentioned in this letter was located at Cavendish Street, perhaps where Olive lived during this time. It appears from a further letter that the owner or renter of the flat had decided to help him by keeping the furniture for him for 5 shillings per month. The full address given in a subsequent letter when he was stationed in France in May 1940 was No. 8 Chester House, Cavendish Street.[144] In a further letter he wrote about not being worried that Olive had disappeared (she had walked out of her accommodation at Cavendish Street) but he was worried that Olive might do something to hurt him and that the RAF would not accept any scandal – presumably he was worried that Olive would reveal to the RAF that he was a queer man. This period of time was stressful for Patrick; he reported in his letter that he was a 'little easier in his mind', and that he was glad to have Duncan, Robin and Jim in his life, 'With all my might & a little strength I am trying to do my work.' He also wrote that if there was anything he could do for Duncan's happiness, he could count on him 'without the slightest delay'.[145]

In another undated letter to Duncan he wrote, 'If you were still in London there would be no need for me to be fond of the girl nor any one else it is only because we can't see each other as we use to at the old Studio O-Duncan I wish we could once again be intimate and once more enjoy life – d[o] you think the days gone by will ever come again? We must hope.'[146] In November 1939, after telling Duncan of his plan to move back to London and then return to Jamaica (more details on this are explored in the next chapter) he reported that 'the girl', presumably Olive, would never know where he was and if she did write to his parents they would not believe her story.[147]

Duncan and Patrick's friendship and romantic relationship before the war was situated mainly within London queer male social networks but also, at least peripherally, within networks of those associated with the Bloomsbury group, particularly other queer members. For example, in a letter dated 9 February 1948 Patrick asked Duncan to 'give my usual address to Edward, and the Bells and if you see Mr. David Garnett you could please say how much I remember the restful time I had at his home before the war'.[148] Throughout

Patrick's letters there are remarks which show that he was acquainted with different members of the 'group' and other related interwar artists including David Garnett, Edward Le Bas, Edward Woolf and Ethel Walker. However, Patrick, it appears, was not connected to other key members of this group such as Leonard Woolf and Virginia Woolf. Several of Patrick's letters provide clues as to where Patrick and Duncan may have first met – at a party (perhaps a party Duncan Grant's mother held). After hearing of a bereavement, probably Duncan's mother who died in January 1948, Patrick wrote from Jamaica of his sadness, and how deeply he felt for Duncan over this bereavement.[149] He further recalled in this same letter how happy everyone at 'the party' had been and 'it also made me sad to think that it is only you and I are left out of that group of people at the party, I can remember how lovely everybody looked'.[150] Patrick also seems to have known about Duncan being Angelica's father and to have met Angelica. In one 1949 letter he asked 'I hope that Mrs Bell is still keeping good. And that Quentin is still at Oxford University. I will never forget beautiful Angellica whom I know you love … . Is Mr David Garnett still a writer? and has he written anything about your mother?'[151] In a later letter Patrick wrote to Duncan with further details on some of the friends they had in common, 'If you see the Duke of Norfolk Ethel Walker or Edward give them my kind regards.'[152]

Patrick, Duncan and portraiture

Soon after they met, Duncan and Patrick became lovers. During his first months with Duncan, Patrick posed for a series of portraits. Portraits surviving include pencil drawings and a 1938 oil on canvas of Patrick entitled 'Patrick Nelson' (Figure 4.7). In this 1938 painting he is painted wearing a white formal cocktail suit and is perhaps represented as a waiter. The painting was included in the May 1940 *Nine Painters* exhibition at the Lefevre Gallery.[153] It was also displayed in 'British Painting 1925–50 (Second Anthology)', a 1951 Arts Council exhibition under the title 'The Jamaican'. It was then included in 'Portraits by Duncan Grant: an Arts Council Exhibition' which took place in 1969. In this exhibition the painting was known as 'Portrait of Pat Nelson'. In the exhibition catalogue the painting was described as lent by the artist, thus still in Duncan Grant's personal collection. The catalogue description stated that 'he was working as a barman at the time of this portrait'. Presumably this information came from Duncan Grant himself. [154]

Perhaps he carried out this bar work at the Cafe Royal. The Cafe Royal was also a place where artists and artist models met. Guy Deghy and Keith Waterhouse described it as being similar to a labour exchange between artists and models.[155] Patrick might have first modelled for artists such as Edward Wolfe and Duncan through meeting them at the cafe. Along with archival material in the form of letters, these visual records of Patrick are significant for exploring not only his experiences but also his interaction with artists and his experiences in working as an artist model.

Duncan's representations of Patrick are all important as visual documents revealing histories of black Britain which need to be documented in black, queer and modern art historiographies. In these portraits Patrick enters a tradition of diverse artist models being represented in modern European artwork. Significant work on this subject has been undertaken by David Bindman, David Dabydeen and Beth Fowkes Tobin. However, not enough attention is paid to the intersections of black British history and art history within the discipline as a whole.[156] Recent curatorial research and exhibitions seeking to combat this neglect and focus on exploring black people in British portraiture include Paul Gilroy's Tate Britain 1995 *Picturing Blackness in British Art*, Jan Marsh's 2005 exhibition on black people in Victorian art and the 2014 Autograph ABP (Association of Black Photographers) exhibition and research project *Black Chronicles II* on Black Victorians in art curated by Renée Mussai and Mark Sealey.[157] The key pioneering publication and project on black people in European portraiture history is the Harvard-run *Image of the Black in Western Art* led by David Bindman and Henry Louis Gates Jr, first started in the 1960s by John and Dominique de Menil.[158] A recent publication from this project has explored black artists, models and visual representations of black individuals in twentieth-century art.[159] Recently, as explored in the introduction to this book, Caroline Bressey and myself have worked on the project *Drawing over the Colour Line* documenting and exploring the history and experiences of black artist models in interwar Britain. In our work we uncovered hundreds of interwar portraits and artist models of African and Asian heritage, many whose names we do not as to date know. Some of these portraits, including one of Edward Wolfe's 1930s paintings of Patrick Nelson, were included in the 2014–2015 Tate Britain display *Spaces of Black Modernism: London 1919–39* curated by myself and Caroline Bressey with Tate Britain curators Emma Chambers and Inga Fraser.[160] These representations are an important historical source to challenge ideas of black history in Britain being a post-1945 experience, and also are important in their enabling us to explore how and to what extent black people were part of the interwar artworld.

The relationship between models and artists in interwar London has not been explored to a great extent in historiography, though there have been significant recent publications exploring the lives of models.[161] Within *Drawing over the Colour Line* we uncovered how members of the Bloomsbury group and other London-based interwar artists painted and drew artist models of diverse backgrounds. For example, Fitzrovia-based artists such as Nina Hamnett, Duncan Grant, Roger Fry and Vanessa Bell created portraits of models of African heritage. Jacob Epstein and others such as Banting and Ker-Seymer painted and took pictures of close friends of African heritage and it can be said that their artwork is indicative of their socializing within London's ethnically diverse environment far more than individuals such as Grant. In particular, for Epstein, representing ethnic diversity in artwork was an important and deliberate endeavour.

Duncan Grant did not often work with black models as compared to artists such as Epstein and Glyn Philpot. Spalding states, however, that 'as a painter, Duncan was fascinated by the colouristic possibilities of dark skin tones, but it also had for him an erotic attraction, that of the forbidden other'.[162] In what way did racialized ideas of the 'other' permeate Duncan's artistic expression in the 1930s and how did his imperial and colonial background shape how he viewed men of African heritage such as Patrick? Grant's lovers, in addition to Patrick, also later included men of African heritage such as Jack Moore and Charles Boyle.[163] When referring to post-war Soho, race and sexuality within a discussion of John Minton's London and Jamaica, Simon Faulkner argues, 'The erotic images of interracial gay sex produced by Grant during the 1960s point to an ongoing fixation with blackness on his part that fits with the racial-sexual dynamics of the Soho delineated here'.[164]

The looming war changed the relationship between Patrick and Duncan as Duncan visited London less often. More significantly, Patrick's life was to take a tremendous turn when in late 1939/early 1940 he signed up to serve with the Auxiliary Military Pioneer Corps and was posted to France with the British Expeditionary Force. The next chapter explores Patrick's life in 1940s France, including his training before being posted abroad, his work at the AMPC headquarters, and the traumatic experiences of May 1940 when trying to escape France and being captured by the German forces.

A Jamaican Serviceman in the British Expeditionary Force in 1940 France

In early 1940 Patrick enlisted in the Auxiliary Military Pioneer Corps and as a member of this corps served in the British Expeditionary Force in France. He was thus one of many black individuals serving for the Allied forces in France, and one of the tens of thousands of servicemen within the British armed forces not rescued in Operation Dynamo, the evacuations of Allied forces from France in May and June 1940. Injured in the fighting and taken POW by the German forces in May 1940, he remained a POW for the next four years. This chapter contextualizes Patrick's experiences within wider historiographies, focusing on the establishment of the Pioneer Corps and its role within the British Army and the British Expeditionary Force and on the experiences of black British individuals during the Second World War. Most of the chapter consists of a descriptive summary of the deployment and day-to-day activities of Patrick's AMPC Company (the 76 Company) during March to May 1940 based upon a detailed examination of the Company's War Diary. The diary was compiled to comprehensively note the activities of the Company and provides an official, dry recording of the Company's experiences during May 1940. However, through examining these details, we can gain some understanding of the struggles, loss and pain faced by those troops. The War Diary is explored at length in order to highlight the experiences of the troops, including Patrick, and what they endured trying to escape France.

As mentioned in the last chapter, previous to Patrick joining the AMPC he worked for the Royal Air Force, it appears, in a civilian position. The same week he returned from Copenhagen he moved to Sedgewick Avenue in Uxbridge and obtained a job as a general assistant in the food department at Royal Air Force Uxbridge.[1] He wrote that he might be sent to France at some point as part of this employment. His room at 52 Sedgewick Avenue was a furnished room and he intended to eventually rent a house. His wages were '£1.5' (probably meaning £1 and 5 shillings) per week including four substantial meals per day. He worked from 9 am until 6 pm, with half a day off each week and a weekend off every other week. He was able to save 11 shillings 4 pence a week which he was saving for times to come. He also wrote about not being able to go out at night because of the blackout.[2] He felt very lonely during this period of time, away from London and his important queer friendship network. He thought of Duncan greatly and wanted to arrange to see him soon. It was during the time he was employed at Uxbridge that he was conducting his relationship with Olive and then after the relationship finished he worried (it appears, though it is not directly mentioned) that she would tell the RAF about his sexual relationships with men.

In a letter he wrote on 20 November 1939, Patrick reported that he was returning to London as his doctor had passed him as unfit for the type of work he was carrying out. He had decided to leave Uxbridge that Saturday, return to London and thereafter wanted to 'by all means' get back to Jamaica. His health problems were bad at this time and he reported that he was getting thinner. After returning to London he planned on the Monday afterwards to visit the Home Office, the British Council and perhaps the Foreign Office in order to try to find a way to return to Jamaica. If this plan did not work out, he wrote that he must find another job that could support him for the duration of the war. However, if he was to return to Jamaica he would find it hard to leave a life that was 'once was packed with friends' and that he would miss Duncan the most.[3] After leaving Uxbridge he found accommodation at 95 Camden Road and wrote to Duncan that the year had been confusing with so many disappointments, uncertain living and that he 'must find means & wages of getting help from the Government – really I will be glad to get back to my native land'.[4]

The Pioneer Corps and enlistment

Instead of returning to Jamaica, Patrick joined the AMPC in late 1939 or early 1940. In a letter sent to the Pioneer Records office in 1944, Patrick recalled,

> I joined up at the Seven Sisters Road in London, on the second of Dec. 1939 I stayed for a little at Caister on Sea, Great Yarmouth, then to Essex South end on Sea, then over to France early 1940.[5]

However, official military documentation registers that he joined the Auxiliary Military Pioneer Corps on 11 January 1940 at Holloway.[6] Patrick's father Leopold recalled in September 1940 that Patrick had 'joined the R.A.F. in England last November went to France to do "active service" was later transferred to the A.M.P.C. and was attached to the B.E.F. in France doing pioneer work'.[7] Although Patrick worked for the RAF for a short while, his main military career was as a private in the AMPC. Patrick may have been asked or requested to join the Pioneers instead of the RAF because of a visual impairment, which was not a barrier to joining the Pioneers. However, racism in the military was prevalent and there was racist colour bar operating in the Royal Air Force and so Patrick might well have been turned away by the RAF for this reason.

Roger Lambo states, 'In 1939, the peacetime recruiting regulations, which were issued under the authority of the Air Force (Constitution) Act of 1917, restricted entry into the RAF to men of "pure European descent". Under the Act, all "men of colour" were automatically debarred from enlisting either as officers, or in the ranks.'[8] In August 1923 an internal Air Ministry document 'Recruiting Regulations for the Royal Air Force' was published in which the nationality of recruits was limited to those of 'pure European descent and the sons of natural born or naturalized British subjects'.[9] Though this colour bar was officially lifted for wartime on 19 October 1939, it still continued in practice. Lambo states, 'In spite of this announcement, however, Black volunteers were, for the first six months of 1940, still being turned away by recruiting officers.'[10] The de facto continuation of the colour bar was protested against by a number of black British individuals in organizations such as the League of Coloured Peoples. Cy Grant, a Guyanese man who in post-war Britain had a successful career as a singer, actor, arts director, writer, broadcaster and activist, had direct experience of this racism.[11] In 1941 he was recruited by the Royal Air Force. Grant wanted to be a fighter pilot but after completing his training he was informed that he had to serve as a navigator. Years later after being shown Air Ministry records researched by Roger Lambo he was to painfully learn of the racism within informal Air Ministry policies.[12]

Patrick was one of many black men and women who were enlisted in the British armed services during the Second World War. As can be seen in Chapter 4 of this book, there was a diverse black presence in pre-war 1930s Britain and many black British individuals served in British units in the war. Recently a number of historical reclamation and heritage projects have worked on documenting the experiences of black people in the Second World War, including those of black British servicemen and women. Though still a neglected subject, historians including Marika Sherwood, David Olusoga and Stephen Bourne have done much to document and explore black history in relation to the two world wars.[13] Amelia King, her brother and father were one such black British family who served in the Second World War. Amelia King was born in Limehouse in 1917 and before the war worked as a fancy box maker. She volunteered to join the Land Army but was refused, being told that farmers objected to her due to her colour.[14] She took her case to her local representative Walter Edwards MP who then brought up the subject of racism within the Land Army in the House of Commons. She was also interviewed by activist George Padmore, who worked for the African American publication, *The Chicago Defender*. In the interview with Padmore she reflected on being rejected by the army and offered work in a munitions factory, stating 'I said to them, if I'm not good enough to work on the land, then I am not good enough to make munitions. No one has ever suggested that my father and brother were not good enough to fight for the freedom of England.'[15] Amelia King's father, Henry King, served in the merchant navy and her brother Fitzherbert King served in the Royal Navy. Henry King was born on 16 July 1887 in George Town, British Guiana.[16] In the *Chicago Defender* article of 1943 she reported that her father had been a fireman in the merchant navy for thirty-eight years and her brother had joined the Royal Navy a year before and was in service in the Mediterranean.[17] In the 1939 register Henry King was cited as working as a greaser on the SS *Lombardy* from 26 September 1939.[18] As a result of reading a newspaper article in the *Daily Express*, farmer Alfred Roberts offered Amelia King work on his farm and after being assured by the Land Army she could undertake this employment within the army, Amelia King accepted.[19]

Charles Arundel 'Joe' Moody, the son of Dr Harold Moody, the founder of the League of Coloured Peoples (LCP) was rejected from becoming an officer of the British Army due to racism.[20] As a result the LCP, together with the International African Service Bureau and the West African Students' Union, campaigned and lobbied the government. David Killingray states, 'Partly as a result of this pressure in April 1940 Arundel Moody, son of Dr Harold Moody of the LCP, who had already been rejected by an OTC on account of his colour, was gazetted as a second lieutenant in the Queen's Own Royal West Kent Regiment, the Buffs, thus becoming the first Black Briton to receive a commission in the British Army.'[21]

Thousands of Caribbean people from various countries volunteered to serve in the Second World War, with the majority enlisting in the Royal Air Force. Various Caribbean people also volunteered in non-military capacities.

For example, Ann Spry Rush has noted that 'about a thousand West Indians were recruited for war factories in Lancashire and Merseyside' and '1200 British Hondurans went to do forestry work in Scotland, and a smaller number joined the merchant marine'.[22]

Dudley Thompson, a Jamaican man who volunteered for the RAF, travelled to England as a civilian and enlisted in the British Army. Dudley Thompson grew up in rural Jamaica in Darliston, in a family that cultivated sugar cane and other crops.[23] He was Roman Catholic but attended various other denominations of churches.[24] His early years were spent in Panama, where he was born as his father was contracted as a teacher.[25] In Jamaica his father continued to work as a teacher and his mother as a seamstress. Thompson studied at the Mico College in Kingston, starting there in 1934. In Kingston he saw that 'the social barriers of race prejudice showed themselves much more sharply' than in rural Jamaica.[26] As a child he read his father's magazines, particularly Du Bois' *The Crisis* and he recalled 'It was with this background, all that I had been exposed to in Kingston and at the Mico, and the burgeoning ideas about my country and my race, that I set out to teach in the countryside'. His first teaching job was as schoolmaster in the parish of St Mary.[27] He recalled that he 'was teaching and learning at the same time' and 'longed to know, and to be able to teach my students, what was happening to Black people in other parts of the world'.[28] He also remembered the 1938 labour protests, as the school where he was working at the time was nearby the Frome Sugar Estate, where the labour uprisings of May and June started.[29]

At the outbreak of war, Thompson recalled, there was much demand to fight in the war and in Trinidad there were demonstrations because of Britain's 'hesitation ... to let Black men enlist in numbers to fight the war'.[30] Thompson remembered picking up *Mein Kampf* one day in a dentist's office in Kingston and after reading statements about Jews and 'Negroes' he decided to join up, being 'angry and stung into activity'.[31] He travelled to England as a civilian with other recruits who were then 'split up to join the various divisions of the army, air force, etc.'.[32] Thompson confronted and challenged the racism within the RAF. He recalled, 'Volunteering for the RAF had its difficulties. One of the questions on the form which I had to fill out was "Are you of pure European descent?" I answered "yes." When the recruiting officer queried me – thinking I hadn't understood the question – I challenged him to prove otherwise by a blood test. I think he gave up in disgust or frustration. This overt racism existed even under the stress of war, in the early stages'.[33] He was determined to train to fly, passed the required tests and after about three months of training was promoted to Leading Aircraftman.[34] Flying over Germany, he remembered they 'were suffering many losses; many planes were shot down' and he 'was wounded in the leg, flying over Nuremberg'.[35] He remembered meeting great friends during his period in wartime England, stating 'I was treated fairly throughout my training by those in command, and warmly by the Englishmen in ranks, including those under me'.[36] He also remembered meeting a number of activists in Britain from the African diaspora, including George Padmore. He recalled

> One lasting effect on me of this war period was that by 1945, I was coming into contact for the first time with West Indian, African and Black American soldiers, and with students, writers and blue-collar workers from the British colonies – all of us meeting in the Mother Country, the seat of the Empire. Being in England, fighting and suffering with her during the war, had truly opened the eye of the colonials. Having lain side by side with the English in the trenches and shelters, we felt we had more than proved our equality and had earned the chance for self-government.[37]

The Auxiliary Military Pioneer Corps which Patrick joined had its history in the Labour Corps formed during the First World War.[38] E. H. Rhodes-Woods states,

> The title given to the Corps was both unfortunate and lacking in imagination for, by implication, it divorced the fighting man from hard work, which was nonsense, and by the same implication segregated men capable of carrying out arduous duties from possible combat efficiency, which bore no relation to fact. Inevitably a lower military caste was created and when the Corps was eventually disbanded its name was removed from the Army List without notice or regret.[39]

Rhodes-Wood argued that decades following the war the lessons learned of the 'indispensability of trained, disciplined and armed labour units in any modern army were largely forgotten, or at best received no more than lip service'.[40] By September 1939 the army had created two divisions of Reservist labour battalions that, Rhodes-Wood describes, were 'trained and partly equipped', 'two divisions half trained and not equipped' and a 'paper' army of militiamen who had only joined for duty a few weeks previously'.[41] An expeditionary force went into France in September and by the end of the month there were four group headquarters, '26 companies of Reservists, mostly men from infantry regiments with some from cavalry units, performing labour duties with the Expeditionary Force'.[42]

Rhodes-Wood describes the initial problems in relations between labour and other services and the eventual formation on the Auxiliary Military Pioneer Corps on 17 October 1939:

> The Reservists detailed for labour duties, whilst largely resenting the divorce from their parent units, went overseas filled with enthusiasm, but it was not long before the continuous seven-days-a-week work, lack of welfare, poor clothing issue and the feeling that other units regarded them as inferiors reduced their morale badly and it is safe to say that when on 17th October, 1939, the Auxiliary Military Pioneer Corps was created no formation of the Army started its existence in less auspicious circumstances and suffering such severe handicaps.[43]

On 26 October 1939 the War Office opened the AMPC for recruitment. Recruitment took place throughout the country and the corps was initially designed for men normally between the ages of thirty-five and fifty.[44] Ten recruiting centres enlisted men, including the Seven Sisters Road centre where Patrick joined up and was placed in Grade II.[45] The duties intended for the AMPC were described in *The Times* as 'to ensure the proper maintenance of all kinds of supplies to our armies at home and abroad', in particular in 'the handling at docks, bases, and depôts of a vast amount of stores, and, to ensure the smooth transportation of such stores, roads and railways on lines of communication must be maintained in a fit condition. In addition, new roads may require to be constructed and light railways laid.'[46] *The Manchester Guardian* reported that on the first day of recruiting for the AMPC, 'over a hundred went to the Hulme Town Hall and comparable numbers to the Free Trade Hall and to the Mount Street Schools, Salford'.[47] Queues were also reported in London. *The Times* wrote on the recruitment for the Pioneers and also for the 'Cavalry of the Line, Royal Armoured Corps, the Royal Artillery, the Royal Engineers (for a variety of trades), and Infantry of the Line'. In London, there was 'a very large response among men wishing to join the new Pioneer Corps, formed with the main object of ensuring the proper maintenance of all kinds of supplies to our armies at home and abroad'.[48]

It is not known to the author whether many other black British individuals living in Britain joined the AMPC in late 1939–early 1940, but it was probably so, as it was during this period of time when the RAF was explicitly carrying out racism in its recruiting practices (despite the official October 1939 policy change). In England the recruits for the AMPC, such as Patrick, were trained and equipped at reception centres. The training took about four or five weeks and thereafter the Pioneers would be sent into service.[49] AMPC's Reception Centre

No. 1 in Folkstone was opened in October 1939. Again, initially the conditions at the Folkestone centre were bad. Rhodes-Wood states

> It is not suggested that any of these conditions were the fault of the Centre Commander, Lieutenant-Colonel J. Crookenden, D.S.O., who was faced with the herculean task of receiving and despatching an ever-growing flood of men, a flood which quickly developed into a torrent, without being supplied with the staff, accommodation or equipment with which to carry out the work in its early stages, but the inevitable consequences were quickly felt in the B.E.F. in November when it was decided to begin the return of the Reservists to their own units and replace them by recruits to the new-born Corps.[50]

The No. 2 Centre based at Caister was run by Lieutenant-Colonel G. H. Parker, M. C.[51] Patrick was posted to Caister on 11 January 1940 and, as stated by Patrick, he also spent time in Great Yarmouth, then Southend-on-Sea (Figures 5.1 and 5.2).[52] Thereafter, on 29 March 1940 Patrick was posted, along with the rest of the 76 Company, to the BEF in France, arriving at their destination on 30 March 1940.[53]

Figure 5.1 Patrick Nelson in military uniform. Scan of a photograph from Spalding, Frances. *Duncan Grant*. London: Pimlico, 1998 (first published 1997).

Figure 5.2 Four members of the Auxiliary Military Pioneer Corps at No. 2 Training Centre, Caister, Norfolk, 1939, Imperial War Museum, H 840.

The BEF, AMPC and Patrick

Previously, in October 1939 sixteen further Pioneer Companies and reinforcements were sent to France. None of the 123 skilled ship-worker recruits (reinforcements sent to France in October) posted to No. 11 Docks Labour Company had received any military training.[54] During November 1939 fifteen more AMPC companies joined the BEF in France, along with No. 11 and No. 12 Group.[55] By December there were 20,000 officers and men serving in the AMPC.[56] By the end of 1939 the AMPC serving in the BEF consisted of ten Group Headquarters and seventy-two companies.[57] That month No. 5 Group arrived, led by Lieutenant-Colonel D. J. Dean, V.C., T.D.[58] No. 5 Group operated in Doullens and it was this group that Patrick was to join on his arrival in France.

With the realization that the need for labour was seriously underestimated, the Pioneer Corps opened up during the end of 1939 to non-British Companies.[59] In February 1940 four new companies arrived in France, including No. 1 (Palestinian) Company led by Major H. J. Cator, M.C., which consisted of about 650 individuals from twenty-six different nationalities.[60] In addition to these Companies, the AMPC formed 'Alien Companies' consisting of refugees from

Nazism, mainly German and Austrian Jews.[61] These companies were formed during the period of internment, where refugees from Nazi Germany and Austria were confined as 'aliens' from enemy countries. These refugee companies also had separate training centres.[62] In November 1940 the *Manchester Guardian* reported that the

> Home Secretary is at last 'getting somewhere' in his aliens' policy. It has taken five months to get fully established the principle that friendly aliens should be utilised on war work for their country of refuge and not condemned to eat their heads off in prison camps and that on 26 November it had been announced that the exemption from internment would be opened up to 'all male internees between eighteen and fifty to demonstrate their loyalty by joining the Auxiliary Military Pioneer Corps.[63]

The Pioneer Corps was one of the corps that recruited in African countries in the 'High Commission Territories' (HCT-Basutoland, Bechuanaland and Swaziland), forming the African Pioneer Corps. These countries, Ashley Jackson states, 'contributed thirty-six thousand men to the estimated five hundred thousand Africans who by 1945 were in British uniform, either in fighting regiments like the King's African Rifles (KAR) and Royal West African Frontier Force (RWAFF), or in labour and support units like the African Pioneer Corps (APC), the East African Military Labour Service (EAMLS), and the Royal Army Service Corps (RASC).'[64]

In early 1940 the extra AMPC recruits to the BEF filled gaps made by those who were unable to cope with the conditions of the winter.[65] At the outset of the September 1939 declaration of war the BEF, which had started to be organized months before, was prepared to be sent overseas, and advanced parties of the BEF arrived in France starting on 4 September, a day after the declaration of war on Germany.[66] By 27 September there were 152,031 BEF personnel in France.[67] Edward Smalley has recently undertaken a study of the BEF during the 1939–1940 period. By May 1940, Smalley states, 'BEF strength had reached 394,165; out of this total 237,319 were in combat units and their related headquarters, whilst 156,846 were serving in rearward areas.'[68] In addition to the public memory myth making surrounding the history of Dunkirk, many of the precise details of the campaign have been obscured in memory.[69] The organizational problems within the BEF's campaign, Smalley argues, has left a lasting legacy 'in that it led to fundamental changes such as an increasingly scientific approach to discipline and the transformation of operational command to a brigade basis'.[70]

As stated, within the No. 5 group Patrick was a member of the 76 Company of the Pioneer Corps. During his service from March to May 1940, Patrick was employed as a runner and clerk.[71] It appears that Duncan did not know when Patrick was leaving for France. There are two letters written by Duncan to Patrick preserved in the Tate Archive. One is preserved in an envelope with return to sender and the other one composed on 12 May 1940 was perhaps also posted but never received by Patrick if it was sent to his British address. In the 12 May 1940 letter Duncan wrote that he was glad that Patrick was well and happy and stated that he had a 'rather interesting government job to go & paint ships & sailors. I have a show of drawings & a wall of pictures at Lefévers gallery. One is a portrait of you in a white cocktail coat. Do you remember it?' Believing Patrick was still in England, Duncan wrote that he was 'rather annoyed when I heard you had been in England for two months after you had told me you were going to France. In fact that is why I have not written. I wonder how you explain it.' Duncan also wrote that he had received a letter from Patrick and gathered from this letter that Patrick had written three times but he did not get the first letter.[72] It is unclear to which letters Duncan is referring and whether these are preserved in the Tate Archives.

Meanwhile Patrick wrote to Duncan on 11 May 1940 that he had received a letter from Duncan and that he did not understand why he had not previously had any other letters from England and was terribly disappointed in all his friends. He wrote that he was very lonely having no relatives in England and France. Patrick made a will in the event of his death and wrote to Duncan about where to find it, the location of his bank account and that he had given the army his mother's address and Duncan's name as nearest to kin in England. He passed on his mother's Kingston address so that Duncan could inform them if anything was to happen to Patrick. He wrote that 'my Father as a retired and grand old Celebrity' would be grateful to be informed by a 'great man' like Duncan if anything did happen.[73] He also described his work and that though where he was located was not a picnic he had enough of what he needed and had the advantage of a type writer as he was doing office work. He ended his letter telling Duncan about his will that 'my belongings and what I have here is yours who has been a friend to me in sickness and in trouble'.[74] The timing of this letter was one of the first few days of the 'Battle of France', when Germany invaded France and the Low Countries.

As detailed in the official War Diaries for 76 Company housed within the War Office records of The National Archives UK, the unit arrived at Le Havre on 29

March 1940 and then travelled on to Beaumetz the following day.[75] Thereafter the whole company with the exception of six sections left for the journey to Doullens (the No. 5 Group headquarters), with the other sections travelling elsewhere: two sections travelling to Mondecourt, two sections to Amplier and two sections to Candas. Patrick was stationed, as already stated, at the No. 5 Group HQ formally carrying out office work. In Doullens on 31 March, two sections were employed in urgent R.E. (Royal Engineers) works and the remainder alongside out-stationed sections were medically inspected and engaged on work in billets. During April the Company worked on attached duty to R.E. at various places including Candas, Amplier, Marieux Wood, Bully Les Mines, Beauquesne and Doullen. Rarely are names given for the individual 76 Company members in the diaries and returns, except for in the weekly returns where individuals have left the company. Injuries to members are also mentioned. On 18 April it was reported that Private Kilburn was fatally injured in a lorry accident, and Private Butterfield suffered from concussion and a broken arm. On 27 April the 76 Company consisted of two officers (a Major and Captain) and in other ranks 263 individuals including 223 privates, 13 L/CPLS, sixteen corporals, ten sergeants and one WO. Class II and the Company requested fifteen more privates and the return of an officer previously with the Company.[76] In the beginning of May the company continued to work in conjunction with R.E. at Doullens, working on the construction of hutting and roads; at Marieux Wood, clearing hut sites; and at Candas, offloading R.E. material from the railway, and stacking and loading for road transport.[77]

Rhodes-Wood describes what happened to No. 5 Group later in May 1940 during the German invasion and British evacuation:

> An impression of the general state of confusion existing at this period can be gathered from the fact that immediately prior to leaving Doullens the Group was accommodating in the town a battery of Royal Artillery, with guns, moving back from the line and four batteries of artillery, without guns, going into the front line. On 19th May Colonel Dean was instructed to forsake Doullens and take the group to Boulogne by any means possible. Accordingly, with 47, 81, 102, 121, 122 and 123 Companies, plus small detachments of other units which as the OC. Troops he had taken under his charge, the Group moved across the country in six columns to St. Pol, where the night was spent bivouacked outside the town. The total strength of the Group was then about 1,200. The countryside was now in a state of chaos with thousands of hungry, fear-crazed refugees blocking the roads as on foot, by horse transport or in motor vehicles they traversed France in endless streams, aimlessly and panic stricken moving in all directions.[78]

Continuing with an exploration of Rhodes-Woods' research on the No. 5 Group, on 20 May Colonel Dean managed to find, 'by bribery and persuasion', an engine driver who would drive the group to Boulogne but by the time they reached St Pol the railways were no longer functioning.[79] Colonel Dean found food and petrol and with three lorries and an ambulance commandeered they began the journey by road to Boulogne, under the command of Captain R. Bland, M.C. of the 122 Company.[80] However, they then heard that an 'enemy mechanized force' was outside of the town and detachments were 'detrained' to engage the force.[81] When No. 5 Group arrived in Wimereux the Pioneers, Rhodes-Wood states, 'became the largest British force in the area and Colonel Dean began preparations for the defence of the town, detailing a party of 400 men to unload explosives and ammunition from the hold of a ship in the harbour which the civilian dockers would not touch owing to the frequent enemy air raids on the dock area'.[82] Dean wanted to send some of his unarmed men to England but was instructed not to do so.[83] On 22 May orders were given to Dean to despatch a party of men to hold the 'crossings of the River Canche from Etaples to Montreuil'.[84] After being outflanked by German units, they withdrew to Boulogne. Here, Rhodes-Wood states, 'Colonel Dean found that two battalions of the 20th Guards Brigade, the 2nd Irish Guards and 2nd Welsh Guards, under the command of Brigadier W.A.F.L. Fox-Pitt, had arrived from England with orders to hold Boulogne "to the last man and the last round".'[85] Dean reported to Fox-Pitt for his instructions.[86]

On the evening of 22 May, 'by nightfall' Dean, seeing that holding Wimereux became 'untenable', withdrew No. 5 Group into Boulogne.[87] When the group had taken its defensive position there were further German attacks. Colonel Dean travelled to enlist support from Brigadier Fox-Pitt and during this travel his car was attacked. The brigade commander, also receiving a 'similar request' from the Welsh guards, stated that he would try to help but was unsure whether he was equipped. Colonel Dean had to travel back to the group on foot and while he was absent on 23 May Colonel Stanier of the Welsh guards informed No. 5 Group that the 'guards were withdrawing to the harbour for evacuation'.[88] The guards' withdrawal started before they could realign their defence. The group moved to the Gare Maritime where they defended the barricades, under heavy attack. Injuries were sustained by Dean who was knocked unconscious and thereafter Major G. C. Gaden, M.C. took control of the group, thinking Dean had been killed. Regaining consciousness later that evening near to midnight, Dean took back control. The Gare Maritime was on fire and the rearguard of Pioneers who totalled about 600 men withdrew to the quay. In the early hours of 24 May HMS

Vimiera approached the harbour and they sailed for England, together with men from other regiments. It was the last ship to leave before the port fell.[89]

The 76 Company experienced a different end to their service in France as on 11 May instructions were received from the officer commanding the No. 5 Group that the 76 Company were to transfer to P.C. No. 11 Group and proceed immediately to Farbus.[90] A 76 Company rendezvous was arranged at Amplier but two sections under Captain E. B. Methven did not keep to this rendezvous. The company without these two sections continued on to Farbus, arriving later that day though it was reported that the area commandant had not been told to expect them. The two sections under Captain Methven arrived later that evening. From 12 May most of the company were employed at Farbus offloading R.E. material and loading trains. On 18 May the 76 Company received instructions from the officer commanding the No. 11 Group to march starting at 9 am to Liévin. At Liévin they were instructed to carry out an infantry role and act as part of the British force defending Lens. The officer commanding the 76 Company decided to position in depth in Bois de Hirondelle. On 19 May they consolidated the forward positions, established secondary strong points and the officer commanding the Company assumed the duty of the officer commanding the troops and established a heavy road-block on Arras-Liévin road and from the rear of the main defence position.

The refugee situation surrounding them was extremely serious, with 'packed masses of Dutch, Belgian and French refugees'. The War Diary noted that the Company's movement was impeded as a result. Additionally, there were 'continuous air raids on position and towns of Liévin and Lens'.[91] On 22 May it was stated that they were still out of touch with any British or French troops and were living in the country and abandoned RASC Dumps. The officer commanding the Company then decided to try to make contact with the officer commanding the No. 11 Group and left the Company with Captain Rea with a rendezvous and a route for the retirement of the Company in case the situation became untenable. However, the OC of the Company did not make contact with No. 11 Group 'which appeared to have left its Hq as adjacent village of Liebercourt was found to have been heavily bombed and was in flames'. The OC of the Company then found 1 Corps and reported the loss of contact with higher formations (i.e. Groups). 1 Corps contacted GHQ and thereafter the OC of the Company was instructed to remain in a defensive position and the OC of the Company found the main body of the Company who were by then entering Lens. Captain Rea reported that British artillery had left the reverse slope of

Vimy Ridge and it was therefore necessary to retire. The OC of the Company then instructed the Company to return immediately under Captain Rea to Liévin. The bombing during this time was reported to be very heavy but there were no company casualties. It was then found that Liévin had been evacuated. The OC of the Company made contact with GOC 50 Division and they instructed the OC to ignore their last orders and retire immediately to the original intended rendezvous, Loison, and if possible, to go beyond this location. As they had been marching for several hours they decided to billet for the night at Loison.[92]

On 23 May the Company left under the command of Captain Rea and when the OC of the Company attempted to contact 1 Corps, they found that they had left the headquarters and after exploring Lille the 1 Corps' headquarters were found in Armentieres. Thereafter GHQ instructed the OC of the Company to place the Company under Pol Force at Sailly. On the way he encountered a severe air raid and a British plane crashed close to the car with the pilot killed. The OC traced the Pol Force headquarters at Sailly on the Armentières-Béthune road and reported to General Curtis. The OC then received instructions from General Curtis to report to Brigadier General Ramsden operating with Pol Force. After reporting to Brigadier Ramsden he received instructions to report to 2 BN Essex Regiment immediately and was told that the bridge at Pont-à-Vendin would be left available for the company to use until 7 pm that evening, but thereafter it would be destroyed. The OC returned to the Company rendezvous and instructed Captain Rea to immediately travel as ordered. Contact was then made with the OC of the 2 Essex and the defensive area in a big mine compound at Estevelles was assigned to the Company to occupy immediately. The OC of the Company carried out reconnaissance of the area and posts to cover the night of 23 to 24 May before full defence dispositions were to be carried out at dawn. There were very severe air raids at 6.45 pm that evening and Pont-à-Vendin station was bombed and set on fire causing explosions. The Company had not crossed the bridge by 7 pm and so the OC of the Company considered the roads, and saw that the road to be taken by the Company, despite damage, was feasible for the troops to use.

The OC then made contact with the Company in the main Lens-Carvin road and Captain Rea had heard unconfirmed reports that Pont au Vendin bridge had been blown up. Due to time concerns, the OC of the Company decided to alter the route and try to use the bridge on the main Lens-Carvin road. They crossed the bridge and arrived in the defensive area at 10.30 pm that evening. The night positions were then taken up immediately.[93] AMPC recruits near

Arras were mentioned in *The Times* on 24 May 1940. The newspaper stated, 'An exploit by members of the Auxiliary Military Pioneer Corps (Labour Corps) in capturing two German tanks near Arras was described in London yesterday. Several German tanks entered a village and pulled up at a petrol station to refuel. Groups of pioneers working by the wayside with picks and shovels attacked the tanks and damaged the tracks. Then they disarmed the crews and captured them.'[94]

Continuing with information gleaned from the War Diary, on 24 May 1940 consolidated positions were occupied, splinter-proof shelters were dug, and other defensive actions were carried out such as arranging road blocks and reconnoitred lines of retreat, in case they were needed.[95] On 25 May the 76 Company continued in improving the defences. After reporting to 2 Essex the OC received instructions to act under the orders of the Leicester Regiment, who were relieving 2 Essex. He was told that the Leicester Regiment would make contact and the Company despatch rider was instructed to remain at the battalion headquarters for communication. By 5 pm, however, the Leicester Regiment had not made contact and so the OC of the Company reported to the late 2 Essex headquarters. At 5.30 pm the OC of the Company had traced the second lieutenant representing the Advanced Battalion headquarters in the village and this official promised to liaise with 76 Company when the battalion headquarters arrived. The diary records that evening that it was obvious that the French and British canal line was giving way, the French African troops had retired, British anti-tank guns had withdrawn and demoralized British troops retired into 76 Company's defence position. By 8.30 pm the French African unit and horsed anti-tank gun moved into a defence position. As explored in the following chapter, West African troops in France played a significant role in the Second World War. Raffael Scheck states, 'In 1940, Africans constituted nearly 9 percent of the French army serving in France. In the spring of that year, the forces that attempted to hold the line against the German onslaught included large numbers of French West African troops in five colonial infantry divisions. In the final days of May, French West African troops protected the retreating French and British forces as they made their way to the beaches of Dunkirk for evacuation to Britain.'[96]

By 9.30 pm on 25 May there had still been no contact or instructions given from the Leicester Regiment and as their position was becoming unsustainable a runner was sent to the battalion headquarters to report their intention to evacuate at 10.30 pm if no instructions were received. Previously at 8.15 pm that evening Cuthbert and 49 other ranks who were not armed were placed under Sergeant Tyler's command and left with instructions to march and report to Neuve Chapelle. At 11 pm they destroyed the French anti-tank gun and left the area with a 'number of stragglers from British and French units'. At this time the British line of front or retirement was unknown to the OC of the 76 Company because of not hearing from the Leicester Regiment but they presumed that the route taken was across the country to the north of Lens. They marched through the night and at 2 am on the morning of 26 May they made contact with 2 Essex and arranged to co-operate with them instead. At 4am the march was resumed, with the 76 Company marching behind 2 Essex and at 6 o'clock in the morning they occupied a defensive area in a village south of Annoellin. At 8am they were ordered to leave the village; they marched all day and by 4 pm occupied a defensive area on the south side of Fromelles alongside 2 Essex. That evening they received instructions to report to 139 Bde at Salome on 27 May. The OC of the Company went to report to the Bde (before the whole company were to march) and arrived there at 7.45 am. The town was under heavy fire and the OC was unable to find any British or allied troops among the flames. The unit car was followed by enemy artillery when it left the town. The OC returned to Fromelles and reported back. At 10 am that morning the village and roads were bombed heavily and the battalion headquarters were damaged. The unit had left the village without instructions to 76 Company.

At midday on 27 May the Company was left under the command of Captain Rea with a rendezvous and route to leave arranged in case it was needed. At this time it appeared there was a general retirement of French troops. The OC of 76 Company was unable to find 2 Essex Battalion on the roads to La Bassee, Sailly or Estaires. On returning to the Company the OC found they had evacuated and then rendezvoused with them. At this place Captain Rea informed the OC that the brigade commander had telegraphed instructions to continue to a map reference via Laventie. This journey involved five more hours of marching. The Company was left under the command of Captain Rea who continued the march to the map reference via Estaires, which was being heavily bombed and which was reported to be very difficult to travel through due to debris and cratered roads.

Contact was then made at the map reference and the OC was told that 76 Company had been left out of an operation order for retirement. They were assigned a defensive area and after reconnaissance the OC travelled in order to make contact with the Company as speed was needed due to a proposed demolition of canal bridges at Estaires. The OC of the Company then continued with lorries and a unit car. The company personnel failed to report and it was presumed they had been diverted to a more easterly bridge in order to cross the canal. The defence position given to the Company was held by the OC of the Company and eight men, under torrential rain which started that evening at 11.30 pm. At 1 am on 28 May the runner reported to 2 Essex Battalion headquarters that the defence position was very thin and 'that large parties of demoralized British troops were filtering through area'. They received an acknowledgement and order at 2 am to retire to a map reference near Le Verrier with the battalion. After consulting with the battalion commander at Le Verrier it was decided to continue travelling to Doulieu and try to contact the Company. The Company was contacted but with several men missing and thereafter men were placed in billets for a few hours of rest. Food and clothing from the stores was also found.

The OC then received instructions to march at 11.30 am and he was told that the rearguard had already moved. The diary reports, '76 Company had apparently again been overlooked when operation order issued.'[97] As no orders were given to the 76 Company they marched independently to Méteren, via Godewaerswelde. At Godewaerswelde they met with many demoralized Belgian troops. They left the village but then came across a motorcyclist who was an OC and the only member of his Artillery Regiment not taken prisoner when the regiment was ambushed north of the village. They then went back to Godewaerswelde and established road blocks. The OC of the Company instructed Captain Rea to continue the journey to Méteren and then the OC reported their position to the Brigadier at Méteren. The Brigadier instructed the OC to go with him on a reconnaissance to ascertain the enemy tank concentration position, and the Company was ordered to remain at rendezvous at the North end of Méteren and wait for the OC's return. However, after the reconnaissance the Company was not at the rendezvous point. Méteren was 'completely choked on all roads with British & French troops'. One of the Company NCOs told the OC that the Company had marched towards Bailleul under the orders of Captain Rea. Thereafter the unit car was sent to contact the Company and they were able to collect 50 men.

The brigadier then ordered all units to send vehicles by road to the east of the roads used by the men who were on foot. From this time contact was lost with the unit vehicle and other vehicles. The march continued towards Furnes and at about 8pm an order came that all transport on roads exceeding fifteen cwt should be abandoned and thereafter the march continued on foot for all personnel. There torrential rain continued, soaking the maps of men 'unfamiliar with Belgian place names and language'. At 1 am on 29 May they arrived at the village of Watou and the men were sent to empty homes for a few hours. This village had been bombed and the diary reports that it was 'completely without food or water'.[98] At 8 am they continued the march to the coast with 2 Essex. At about five miles outside of Dunkirk a lorry transport was found but there was a block in the village a few miles outside of Dunkirk and there was also heavy German bombing of the lorries. Due to the lorry formation seen as an incentive to bomb, the OC of 76 Company advised other senior officers that he intended to order lorries to continue moving with fifty-yard gaps between them. The vehicles arrived at the outskirts of Dunkirk at midday and there encountered an 'exceptionally heavy aid raid'. The men then marched to sand dunes and were made to be still during the raids. On 30 May it was arranged to embark the troops in groups of fifty in order of the time they arrived at Dunkirk. The 76 Company evacuated late that afternoon and arrived in Dover late in the evening, where they were immediately sent to Chiseldon, Wiltshire, arriving at 3 am on 31 May where the men who made it home were given a 'good meal and accommodation for rest'.[99]

Operation Dynamo resulted in a far more successful evacuation of Allied forces imagined or expected, with 338, 226 troops evacuated.[100] Despite the success many were taken prisoners during and after the operation. Neville Wylie states, 'By the time the remnants of Britain's expeditionary force had been rounded up and escorted to their prison camps in Germany, some 44,800 British servicemen had been lost to German captivity, including over 1,500 army officers, 291 pilots and 436 aircrew'.[101] Patrick was one of these BEF prisoners. Wounded in both feet, he was taken prisoner he remembered on 24 May 1940, six days before his Company was evacuated. Details of his capture, imprisonment and survival are recorded in his many POW letters to Duncan Grant, to his family, to military officials in the Pioneer Corps and to the West India Committee. The following chapter explores these sources, examining as much as possible Patrick's experiences during his capture and imprisonment as well as his reflections on these experiences.

Imprisonment and Survival in the German Prisoner of War Camps

This chapter reconstructs Patrick's POW experiences, in particular by exploring his attempts to maintain his spirits through the letters and postcards he wrote to Duncan during his time in captivity. It also explores the letters sent by his parents Leopold and Gertrude, the International Red Cross and the West India Committee to Duncan Grant, who acted as his next of kin. Examining Patrick's experiences in the various Stalags in which he was captive, it assesses his experiences as a black POW, the role of education and learning in Patrick's survival in the camps, and his emotional life in the Stalags. Patrick's POW letters are incredibly rich in detail and emotion, and are a significant source not just for constructing his biography but also for revealing important, broad insights into the POW experience. This chapter explores his identity as a Jamaican serving in the British armed forces, and compares his experiences to other black people serving and black POWs. It explores the POW cultural and educational life in addition to developments and issues surrounding wartime psychiatry, including developments in psychiatry by British POW doctors. It also explores Patrick's life in the context of other POW writers, utilizing memoirs, biographies, photographs and contemporary newsletters created by POWs.

Patrick reflected on his experiences during the horrific days of his capture in late May in letters to Duncan Grant, to the Pioneer Records Office, and in an interview to the *Gleaner* in June 1945 after his return to Jamaica. He reflected to the *Gleaner* interviewer that he hoped to write down his thoughts and experiences of the war on to paper.[1] If he did write down these thoughts, the document is yet to be found but in the interview he remembered the German attack which 'swooped down on them with overwhelming might' in the small

French town of Doullens, at the Pioneer HQ. He recalled, 'They attacked us with incendiaries, bombs, long range artillery and tanks' and

> We fought it out with them and for a time it was rather grim but naturally as they had many divisions advancing in that territory they overpowered us less than no time. We were then marched all the way for some 800 miles across Belgium and France and then Germany to prison.[2]

During the march Patrick collapsed and was sent to a hospital in northern France and, he recalled, 'As I was not fully recovered, the Germans gave me a lift in one of their lorries going to Belgium; from Belgium, I was transported to Germany.'[3]

Patrick also detailed his initial capture in letters sent to Duncan Grant. The first letter Duncan received was during late 1940. In it Patrick wrote, according to Gertrude (to whom Duncan sent the original letter) that 'he was wounded during the evacuation at Dunkirk and was made a prisoner of war.'[4] In a letter sent in late 1944 to the Pioneer Records Office asking what ribbons and title he was entitled to, Patrick reported he was 'taken prisoner of war on the 24th of May 1940 in France, near Dunkirk' and 'last was with Col. Deane of the 76 Com. A.M.P.C. H.Q. at Doullons, in France, before captivity'.[5] As Patrick mentioned Colonel Dean, does this mean he stayed with No. 5 Group travelling to Boulogne until he was captured or did he continue with his own company, 76 Company, when they were ordered to move from No. 5 Group to No. 11 Group? As the 76 Company were transferred to No. 11 Group just a few weeks before capture, it is possible that he may have conflated his experiences and left out of his written memories that Colonel Dean was not his last group commander. It is also possible that as his job involved working as a typist at HQ, the No. 5 Group required that he stay on with them instead of travelling on with his Company. A February 1941 short article in the *Gleaner* entitled 'Mr Patrick Nelson. War Prisoner in Germany' reported 'it now transpires that the young Jamaican soldier was captured by the Germans in Bologne [*sic*], to which port he had gone with his regiment to be evacuated to England. He was among the last lot to arrive and with several other soldiers evidently fell asleep from sheer exhaustion while the harbour was under heavy bombardment from German air and land forces, and was unfortunately left behind'.[6] In an article in July 1941 it was reported that 'Mr and Mrs Leopold Nelson have received word that their son, Patrick Nelson, who was a unit of the British Expeditionary force to France and Belgium, and was taken prisoner at Bologne [*sic*] on May 24 1940, was, wounded in both feet, which necessitated his being taken to hospital'.[7] Additionally, one of the letters Patrick sent to Duncan with the address given of No. 5 Group HQ is dated 12

May 1940, the day after the 76 Company left the Group HQ. Therefore, he might have either travelled with 76 Company or served and fought with No. 5 Group throughout the rest of May before his capture on 24 May.

Status: Missing

Although Patrick became a prisoner in May 1940, it was many months before Duncan, Leopold and Gertrude found out whether or not he was still alive and it was a whole year before he was officially listed as a POW instead of as 'missing'. It often took a great deal of time for family, friends and officials to find out detailed information about missing personnel.[8] Leopold and Gertrude were informed by the army that Patrick was 'missing' (Figure 6.1) and in September 1940 Leopold Nelson wrote to the Auxiliary Military Pioneer Corps, requesting that they write to him again if any further news arrived. Leopold also wrote that 'we very much

Figure 6.1 The *Gleaner*, 30 September 1940.

regret to hear this bad news and hope that it may be he is some where in France or even a prisoner, but if he is dead we feel *proud* to know that we gave to the mother country our loving son St Patrick who could have died for no worthier cause than for his King and country in suppressing Hitlerism'.[9]

In December 1940, Gertrude Nelson wrote to Duncan Grant to thank him for a recent letter and for trying to find out from Colonel Dean about what could have happened to Patrick. Gertrude told Duncan Grant they had been informed by the government that Patrick was missing but that in November 1940 she had received a copy of a letter from the delegate of 'Croix Rouge de Belgique' in France. This letter, forwarded to Duncan, was sent to Gertrude in September 1940. It reported that Patrick was in good health and 'excellent morale in the Military Hospital at Cambrai'. After receiving this letter Gertrude tried to find out more but had not heard anything further after writing to Patrick. Gertrude asked Duncan to pass on the letter from the delegate to 'Lieut-Colonel Dean or to competent authority, thus making it possible of obtaining more possible truth or certainty as to his where abouts'. She poignantly continued, 'Although we have been informed as much from the Delegate, still we are anxious to be better informed, and I do hope that with the letter much will materialize. Oh! how much do we think of him daily, how much do our anxiety increase. May God bless and keep him wherever he may be, I only hope that he is alive.'[10]

Throughout the war Duncan and Leopold and Gertrude Nelson often wrote to one another with information about Patrick. In a letter sent in September 1940 Leopold wrote to Duncan, 'thanks a thousand times as we would never have known the sad news' and that 'I hope sincerely my dear friend that he is missing and as you have promised to let us know as soon as you hear we, therefore place our entire confidence in your hands'. It appears that Duncan and not a member of the military was the first person to tell Leopold and Gertrude about Patrick being missing.[11] Leopold, Gertrude and Duncan all wrote to a variety of British officials seeking news about Patrick.

Although Leopold and Gertrude had been informed by the Belgian Red Cross about Patrick's status as a POW, the British still had him listed as missing even in early 1941 as they had not received the POW news through official channels. On 27 January 1941 Duncan Grant reported to Colonel Dean about Patrick being found alive.[12] This letter was then forwarded from Colonel Dean to the Bournemouth Pioneer Corps Records Office who then wrote to Duncan in early February 1941 that their records showed him 'unfortunately, as "Missing" and then asked Duncan to 'please to send any letters or evidence which you may have in this respect, when after perusal I should be pleased to officially post him as "Found" instead of the present unhappy state of "Missing."'[13] Duncan then sent on the letter to the Pioneer Corps Record Office on 8 February 1941 stating that he had received a letter from Patrick about a month previously. He had sent the original to Gertrude and then had received a letter from her with the Belgian Red Cross letter.[14] However, the Record Office replied that 'the information given in the letter from the Belgian Red Cross is not accepted as official by the War Office' and that if they could not obtain something written from Patrick Nelson they had to keep his status officially listed as 'missing'.[15]

The Pioneer Corps Record Office also wrote to Gertrude stating 'It gives me pleasure to say it appears as though your boy is safe, but I must have authentic evidence before I officially post him as "Found". If you should have an envelope or postcard in your possession received from him since June, I ask you please to forward same to this office for my perusal, and if such should bear stamps or identifications which tell me they have passed through enemy hands, I should be only too happy to officially post your lad as "Found", instead of the present unhappy state of "missing".'[16] Although this missing status continued in British official records, Patrick's family could breathe a sigh of relief as they now knew what had happened to their son. Leopold Nelson once again wrote to Colonel Dean, and in this letter we see expressed his own experiences and identification with the military as well as a detailed description of what had happened to Patrick based on both Patrick's initial letter to Duncan and the letter sent by the Belgian Red Cross. Leopold Nelson wrote,

> This is indeed a priviledge given me to write a letter of thanks for the interest you have displayed in your men during the evacuation of Dunkerque. Sir, the letter you wrote to Mr Duncan Grant in response to his letter inquiring about Leopold Patrick Nelson, a private in your company was sent on to me the father of Patrick by Mr Grant, and you undoubtedly did your best for all those who were in your company. It, was very unfortunate that my boy had to be left behind but I suppose he was among the tired ones and was captured or maybe was injured and could not get away. I take great pleasure in informing you that Patrick Nelson was wounded and was first in a hospital in occupied France but has been transferred to Deutchland where he is at present a prisoner of war. You have lived up to the high traditions of great English men. No sooner you came back from your unconsciousness you immediately asked about your men. I have served as a military man for years on Home Defence and know what duties are,

and I pray it wont be long when the fruits of your labourers be harvested and Hitlerism be completely crushed. May you be preserved by God to enjoy it.[17]

Before closing this letter to Colonel Dean, Leopold Nelson wrote in a P.S. that 'I received a letter from the British Red Cross Society, Warwick House, St. James, London S.W. dated Dec. 31.1940. which said my son is at Camp of Basta Les Forges, Dox. Landes, France'.[18] In March 1941 Patrick's parents wrote to the Record Office enclosing the British Red Cross letter stating that Patrick was safe and in May 1941 the Pioneer Record Office replied to them and also wrote to Duncan Grant and to Colonel Dean with the news that Patrick was 'now officially posted as Prisoner of War'.[19]

Making contact with Patrick

Prisoners of war from Jamaica and the Caribbean in general who were resident in Britain and serving in the British Army had various complex administrative channels to go through in order to receive help and support, in particular when receiving parcels. For a while, Duncan Grant acted as Patrick Nelson's next of kin as he lived in Britain. Patrick's parents Leopold and Gertrude requested he take on this duty and in early May 1941 Mary Lucie-Smith of the Jamaica Central War Assistance Committee sent on the request of Gertrude Nelson a letter to the Record Office in Bournemouth reporting that she was 'instructed by Mrs Nelson to say that she would like Mr Duncan Grant, Charleston, Firle, Sussex to act as next of kin on her behalf in all matters pertaining to her son's welfare and with whom you should get in touch for the purpose of your records'.[20] The Jamaica Central War Assistance Committee also wrote directly to Duncan Grant asking on behalf of Patrick's parents that he act as next of kin and

> arrange with the Red Cross for parcels to be sent to him if possible. Mr Nelson would be much obliged if you would do this. Previous to receiving this communication I sent forward a parcel of tobacco and cigarettes C/O West India Committee for forwarding to Pte Nelson from Mr Nelson but under the circumstances I suppose he will not get it. We are very much in the dark here as to the possibilities of arranging for parcels of a personal nature or otherwise, being sent to prisoners of war as one minute I get pamphlets from the Postmaster saying the same and the next, I hear from the West India Committee and from this letter from the Red Cross to Mr Nelson that personal parcels may not be sent.[21]

In the Jamaican National Archives files on POWs who were Jamaican is a brief handwritten note referring to Leopold Nelson dated 1 May 1941 which refers to Patrick as being a POW in Stalag VIA and that Leopold would like a parcel returned to him if it cannot be sent to his son. This parcel would have been sent before Leopold had been told that parcels could not be sent from Jamaica to the Stalags.[22] By October 1942 Leopold Nelson had been informed by the Jamaica Central War Assistance Committee that he would not be able to send parcels directly to Patrick, Leopold wrote to Duncan that he was very grateful that he was sending parcels quarterly to him.[23]

There was much confusion over how parcels would be sent to POWs. In general Britain's administrative response to POWs in the earlier part of the war has been described by Neville Wylie as 'benign neglect'.[24] Prior to Dunkirk there were about 3,000 British POWs in the German camps, and British authorities were not prepared for the administration involved in seeking to look after the interests and welfare of so many POWs post-May 1940.[25] As seen in the correspondence with Jamaican war organizations over Patrick, it appears the initial problems with bureaucracy were even more complicated for organizations who represented colonial POWs who had to liaise and first go through British authorities in order to organize and facilitate family and friends to be able to make contact with loved ones.

Duncan's formal next-of-kin relationship highlights a significant way in which Duncan and Patrick's relationship was further cemented through the practical needs of wartime and is an example of queer family. For Patrick, Duncan was an important member of his non-related family. Interestingly, Patrick appears to have explained or contextualized the relationship between himself and Duncan to those in military authority by stressing Duncan Grant's links to Jamaica. For example, the Pioneer Corps Record Office wrote to Major T. H. Woodland with a regimental question Patrick had asked him, stating 'his parents are resident in Jamaica and his recorded Acting next of kin (friend) in this Country is Mr Duncan Grant, Charleston, Firle, Lewes, Sussex. This gentleman was a former Governor of Jamaica'.[26] In this last reference the Pioneer Corps Record Office officials confused Duncan Grant with his grandfather, who was a governor of Jamaica in the late nineteenth century. Nevertheless, Patrick passed on information about Duncan's links to Jamaica to those in charge possibly because they might have wanted to know why Duncan Grant was Patrick's next of kin.

The confusion for Duncan during the first year of Patrick's captivity arose because he did not know Patrick's location. During this first year (after his initial captivity in France) Patrick was sent to Germany but was then moved back to France from one Frontstalag to another before being transported back to Stalags in Germany including 8b/344. In the first POW letter received by Duncan in early 1941, Patrick reported that he was a POW and he was being held at Stalag VI.A. Germany. Duncan passed on this information to Colonel Dean who then passed it on to the Record Office in Bournemouth.[27] After receiving this information he sent Patrick's letter on to Gertrude Nelson but then mislaid the address contained within it as to where he should send parcels, so there was a delay while he retrieved this. On 22 June 1941 Duncan wrote to the Record Office confused about the camp in which Patrick was then being held. He also requested to know whether Patrick's POW number was 57167, or, as stated in a letter sent in May 1941, 37167.[28] The last address Gertrude and Leopold had for Patrick during June 1941 was Camp Stalag VIA with POW number 37167.[29] In reply to Duncan Grant the Pioneer Corps Record Office outlined the different camps to which Patrick had been imprisoned, stating,

> In the first place he was reported to have been at Stalag VI.A. Then the report was received to the effect that he was transferred from Front Stalag 222 to Front Stalag 221 on 14.1.41. The fact that we received no advice that he had left Stalag VI.A or Front Stalag 222 conveys nothing, as we do not receive much detailed information from that source. I think you will be quite safe in accepting my last notification, namely: Front Stalag 221. His correct Prisoner of War Number is 37167.[30]

Patrick and Duncan sent various letters to one another. One of the first letters Duncan received, postmarked 16 October 1940, was sent from Stalag VIA.[31] After receiving this letter from Patrick, Duncan sent various letters to Stalag VI A (but not as far as I am aware to Front Stalag 221) but received no reply. Duncan and Patrick eventually managed to make contact with one another, but not until 1942.

It appears that Patrick might have been one of the prisoners sent from Germany to France in 1941 to be repatriated. In around early February 1942 Duncan Grant again wrote to find out the current address of Patrick, stating he 'had a letter from him a few days ago to say he was well & now in France ... . But I have stupidly burned the letter by mistake. The address I had always written to him was Stalag VI A Germany & never had any reply.'[32] The Pioneer Corps Record Office wrote in reply to Duncan's letter, that 'as you mention the fact that he wrote to you from an address in France, coupled together with the fact that he was wounded in the feet, would seem to indicate that he was sent to the

Repatriation Concentration Camp, the address which is Heilag, Rouen, France. I have reason to believe that quite a number of men are still there awaiting decision regarding repatriation, which, as you know, unfortunately fell through at the last moment. I also know that some men who were at Heilag, have been moved back to Stalags.'[33] Patrick was one of the men eventually returned to the prison camps in Germany as he was in German Stalags until late 1944.

The first sentence of Article 68 of the 1929 Prisoner of War Convention states: 'Belligerents shall be required to send back to their own country, without regard to rank or numbers, after rendering them in a fit condition for transport, prisoners of war who are seriously ill or seriously wounded.'[34] Arieh Kochavi states

> Negotiations between the British and the Germans over the exchange of seriously sick and wounded POWs had begun already in 1940, but the two countries were close to carrying out a first exchange only in the fall of 1941. Shortly before the exchange was to take place, however, the Germans changed their minds, mainly because they were to receive no more than 50 men while the British stood to recover over 1,100 POWs. The British were thus forced to wait until they had captured a substantial number of German soldiers, especially those who had been seriously hurt, before they found Berlin ready to agree to an exchange. This happened in May 1943, when the German forces in North Africa surrendered. In October 1943, the first mutual exchange of seriously wounded and sick POWs took place, involving British, American, and German former prisoners.[35]

In June 1942 Duncan reported to the Pioneer Corps that he heard from Leopold Nelson that Patrick was in France, in Front Stalag 221, St Médard in the South West.[36] Leopold wrote to Duncan with this news in April 1942 also telling Duncan 'I have given all information concerning him to the Red Cross Society in Jamaica. I think you could write to him care of the Red Cross Society in the South of France to ensure its delivery for, in his letter to me he says he has never received a letter or parcel from you or anyone, & he had written over 28 letters to England & has no replies.'[37] By Summer 1942 Patrick had been sent to the German Stalags as the War Office reported his present address was Stalag VII A.[38] Duncan was also in correspondence with the British Red Cross seeking to find out where to send parcels. In July 1942 they wrote to Duncan stating 'I find that the special label and 40 clothing coupons were sent to you in October, but that you have not so far made use of these for the purpose of sending Private Nelson a parcel.'[39] It appears likely that Duncan sent parcels but to the wrong camp.

News of Patrick serving in the BEF and his confinement was reported in the *Gleaner*, as was news relating to many Caribbean people serving in the war. The news that Patrick was a POW was reported in the *Gleaner* in November 1940, before Patrick had been officially declared a POW. The report stated:

> Mr E. Leo Nelson received the welcome information yesterday that his son, Mr Patrick Nelson, who went to France with the British Expeditionary Force and disappeared after the June withdrawal, is alive and well in France. The notification came to Mr Nelson from the Red Cross Sisters at the Hospital at Cambrai (which is a part of France occupied by the Germans) and stated that 'Sub-Lieutenant Nelson was in good health and in excellent morale'. His family can communicate with him by open letter or postcard. Although not specifically stated, it appears that the young soldier is a prisoner of war of the Germans.[40]

Captivity in Frontstalags

Frontstalags such as 222 and 221 were POW camps situated in occupied countries such as France. Raffael Scheck has explored the experiences of French colonial soldiers who were POWs in German captivity in the Second World War, including the treatment of black POWs in Frontstalags.[41] Scheck's exploration of the experiences of Senegalese poet, academic, theorist and politician Leopold Senghor is particularly relevant to Patrick's experiences as a black POW in occupied Europe. Senghor was imprisoned in various POW camps in France and Scheck describes that 'he suffered in these overcrowded and undersupplied camps, but he was spared the harsh transfer to Germany that 40,000 prisoners from the French empire had to endure in June and July 1940 before most of them were sent back on Hitler's orders'.[42] Patrick was one of these individuals who was sent from France to Germany then back to France again then back to Germany (as he was listed as being in a German Stalag before Frontstalags 222 and 221). In October 1940 Senghor was registered as a POW in Frontstalag 230.[43] Scheck identified an anonymous report as being authored by Senghor in June 1942 which documents his experiences as a POW. In this report Senghor wrote about the terrible accommodation given to the colonial soldiers and the abuses of a camp commander who ordered a guard to kill a black prisoner who took a potato. He also reflected on the importance to the colonial soldiers of French women who agreed to work as 'war godmothers' and send them letters and packages. By February 1941 a new commander had arrived and there were improvements in the camps' facilities, and Senghor was appointed as prison secretary of the camp.[44]

Patrick did not reflect on POW experiences of racism, including racial violence, in post-war letters to Grant and could not mention conditions of the camps in his surveilled POW letters but that obviously does not mean he did not experience violence from the guards. In fact, during this period of time black soldiers were in great danger. During the invasion of mainland France, Germany initiated a propaganda campaign against black troops and German soldiers massacred several thousand black POWs in the French Army. Raffael Scheck has observed that 'most scholarly accounts represent the German army's western campaign in 1940 as a military affair devoid of the racially motivated atrocities connected to the German wars in Eastern Europe and the Balkans' but black people serving in the French Army were the victims of racial violence and murder. About 100,000 soldiers from French colonies in West Africa served in France in Spring 1940, and when captured these soldiers were subjected to abuses which included massacres.[45] K. H. Adler writes of these massacres, 'In failing to prosecute Germany for these war crimes after 1945, the restored French Republic misplaced their memory and it became one of the "forgotten" episodes of the fall of France.'[46] Patrick briefly reflects on the comparison between life as a POW in France and Germany when he was a POW in Stalag VIIA, writing 'one of the officers here has promised me to send you a letter just to assure you that I am well and living better than I was in France'.[47]

French POWs categorized as European were sent to camps in Germany while African soldiers were sent to Frontstalag camps in occupied France.[48] Additionally, as Scheck states, most white prisoners were dismissed from French Frontstalags on 3 July 1941.[49] As previously mentioned, at some point after his initial captivity in France, Patrick was held in Germany in Stalag VI A before being sent back to France. His race was possibly the reason why he was sent back to France from Germany (though it is possible he was sent back to France because he might have been a candidate for repatriation on medical grounds). As well as British and French colonial POWs of African heritage, there were also African American POWs in Frontstalags.[50] Clarence Lusane has explored documentation relating to the experiences of black POWs in Frontstalags in the 2003 work *Hitler's Black Victims,* including examples of racism by US officials in seeking the release of white American troops as opposed to African American troops. Lusane states that the 'already desperate situation for black prisoners was compounded by the racism they experienced from their Allied fellow white soldiers and white officers'.[51]

Captivity in Germany

After his return to Germany (perhaps to be held alongside other British Army POWs) in Spring/Summer 1942 Patrick was imprisoned in Stalag VII A. The second POW letter we find from Patrick to Duncan in the Tate Archives is postmarked 16 July 1942. In this letter Patrick wrote 'Today is sunday and I am two weeks in this new Camp so I am writing to give you my news. I have been all last year and most of this spring in France in a French camp untill [sic] Apr. they decided to send me back to Germany. Have you been getting my letters? I think not, I did my utmost to get in toch [sic] with you and few others but never get a single reply.'[52] As Patrick feared, most of these letters were never received by Duncan. Similarly, Duncan sent replies which Patrick never received. The first letter Patrick received from Duncan was one dated 6 August 1942, which arrived on 18 October 1942. In fact, this was the first letter Patrick had received from any friends or family, despite many letters being sent to him.[53] Patrick later reflected on these missing parcels and letters in a letter postmarked 30 October 1942, stating 'I only wished the Germans did not send me to France, I should have had all my letters and parcels then.'[54]

During his captivity Leopold and Gertrude also wrote to Patrick, although we do not get a sense of what these letters included as they are not preserved, as far as my research can confirm, in the Tate Archives, Jamaica Archives or the Ministry of Defence records. What gets saved in archives has profound consequences for relaying a person's life in a book or study such as this. A life-as-lived can never be recalled by a historian with completeness, particularly in seeking to reconstruct a person's inner life. Additionally, in exploring Patrick's letters to Duncan but not having access to his letters to other individuals, we cannot explore the different manner in which Patrick would have articulated his feelings or discussed particular topics with someone else besides Duncan. These various familial, friendship and romantic links surrounding Patrick, Duncan, Leopold and Gertrude can be compared with the connections explored by historians such as Clare Makepeace and Neville Wylie. Wylie states, 'Throughout the war POW families supported their loved ones as best they could; composing letters, assembling next-of-kin parcels and, when necessary, mobilizing opinion to hold the government to account for its actions.'[55]

Duncan acted as next of kin for a while and continued to write and send parcels to Patrick. In Duncan's papers within the Tate Archive is an information sheet entitled 'Communication with Prisoners of War Interned Abroad' which outlines information on what could and could not be sent to POWS and how letters and parcels should be sent. For example, letters and postcards could be sent free of charge through the 'ordinary post'. They were to be 'clearly written or typed, and letters should not exceed two sides of a normal sized sheet of notepaper'. They could only deal with 'personal matters' and 'no references to naval, military, aerial, economic or political matters [were] allowed, and movements of any members of His Majesty's Forces or any warship merchant ship must not be mentioned'. Parcels could not be sent directly by relatives and 'food, soap, cigarettes and tobacco at the cost of 10s. per parcel [were] sent to British, Dominion and Colonial prisoners of war in enemy territory by the British Red Cross and St John War Organisation'. Individuals could contribute funds to the Prisoner of War Department towards defraying these parcel costs. In addition to these official parcels, people could order from 'firms holding special permits for the DIRECT despatch of parcels containing books, music, packs of cards, games, tobacco and cigarettes' and parcels could not be sent by air mail.[56]

From around late 1942 to early 1943 official next-of-kin duties were carried out by Lady Davson of the West India Committee. Lady Davson forwarded one of the letters sent to her from Patrick on to Duncan, where he thanked her for the clothing parcel sent in December 1942 and the books which she ordered for him.[57] Writing to let Duncan know about the next-of-kin arrangements with the WIC, Leopold expressed his gratitude for Duncan's support for Patrick, stating 'I have now to thank you exceedingly for your continuous services of kindness to my son since you have known him & I do hope you shall be spared to see him after the war is over & that you shall hear from him in the meantime'.[58] Patrick mentioned that the WIC had been supportive and also believed that Duncan's involvement or intervention might have increased this support, stating in late 1942 'the Christmas card from the West Indian people is also very nice I did not know you knew them, how kind of you to have got in touch with them on my behalf; no wonder they are anxious to do me favours'.[59]

Patrick received packages consisting of books, clothes and cigarettes.[60] On 17 March 1943, Patrick wrote to Duncan that Lady Davson has accepted 'responsibility as my next of kin for the duration, her name will always remain dear to me she has been sending me cloths chocolate, books Latin Dic. & I am now receiving monthly cig. through the British American tobacco'.[61] In an undated note from the WIC to Duncan they listed the contents of the No. 14 parcel they had sent to Patrick. It included '2 shirts with collars, 2 vests, 2 pants, 2 prs, socks, tooth brush, dentrifice, vaseline, shoepolish, shaving soap, comb, pencil, face-cloth, 3 razorblades, darning wool, needles, 2 lbs. Chocolate, ½ lb soap'.[62] The West India Committee also acted as next of kin for other Caribbean Prisoners of war. In June 1942 it was reported in the *Gleaner* that Lady Davson of the West India Committee had sent to the secretary of the Jamaica Central War Assistance Committee the names of two civilian Prisoners of war, asking if she could find out if any of their relatives lived in Jamaica. If they were resident there, the *Gleaner* reported, Davson had

> kindly offered to send quarterly personal parcels to all Jamaican Prisoners of War on receipt of a written authorization from the next-of-kin authorizing her to receive the special labels from the Red Cross which are necessary before such parcels can be sent. She keeps meticulous records of all correspondence concerning West Indian Prisoners of War, and the parcels which have been sent to them, and has sent copies of these to the Secretary, Jamaica Central War Assistance Committee, who will be glad to furnish these details to any relatives of Jamaican prisoners if they will communicate with her C/O G/P/O Kingston. The Secretary would also be glad to hear from the relatives of the above-named two prisoners, if they reside in Jamaica, and would like Lady Davson to undertake the next-of-kin quarterly parcels service for them. This service is free of charge, though relatives may contribute if they wish to do so. In the meantime, the parcels are being sent from the West India Committee to these two prisoners.[63]

Correspondence in the Jamaican National Archives highlights that the Jamaican colonial secretary was involved in passing on information from the British Red Cross and the Colonial Office to family members and also involved local authorities in finding possible relatives of POWs. For example, in August 1943 the acting colonial secretary wrote under the orders of the governor's office to Mrs Herrick to inform her that her uncle Frank Rowan Ward had been officially reported a POW at Stalag VII.[64]

In April 1943 Patrick was moved to Stalag VIIIB, which was later renamed Stalag 344. This Stalag was situated in Lamsdorf in Silesia. Due to overcrowding by the end of 1943 two new camps were created and the original camp was renamed Stalag 344.[65] A Stalag (short for Stammlager) was a main prison camp for enlisted and non-commissioned officers from the army.[66] In addition, there were also attached work camps (Arbeitskommandos) and Lazarettes (hospitals).[67] The Stalags were numbered by using Roman numerals which corresponded to the military district where they were situated, so Stalag VIA (the first German camp where Patrick was imprisoned in-between the two periods of French confinement) was in District VI.[68]

The POW camps run by countries who had signed the 1929 Geneva Convention were in principle subject to the articles of the convention concerning food, hygiene, labour and shelter as well as providing the Red Cross access to the camps for inspections.[69] Clifford Westland Annis was repatriated at the same time as Patrick and in September 1944 gave an interview to *The Lincolnshire Standard* which reported that 'the rations issued to the prisoners by the German authorities were meagre in the extreme and without the Red Cross parcels they could not have existed'.[70] Similarly, Patrick reflected on the conditions in Stalag VIIIB/344 in his post-war interview with the *Gleaner*. The newspaper reported,

> Life in camp was not in any way a bed of roses. In the first place sanitation was bad – they often had to spend a great part of the day killing the flies that congregated and bred in the camp compounds. Then the food was not always digestible and the dishes unlike English dishes – cabbage, sauerkraut, very little meat, a sort of margarine, heavy black bread. The winters were almost unendurable; most of the time there were no fires and the clothing was inadequate to keep out the biting cold; neither was it possible to obtain regular hot drinks or food.[71]

John Jay wrote a book about his father's experiences of captivity, paying tribute to his father, who had previously started to write his own memoir.[72] Alec Jay was a POW for five years and on his return to Britain in 1945 weighed seven stones, two stones less than John Jay described as 'his natural weight'. His father was a POW at Lamsdorf before Patrick's arrival and then during 1944 the last year of Patrick's captivity. Jay served with the Queen Victoria's Rifles as a 9 Platoon, C Company Bren gunner. His battalion left Kent on 22 May 1940 and they served defending the Calais garrison in a motorcycle unit within the 30th Infantry Brigade, which was hastily put together. They fought, John Jay describes, 'until their ammunition ran out, surrendering only when they realized resistance would cause loss of life to no purpose'.[73] Alec Jay was imprisoned at Stalag VIIIB on 21 June 1940.[74] Stalag VIIIB (later to be known as Stalag 344) was Germany's largest POW camp, which became known for its terrible conditions. The camp was surrounded by two barbed-wire fences with long spikes, which were nine feet high. There were armed watchtowers at corners and every hundred yards, and a trip wire inside the inner fence.[75] John Jay reflected on his father being a Jewish POW, stating, 'About 135,000 Britons were captured by the Germans so my father's was not a singular experience. It did, however, have an unusual texture – he was Jewish, and in the lottery of POW life this meant the odds he might die were greater than for most Kriegsgefangene – or 'Kriegies' as they called themselves.[76]

Clare Makepeace has explored the crucial connections maintained between POWs and loved ones, looking 'beyond the barbed wire' to the intimate bonds maintained through letter writing and the importance of these connections to the mental sustenance of surviving as a prisoner. Makepeace explores the 'escapism' through these connections, the importance and joy at receiving letters and parcels, and the worry and anxiety for loved ones when not receiving letters. These themes can certainly be seen in Patrick's letters to Duncan.[77] Patrick and Duncan's emotional relationship during the war was sustained through letter writing and Patrick's letters highlight and provide insight into the particularities and emotional bonds of their relationship. They discussed day-to-day events, including those in the artworld. In 1942 Patrick wrote about the fire which struck Duncan's studio in Fitzrovia, the studio where they met when they were lovers in the late 1930s.[78] Patrick asked about Duncan's painting, stating 'I know how energetic you are, so I am expecting to see more of your genius on canvas when I come back.'[79] Patrick also wrote about his own study of art. On a POW card in April 1944 he wrote 'I read a lot and think of pictures. I was ammused yesterday when I came across some of Whistlers works in a little book.'[80] Patrick expressed his emotions towards Duncan in various ways within his correspondence. In a letter dated March 1943 Patrick wrote to Duncan 'I am so glad to hear of your work & healthy life, you shall never have a long grey beard nor white hair, your noble heart will always be young.'[81] Duncan wrote to him in 1944 with news about a baby, presumably Amaryllis Virginia (Angelica Garnett's daughter and Duncan's granddaughter) as Patrick reported he was delighted to hear of the baby.[82] As well as passing on news about daily life, Patrick also passed on the news, as far as possible, to Duncan about the emotional and physical ramifications of the war and his capture. In a letter sent in 1942 he reflected about the day of his capture:

> Fate struck me on that hot May morning and blasted my life, for months I saw red and lived in hell while I thought of us failing in France. I have been wounded, I am sorry to say I was parallized now I am better it has left me with bad eyes however I have helped to stem the tide of our Nations decendance and here in captivity I can bear anything for the duration the end is near. I can't give you an account of the Battle, but in brief words it was exactly like the stories of hell we read in our childhood, fire pains and horror.[83]

Similarly, Duncan provided emotional support for Patrick in his letters. Though I have not had access to any copies of the letters Duncan sent to the POW camps,

Patrick's replies provide clues as to their content. In a letter postmarked 30 October 1942 Patrick wrote to Duncan 'Thanks for describing me as an Hero, I can't see anything Heroic about myself.'[84]

Education in the camps was an important way for POWs to keep mentally active and survive as well as plan and prepare for the future. POWs created universities, and the Red Cross would send educational material to the camps. Prisoners themselves contributed towards funds for this initiative. The Dundee *Evening Telegraph* of 5 July 1944 reported that 'a gift has been made by 255 British, Dominion, and U.S. Prisoners of War at Stalag 344 to the educational books section of Red Cross and St John.'[85] Patrick spent time in the camps continuing his education, with the hope that he would complete a law degree at London University after the war. In one letter postmarked July 1942 Patrick reported that his 'new prison life is teaching me many things every moment is an education to me'.[86] In a further letter postmarked December 1942 he told Duncan that he had not wasted a single day since his captivity: 'I speak perfect French, with a good book knowledge and I am able to read and write it, I also know enough German to be interpreter when necessary. I have been working hard on latin, as I intend to take a law degree at the London University on my return, I am reading local laws of the United Kingdom now and hope to get a better book later on.'[87] The *Gleaner* reported 'through it all Nelson drew a measure of comfort from the fact that he was able to read and study and improve his education ... . The books he got to read were sent by the Bodleian Library of Oxford University.'[88] The *Gleaner* interview, however, did not refer to Duncan's role in providing Patrick with books and educational materials from the Bodleian. Perhaps Patrick deliberately did not mention him, wanting to keep his relationship and connection to Duncan outside the purview of the Jamaican press.

But these Bodleian library book parcels were arranged by Duncan. In February 1943 Duncan wrote to the Educational Books Section, Prisoners of War Department of the Red Cross and St John War Organisation at New Bodleian Library, Oxford ordering books to be despatched to Patrick.[89] On 26 March, 1943 the West India Committee wrote to Duncan, replying to a letter he had sent them with a letter enclosed from the New Bodleian Library to the British Red Cross Society. This confirmed that the books Duncan requested were being despatched to Patrick immediately.[90] Dated 15 March 1943 it stated 'We have here as gift books copies of Harris and Wilshere's Criminal Law, and Kenny's Cases on Criminal Law, which our Law Adviser tells us would be just the books Mr Nelson would require, and we are despatching them.'[91] Another of these books, mentioned as being 'on order' was Cassell's Spanish Dictionary.[92]

Prior to this, Patrick had requested other books. In a letter postmarked October 1942 Patrick asked Duncan to obtain for him a Latin dictionary with 'the largest prints you can get hold of'.[93] In a further letter dated 21 November 1942, Patrick informed Duncan he had a very good 'prof' (proficiency) in Latin, French and German, but he really needed some law books sent to him, ending 'please do not neglect this, it means so much to me right now'.[94] In August 1943 Patrick wrote to Duncan to thank him for the two law books he ordered for him from B.H. Blackwell Ltd.[95]

Patrick also had, perhaps, informal religious education in the camps by learning more about Catholicism, a religion that played an increasingly important role in his life after the war. In March 1943 he reported to Duncan that he was learning from an old priest who was teaching him 'educational things I want to know' and as a result he was more 'learned' and 'intelligent' than when he had last seen Duncan.[96] He mentioned his spirituality on other occasions. In one letter he told Duncan 'I think of you continually and have taken up spiritualism and clairvoyance so that I am able to telephone to you when I want to.'[97] This could be a light-hearted and not serious reference, but at other points in his correspondence Patrick references his spiritual belief and his linking of this belief to Catholicism. This reference could be another indication of the importance and centrality of spiritual life to him and the different ways in which this belief was expressed.

As well as connections to life outside of the camp through Duncan and his family, connections inside would have undoubtedly been important for his mental and physical health. He did not mention any friends, lovers or acquaintances in the camps with the exception of the priest who was instructing him. Patrick did, however, send Duncan a photograph of himself with, it appears, other POWs, perhaps friends of his in the camp (Figure 6.2). Obviously with official censors he was unable to write in the way he did in his late 1930s letters or his later post-war letters about queer romances and feelings of desire, possible romances or whether he was able to form close emotional bonds with anyone in the camp. The correspondence with Duncan, along with packages and books Duncan sent to him, provides an important articulation of his queer identity and romantic connection with Duncan while in confinement. There are a couple of times in their correspondence that obviously reference his and Duncan's relationship, such as the reference about spiritualism in order to communicate with Duncan and thinking of him continuously.[98]

Recent important work has explored the experiences of queer men, same-sex relationships and desire among men in the Second World War including in the military, in particular Paul Jackson's 2004 book *One of the Boys*.[99] Paul Jackson has documented that 'few historical accounts of POW camps, either scholarly or autobiographical, address the issue of homosexuality in any depth'. Jackson points to writers who have referenced homosexuality and the POW experience in a defensive manner by seeking to highlight and assure 'the reader that homosexuality was not widespread', citing Kingsley Brown who in his 1989 memoir stated that 'there were instances of such relationships; we were aware but they were few'.[100] Jackson has carried out research into the close friendship bonds, homosociality, romances and same-sex relationships in POW camps. Jackson found that 'the development of male marriages among prisoners of war and many others who served in the Canadian forces suggests that intimate emotional and psychological bonds were not restricted to homosexual relationships' and 'in fact homosexual relationships did not necessarily entail emotional bonds'.[101] Jackson points to a weekly journal *Daily Louse* published by Sapper Victor Croxford who was a POW in Stalag VIIIB, the same camp as Patrick. The journal, in its early editions contains 'playful references to homosexual relationships in the camp', which commented on rumours of relationships. After an article in the 1942 edition was charged with being libellous, the journal was censored and thereafter homosexuality was alluded to 'more warily'.[102] Another magazine, *Stimmt*, also created in Stalag VIIIB by POWs including Ian Sabey, a pre-war journalist, was printed on stolen German official paper.[103] Sabey described the paper as summing up 'for the news hungry camp the factual news of the camp itself'. [104] Amanda Laugesen stated of the paper that 'it was also used to attack homosexual behaviour in the camp'.[105]

Along with education as a tool of survival, POWs were engaged in various cultural activities, carrying out theatre productions, sporting contests, art contests, and at Stalag VIII B/344 the POWs produced their own magazine called *The Clarion*, which included a range of articles on subjects such as news from home, advice on keeping healthy, English language lessons and activities in the camps.[106] The newspaper acted as an essential medium to communicate important information to others in the camp. The May 1943 edition of the magazine included reports on toys sent to children of Channel Island POWs, information on correctly filling in allotment and remittance forms, on topical diseases, next-of-kin parcels, a statement of accounts for a welfare fund, recipes and medical advice. It also posted obituary notices about POWs who had died in the camps with reports that messages of sympathy had been sent on behalf of Stalag VIIIB POWs in personal letters to relatives of deceased POWs.[107]

Figure 6.2 Photograph of Patrick Nelson sent from Stalag VIIIB.

The Clarion also included sporting news from home (which included reports from Britain, Australia and New Zealand) and the May 1943 edition included news of a football match between Lamsdorf POW footballers and recent POW arrivals from Stalag VII A (Patrick was one of these new arrivals, having been transferred in April 1943).[108] Sporting events were an essential aspect of camp life and the YMCA played a key role in supporting these activities in the Stalag camps. In his September 1944 interview Clifford Westland Annis recalled, 'We passed most of our time playing various kinds of sports. The equipment for practically every known games was supplied by the Y.M.C.A. and I can definitely say that all of us greatly appreciated this.'[109] In a 1943 POW letter to Lady Davson, Patrick reported on the sports played in the camp, stating, 'Winter here has been very mild except for a nasty north wind which blew during the early part of the passing month, to-day is fine and the British are able to play Rugby. We are fairly established for sports here and ran a great deal of competition against the foreign troops.'[110] In the *Gleaner* in 1945 he reported that sport was personally important to him and that 'many people wondered why I have kept up so well physically. You see I did a great deal of P.T. and other forms of athletics; I washed my clothes regularly and saw to it that the food I ate was as clean as possible.'[111]

Reading through *The Clarion* there is evidence of some of the ethnic diversity within Stalag 344. The 'Around the Camp' column in the June–July 1943 edition reported that 'Victor Ludorum at the Whitsun sports was Dafalder-Major Mohammed Khan, an Indian, who received his prize at the hands of Surg.-Cdr. W. Greaves, R.N., before the Boxing in the evening. The presentation was ordinary enough, but afterwards the winner returned to the Surgeon-Commander and handed to him necklaces of Lagergelt notes threaded on to cotton, which were in turn hung round the smiling Indian's neck.' The article then went on to explain that 'it is an Indian custom to decorate anyone who has gained a distinction, usually with flowers'.[112] Additionally, there were sporting events such as the August Sports during Summer 1943 where 'British Isles' played against the 'British Empire and Allies'.[113]

Patrick was not the only black POW in Stalag 344, though he recalled being the only Jamaican. Based on his father's memories, John Jay wrote of Stalag 344 POWs during 1944 as 'alongside the Brits there were Sikhs and Gurkhas, Maoris, Canadians, Free French, Spanish Republicans, Belgians, Poles, Czechs, Estonians and Lithuanians, Australasians, Arabs, Palestinian Jews, Rhodesians, Afrikaners and black Africans. There were even a few Russians rescued by South Africans briefly billeted in the Russian camp prior to registration.'[114] Although black colonial POWs were imprisoned in French Frontstalags, there were also black POWs such as Patrick in the German Stalags. As mentioned in the previous chapter, black Guyanese POW Cy Grant served in the RAF. His plane was shot down in 1943 and he spent two years as a POW. After six days of solitary confinement, he was transported and imprisoned at Stalag Luft 3 in Silesia, which he stated 'was one of the largest German prisoner-of-war camps for aircrew personnel'.[115] He recalled how the Nazis used his picture in a German newspaper with the caption 'A member of the Royal Air Force of indeterminate race'.[116] In his post-war *Gleaner* interview, Patrick reported on the ethnic diversity of the camps. After interviewing Patrick, the *Gleaner* wrote of the camp POWs: 'They were a strange mixture in that camp, he said. There were Canadians, Britons, Australians, French, Belgians, Arabs, Indians. Thanks to his knowledge of German he was given the job of interpreter. The men got on well together and lived together, except the Indians who took their meals apart, the Germans respecting their religious scruples.'[117]

Resistance in the camps included escape attempts at Stalag 344. Private Arthur Leak was a twenty-seven-year-old man of the Royal Army Ordnance Corps imprisoned at Stalag 344 who was repatriated at the same time as Patrick. He was interviewed by *The Lincolnshire Standard* in September 1944 where he recalled the ways in which the German guards would try to stop escapes, stating

'Our guards had various ways of trying to locate any tunnels or other means by which attempts to escape are made. One of the laws the Germans had was that we were not allowed out of our huts after ten at night.'[118] Escape attempts were especially difficult for black POWs. In the 1945 *Gleaner* article written about Patrick it was reported 'camp discipline was rigid, said Nelson: anyone caught beyond the enclosure was shot out of hand. Many of his comrades tried to escape and he had been told that the majority were caught and shot. Nelson never made any such attempt. The young pioneer is black with delicate features. He explained to the reporter that it would have been easy to pick up a man of his colour in Germany; so he remained patiently awaiting the Allied victory.'[119]

But captivity affected the mental health of POWs in many ways. In addition to the traumatic stress of captivity, the conditions of the camps, being unable to see loved ones, the length of time of confinement and the stress at wondering if they would ever be free contributed to mental ill health. As Arieh Kochavi observed in letters POWs sent from the camps, prisoners were worried about how much more they could take of confinement.[120] During 1944 Patrick developed mental ill health and as a result spent a period of time in the camp hospital. Duncan received this news in June 1944, through a letter sent by the War Organisation of the British Red Cross Society and Order of St John of Jerusalem, Prisoners of War Department.[121] On 24 March 1944 they received a letter from the senior British medical officer in the Stalag 344 Lazarett, who reported his condition. They also reported that the hospital had a 'block set aside for those suffering with nervous troubles' and that there was a British doctor there who was kind and sympathetic.[122] Duncan wrote to the West India Committee stating that he intended to write to Gertrude Nelson to inform her about Patrick's health. They responded on 27 June 1944 stating they had received a postcard from Patrick dated 28 May addressed to his mother and a Miss D'Costa in Jamaica, where he wrote that he was in good health. As this postcard was sent after the doctor's report the Red Cross stated that was 'every reason to believe' that Patrick was recovering.[123] Patrick wrote to Lady Davson during March 1944 when he was in hospital letting her know that he felt his treatment was being carried out with skill and care and that he was in good hands and hoped to do some work soon after but in the meantime was resting.[124]

Also a POW in Stalag 344 was pioneer forensic psychiatrist Trevor Charles Noel Gibbens, who would have known and probably treated Patrick.[125] In 1994 Graham Robertson published research on the life and career of Gibbens. Gibbens trained at St Thomas's Hospital and graduated in 1939. He was working as a clinical assistant at the Maudsley Hospital (and was due to start working at a hospital in Leicester in October 1939) when war broke out. Thereafter, he wrote to the British Medical Association to offer his services for emergency work in Britain. The letter was passed to the War Office and he then received orders to report to Crookham's Royal Army Medical Corps depot. He went to France in December 1939 with the First Bucks Battalion of the Ox and Bucks Light Infantry.[126]

The first few months of Gibben's posting in France were spent near Le Havre and during spring the following year they were moved to the Belgian border. During the German offensive there was heavy bombing as his regiment travelled through Belgium. Gibbens' regiment was defending a town twenty miles north of Dunkirk called Hazebrouck and he looked after the wounded and dying amidst the town being bombed. Gibbens was captured as a POW in Germany for the next five years, where he worked as a doctor in a number of camps including a repatriation camp and a typhus hospital where he looked after some of the Russian prisoners. At this typhus hospital Gibbens tried to provide chocolate to an English orderly who was given solitary confinement with bread and water rations. As the attempt to provide chocolate was discovered, Gibbens and an English doctor escaped but were recaptured a few days later. From June 1943 he was a prisoner in Stalag 344, where he took over as the head of the psychiatric ward. Two other doctors joined him, including Turner McLardy, a former colleague from the Maudsley.

Gibbens reflected on treating patients in his memoir *Captivity*, quoted by Graham Robertson in his study of Gibbens. These memories provide significant information on the likely experiences of Patrick in the Lazarett. Gibbens states:

> I became completely absorbed in the treatment of the neurotic patients we admitted, going back to the ward after supper so that I could hold psychotherapy sessions in peace, and also to make a trial of hypnosis, since most of them were cases of long delayed battle hysteria.[127]

Pamela Moss has explored how mental health was understood during the Second World War through a reading of documents created by Canadian psychiatrists. At the start of the First World War, understandings of battlefield breakdowns were informed by ideas and debates on the causes of traumatic neuroses and whether they were caused by psychic or physical neurological factors or a combination. Moss states, 'By the onset of the Second World War, military psychiatry subscribed to the idea that breakdown in battle was the effect of a key unresolved tension in the psyche' but that by the end of the war 'military psychiatrists were mostly in agreement that breakdown on the battlefield could happen to anyone.'[128] After the war Gibbens continued with his psychiatric work and completed his MD thesis on 'Psychiatric Disorders in Prisoners-of-War' based on 209 outpatient clinic men and seventy-four who had been treated inside the clinic.[129] Perhaps Patrick was one of these patients.

Repatriation to England

Because of his health, Patrick was one of the prisoners designated to be repatriated from Germany and at Stalag 344 it was Gibbens who worked on preparing cases to be considered for repatriation. He presented cases to the commission which decided which prisoners should be repatriated on grounds of ill health. Gibbens, in fact, accompanied the prisoners to the port.[130] E. T. Perry of the War Office first informed Duncan Grant of Patrick's repatriation in September 1944, stating they were due to arrive in the country on 15 or 16 September and that 'special arrangements have been made to enable the repatriates to communicate direct with their relatives or friends immediately on arrival'.[131] Patrick's experiences during the war were to have a profound effect on him for the rest of his life. The following chapter explores his experiences after September 1944 in both London and Jamaica.

Life After Captivity: Patrick, Politics and Life in Post-1945 London and Jamaica

This chapter explores Patrick's post-war experiences in Britain and homecoming to Jamaica. After seven months of recuperation, hospital operations and army duties within Leicestershire, Scotland and London, Patrick sailed back to Jamaica via New York in April 1945. He lived in Jamaica until approximately 1960–61 (he returned to London briefly during 1947). As mentioned previously, his return to Jamaica was, like his leaving, the subject of a newspaper article in the *Gleaner* in June 1945.[1] After describing his POW experiences, the article ended by stating, 'Now that he was returned to the island, Nelson hopes to settle down and find himself a suitable job right here in Jamaica.'[2] This search for work in post-war Jamaica was incredibly difficult and Patrick's letters to Duncan highlight his and other Jamaicans' experiences of unemployment and temporary employment (some of the reasons for the overall trend in post-war Caribbean migration to Britain). Many of Patrick's post-war letters are descriptions of everyday life, while others concern his viewpoint on subjects including religion and politics. Patrick's letters to Duncan reveal significant personal reflections on the momentous changes occurring in post-war Jamaican (and Caribbean) politics and society and this chapter and the subsequent chapter explore some of these reflections, placing them within their historical context. This chapter follows the course of his letters and although thematic in sections, it is broadly chronological.

Repatriation and London, 1944–5

Patrick was one of a number of sick and wounded POWs repatriated to Britain during September 1944. British national and local newspapers covered the repatriation ships' arrivals extensively and, as mentioned in the previous chapter, local newspapers carried out interviews with POW repatriates from their areas.

Though next of kin were kept informed as to the process of repatriation, they were unable to meet the ships on arrival. E. C. Gepp, the director of Prisoners of war at the War Office wrote that 'owing to the number of men returning from Germany and the desire of the War Office to get them on leave quickly, it will not be possible for relatives to meet the ship'.[3] The September 1944 repatriation convoy arrived in Liverpool and consisted of three ships, the Swedish liners *Gripsholm* and *Drottningholm* and the British liner *Arundel Castle*, altogether bringing 2069 former POWs and 583 civilian internees.[4] On 15 September, *The Times*, reporting on the arrivals expected that day, stated that they would be welcomed by General Sir Ronald Adam, adjutant-general to the Forces who would relay a message to them from the king and queen and 'except for those who require hospital treatment, all the British repatriates will be sent on leave as soon as they have been passed medically fit, documented, and issued with the necessary kit'.[5]

The length of leave given to repatriated POWs was twenty-eight days. E. C. Gepp wrote, 'They will then go before a Medical Board which will examine them carefully and decide whether they need any treatment, are fit to continue to serve, or will have to be discharged. The same rules about discharge or further service in the Army apply to repatriated prisoners of war as to all other men in the Army, both overseas and at home. If they are unfit for further military service, they are treated and helped as far as possible by the Army before discharge, and by the Ministry of Pensions after discharge. If they are fit, they must go on soldiering, as the war is not yet finished.' With the exception of a particular crisis, returned POWs who were deemed fit were 'not liable for any form of overseas service for six months'.[6]

For those men who had to go straight to hospital before being placed on leave, such as Patrick, the next of kin would be told where they were to be located.[7] The day after repatriation, Patrick was admitted to Ashurst Military Hospital.[8] After leaving this hospital, instead of being allocated the usual twenty-eight days, Patrick was placed on leave for forty-two days, starting on 18 October 1944, a month after his repatriation. Patrick arranged to spend his leave at 9 Devonshire Terrace, where he had lived with Robin for a short while before the war.[9] The city Patrick returned to had experienced immense suffering and devastation. From September 1940 to May 1941, as Amy Helen Bell notes in the 2008 *London Was Ours: Diaries and Memoirs of the London Blitz*, German raids on the city resulted in the deaths of 15,775 Londoners and 1,400,000 were made homeless.[10]

After repatriation Patrick had to obtain his rations, which had been delayed and had caused difficulties as a result. He wrote to the Pioneer Record Office in

November 1944, stating that as 'a repatriated prisoner of war I am in urgent need of the twenty five pounds and the ration along with the extras I mentioned'.[11] Before he returned to Jamaica in April 1945 he resided for the most part in London. His first fixed address after staying at Devonshire Terrace appears to have been in Epsom and he reunited with Duncan in London in October 1944. He wrote to Duncan in late 1944 letting him know how much better he felt in Epsom than in London and that Duncan would never know how happy it had made him to have seen Duncan again.[12] He further wrote that he was 'so glad you think that I am looking well and fit'.[13]

Patrick's address in Epsom was 12 Copse Edge Avenue. From the time of his repatriation he continued his connection to the West India Committee and it appears that they arranged for his accommodation in Epsom. In the 1945 electoral registers those listed as living at 12 Copse Edge Avenue were Martha Batten, Onyx P. Brettell, Walter J. Brettell and Rosanna R. Cutajar.[14] Onyx Patti Batten and Walter Brettell married in 1937 and Martha Batten was Onyx's mother.[15] In November 1944 Patrick wrote from this address that 'the people I'm staying with are most kind and have done wonders in helping to restore me'.[16] In a further letter he described them as 'charming people whom have looked after me, and have done so much for my home comfort'.[17] Patrick's father Leopold and Duncan continued to write to one another during this time as in January 1945 Leopold thanked Duncan for his letter. In this letter Leopold provided further information on Walter Brettell, stating he had also heard from

> Mr W. J. Brettell of Copse Edge Ave Epsom, Surry with whom Patrick had spent quite a few weeks who seems quite anxious to help him in any way he can. He suggested in his letter to me to make Pat try his hand at Furniture business & asked for my opinion. I told him, in my reply that I thought a Wholesale & Retail Dry Goods business would be far better as those articles sell daily.[18]

The archives available to me do not show whether Patrick tried his hands at retail, but it does not appear so. Patrick spoke about the Brettell's book collection, stating 'I have been reading a volume of English history and these people have all sorts of books, so I'm able to choose my literature from their collection'.[19] This emotional connection made in Copse Avenue with the Brettell family highlights one of the friendships Patrick made during his time recuperating in England and is also an example of the many everyday and hidden interactions between Londoners that was based on friendship and support.

Patrick also wrote about the ways in which he was spending his time recuperating. He mentioned attending church, presumably a Catholic Church in Epsom. He also carried out some speaking engagements. For example, he was asked by the Red Cross Committee to speak about his experiences in Germany, perhaps for an internal meeting or a public event.[20] He also mentioned a 'young lady' he had started spending time with.[21] It is unclear how and when he met her, whether it was pre- or post-war. In a further letter he wrote 'the young lady rang up to tell me she is well and out of hospital, she is also having a weeks leave when I am planning to see her and most likely spend some time with her somewhere and tell her I must wait and see what my position will be and when I will earn my daily bread, before I can get married.' He also wrote that Edward, presumably Le Bas, had offered them a night at his place and that if Duncan agreed to this he would 'so much like to tell you more, and again to get your advice and opinion of some things'.[22] He continued his connection with Edward Le Bas, meeting him in London for a drink in November 1944, speaking of his wartime experiences and talking about Duncan. Edward Le Bas also showed Patrick a picture of him at this meeting.[23] In November 1944 he was also able to travel to other cities in England, he mentioned having stayed at a manor house in Chichester, seeing much of the city including visiting the cathedral.[24] These visits were especially important to him. Patrick had a love of architecture, in particular the architecture of cathedrals. In 1945 the *Gleaner* reported, 'Nelson is enthusiastic about the various cathedrals he had seen in various parts of Europe, mentioning specially those he had seen in Italy, and Durham Cathedral in England.'[25]

During the latter months of 1944 Patrick mentioned a number of people he spent time with. In December 1944 he mentioned that he had been meeting quite a few Jamaicans, who told him how much Kingston had changed. This sentence was written straight after mentioning his service uniform and it is probable that he met other Jamaicans also in service, perhaps through the West India Committee.[26] In the 1945 *Gleaner* interview he recalled meeting other Jamaicans in England. The reporter wrote that 'back in England, Nelson said he was well treated. He is particularly grateful to the West India Committee for the treatment given him and other West Indian boys in London. They were really very kind. A great many Jamaican boys in England have relatives here, who may be glad to know the fine work the Committee are doing for the boys.' [27]

The West India Committee continued to act as next of kin or at least assist Patrick in Britain after his repatriation. In November 1944 he stated that until the WIC could arrange for the passage back to Jamaica it would cost him '£1.10.0 weekly while I wait for the boat'.[28] In November 1944 they arranged for him to meet with the head of education at the Colonial Office, probably in order to assist him in his legal studies which he still hoped to pursue.[29] He wrote to Duncan about his discussions with the Colonial Office. He reported that they wanted to assist him but advised him against pursuing legal studies 'which I have devoted much of my time to but I think they are right in saying it is not practical at my age'.[30] This short sentence no doubt does not convey the emotions felt by Patrick after being advised to change his career ambitions away from the law. As highlighted previously, his legal studies and hopes and dreams of entering the legal profession sustained him through his time in captivity.

Patrick also made contact with Lyulph Stanley's mother, Lady Stanley, and the two of them had tea together in November 1944. Patrick informed her of the woman he was seeing, whom he described as a soldieress, and Lady Stanley asked him to bring her along the next time they met. Patrick also wanted Duncan to meet her as he was sure Duncan would like her.[31] He mentioned later on in this same letter that 'Miss Buxton' would be on leave two days later and they planned to see Winchester. Presumably this is the woman Patrick had started spending time with.[32] By early December he was not spending time with 'the girl anymore' as she told him she was in love with an American.[33] In January 1945, however, he wrote to Duncan that 'so far I have received no news from my girl, neither my mother or friends have written'.[34] As we see in these letters Patrick talks about and is open with Duncan about other relationships and companionships without raising problems for either Duncan or Patrick.

In early November Patrick was informed by the army that he had to report to Queen Anne's Hospital on 29 November 1944 for his final inspection.[35] Patrick wrote to Pioneer Corps officials from Copse Edge Avenue on 30 November 1944, the day after the final inspection, asking for them to send his ribbons and service stripes as soon as possible. He also asked them to confirm his rank as sergeant as Patrick was a private when he was captured.[36] In giving details to obtain his ribbons he wrote to the Pioneer Record Office 'At the end of my present leave I will have completed five years service so if you could forward to either of my addresses the ribbons you think I am entitled to I would be obliged' and that his commanding officer, whose address he no longer had, 'would know best of what ribbons I am entitled to and if I am a Sgt. Cpl. or my old rank as Pte'.[37] Patrick was declared fit, and he declared 'so glad was I that I celebrated'. Though he would not be discharged from the army immediately, he was prepared to continue serving for the duration of the war as he did not think they would give him difficult duties.[38]

On 9 December P. C. Field, Lieut. Col., RAMC of the Queen Alexandra's Military Hospital in Millbank reported to the Pioneer Record Office that Patrick had been examined at the medical board, was placed in category C2 and they had made arrangements to admit Patrick to 102 Convalescent Depot in Kingston, on 11 December.[39] Convalescent Depots were military centres for the rehabilitation of wounded and ill soldiers. In 1945 it was reported by the *Journal of the Royal Institute of Public Health and Hygiene* that approximately 20,000 men passed through Kingston's Military Convalescent Department each year.[40] Therapy occurred in the depots, including psychiatric therapy, and Patrick probably would have continued his therapy there. Pamela Moss' exploration of the Second World War and Canadian psychiatry is relevant in this context. Exploring reports and documents made in a Convalescent depot, Moss documented the psychotherapy carried out in this institution. The aim of the depot was to treat and recover soldiers in order to make men fit to return either to front line or otherwise Line of Command or base duties and additionally to prevent future breakdowns.[41] Patrick did not mention details of the treatment he underwent in this camp but does specifically reference to being at the camp in Kingston in a 1946 letter to Duncan, by mentioning a book he had taken out from a library nearby.[42]

Patrick spent the rest of December in the depot camp and told Duncan that his C.O. was 'most kind' in finding him a job in the paymaster's office at the depot. However, though things were better for him with this job, he reported to feeling lonely.[43] Patrick went on to spend time with his Company in Darlington and then Durham. He wrote to Duncan in February 1945 from an address in Durham (B Company, 45 D.T.U., Sedgfield), hoping to see Duncan while he was on discharge leave and writing that he intended going to Scotland and seeing the cathedral in Yorkshire before returning to London.[44] By early March 1945 during this leave Patrick travelled to Scotland, where he stayed in a little village in the hills. On the trip he visited Edinburgh, where he explored the castle, walked the Royal mile to the Holyrood Palace, visited the zoo, the gardens, the art gallery and museum.[45]

Duncan and Patrick do not seem to have kept in touch a great deal during this time. They do not see each other on Patrick's return to London during his birthday. Patrick hopes Duncan will visit, stating 'I shall be staying in London, so do please write to tell me when you can come and see me as I have all good news for you.'[46] During this time Duncan's mother was ill. By his next letter, the day after on 19 March 1945, Patrick had received word from Duncan, and began the letter by writing 'My darling Duncan' and continuing 'I am so sorry to hear of your dear Mothers illness, and I wish her a speedy recovery'.[47]

During Patrick's leave before being formally discharged, he was living for a time at a place called the Unicorn Club near Euston, but still using the West India Committee address for correspondence. In this 19-March-1945 letter Patrick told Duncan that he had visited the admiralty and made friends with Lyulph Stanley again. This visit was the impetus for Patrick writing to Duncan stating how the future might bring Lyulph and him closer together but now that he had Duncan he hardly thought he would find a friend like him, and as quoted earlier in the book, 'so I'm afraid I will never give you up and I'm sure you love me too'.[48] Lyulph had been a probationary midshipman in the Royal Navy Volunteer Reserve since September 1934 in the Mersey division, and enrolled in the supplementary reserve on 4 October 1937, also in the Mersey division. He was made a temporary sub-lieutenant in the reserve on 18 January 1940 and temporary lieutenant on 8 December 1940, which was his position in 1945.[49]

In this same 19-March-1945 letter Patrick also referred to their sexual romance before the war, that he had much to tell Duncan and 'that if things were more like pre-war times although you have no where to live like me in London, we could find a lodging for at least 3 days'.[50] He also wrote in the same letter than he had spoken to Edward who said that he would like them to meet at his place. He ended the letter with 'All the best and cheer up and I wish I could be near to you because I'm sure I would make you happier in your depression.'[51] Patrick did not hear from Duncan and in the meantime got an offer to stay on a farm called The Cedars in Normanton-on-Soar, near Loughborough, where he wrote to Duncan on 26 March 1945. He spoke about how glad he was to have gone there as he was having eggs, milk, pure air and quiet.[52] He again longed to see Duncan, suggesting that he could, if Duncan wanted, visit Sussex and see him at the farm, namely Charleston.[53] I do not know whether he did visit Charleston. By this time Patrick had details on when he was to return to Jamaica. He wrote to Duncan 'and if *you* really want to see *me* before I return to Jamaica please write and let me know here *when* and *where*'.[54] He also mentioned again where they might meet, stating 'Edward Le Bas and I held a short telephone conversation he agree that that we may visit at his place for purposes of close contact with each other'.[55] Patrick and Duncan reunited (perhaps at Edward Le Bas' home) on 6 April and Patrick wrote again to Duncan on 8 April from The Cedars, saying that it was good to have seen him and that he would be staying out there for as long as possible, before, he hoped, returning to Jamaica.[56]

Emma Vickers has recently analysed queer life and the experiences of queer servicemen in Second World War London, focusing on a series of interviews with queer men who lived in the city during the war.[57] Vickers cites the memories of John Alcock, a queer man who migrated to London from Birmingham and who, on visiting Leicester Square, saw 'young Air Force boys wearing make-up' and thereafter Alcock 'experienced an epiphany' and London, as Vickers argues, 'represented rebellion and the possibility of spatial and sexual freedom unconfined by the strictures of family life in Birmingham'.[58] Vickers explored the changes which occurred in wartime London, with migrations linked to war service, that 'throughout the duration of the conflict, large numbers of servicemen and women from Britain, the commonwealth and, later, the United States of America continued to drift in and out of London on leave, a movement that ensured a regular stream of queer bodies'.[59] Queer socializing took place in bars and clubs and in homes and private residences, including new clubs and bars which continued to open throughout the wartime period. Vickers states 'aside from bars, clubs and pubs, hotels and hostels continued as sites of queer expression during the war. Police surveillance of these venues was virtually non-existent given that the much of the homosex occurred behind closed doors. Most charitable hostels were willing to accept any servicemen looking for a bed'.[60] Before the war, it appears, Patrick and Duncan had used lodgings such as these. However, they usually met at friends' homes (particularly Edward Le Bas') or their own residences and artist studios.

It was at this time that Leopold Nelson, Patrick's father, passed away, with Patrick never seeing him again. Patrick sent a telegram to Duncan on 11 April 1945, with the sentence 'My father died in Jamaica. Patrick'.[61] A few days before on 5 April 1945 Patrick was contacted by the Colonial Office with queries relating to when he came to Britain, the name of the ship and date embarked.[62] It is not clear whether Patrick decided to be repatriated after initially wanting to stay in London. Perhaps he took the opportunity of being able to return to Jamaica or perhaps he aimed to return temporarily knowing his father was ill.

Patrick was formally discharged on 10 June 1945, just short of nine months since he had been repatriated, though he did not receive the discharge information until 6 August 1945.[63] He wrote to Duncan in February 1945 that he was out of the army, so this was probably when the news was given to him that his discharge was imminent.[64] In the statement of service record it was noted that he was awarded the 1939–43 Star PCRO 134/44 War medal, which was issued in January 1950 and his military conduct was described as exemplary. His statement of service also includes the formal reason for his discharge, stating he was 'permanently unfit for any form of military service'.[65]

One of the printed documents in Patrick's service records included the dates he was discharged, along with details such as name, address and religion, his home town and county. The latter was initially listed as Kingston, Jamaica, but then crossed out and replaced with Lewes, Sussex.[66] This use of Vanessa and Duncan's address is significant; perhaps this is the address where he felt most connected to within Britain. The use of this address shows the nature of the queer family Patrick had formed with Duncan, representing the continuation of a significant emotional connection and the symbolic use of domestic spaces as a constituent of this connection.

Return to Jamaica

Patrick travelled back to Jamaica via New York on 26 April 1945, after having been away from his home country since 1938. He sailed on the S.S. *Castalia* from London to New York.[67] He wrote to Duncan about his voyage in a letter sent in June 1945 that it had been a rough passage from London to New York.[68] He then stayed in New York for a weekend arriving on Victory in Europe day. After leaving New York he then travelled to Barbados and Trinidad, before arriving in Jamaica on 3 June where he had an emotional reunion with his mother, sisters and brothers at their home in Kingston.[69]

Jamaica in the 1940s had continuing economic, political and social inequalities emanating from the injustices of colonial rule. From these first letters onwards, Patrick commented on the changes he had observed in Jamaica since his absence, including the poverty and bad economic conditions. In June 1945 he described Kingston as very unpleasant with no change in the administration.[70] He also wrote that he wanted to leave Jamaica, as he saw no prospects for study but did not know where he intended to migrate.[71] He referred to racism in Jamaican society and in an August 1945 letter he wrote that he did not see any prospects of work for himself and generally for black people in Jamaica.[72] In this same letter he told Duncan that his brother was now out of the army and they were planning to leave Jamaica together. [73]

By October 1945 Patrick was settling back into daily life and to some extent enjoying himself. He wrote of the beauty of Jamaica and the place he was living being too nice for words, with blue skies in the daytime and a brilliant moonlight by night. However, he still wanted to leave Jamaica and wrote about his bad treatment at the hands of the War Office, which was especially upsetting given all he had done for the war effort, stating 'I know you will be surprise to hear of the bad treatment I have received from the War Office they have discharged me without job or even a little money I really did not think that this would occur to me after having done all I could to help the War efforts, however, people do behave badly in the Government.'[74]

There were some fundamental changes in Jamaican politics since Patrick had been absent. Political struggles had taken place throughout the post-emancipation period by Jamaicans of African heritage struggling to overturn white supremacy and gain economic and political rights. As documented in Chapter 2, political power after the 1865 Morant Bay rebellion was in the direct hands of the Imperial government in the form of Crown Colony rule. There were political and cultural movements opposing direct rule and British colonialism. Cultural movements which spoke against colonial injustices included spiritual and religious movements such as Bedwardism.

Trevor Munroe and Arnold Bertram have documented and analysed Jamaican twentieth-century politics in relation to suffrage, constitutional change and the development of political parties and periodicals. Political organizations and newspapers were established to challenge and reform Jamaica's political system. In 1909 Jamaican legislators Alexander Dixon and Sandy Cox organized the National Club, a political organization seeking Jamaican self-government.[75] The National Club was, Robert A. Hill states, Jamaica's first nationalist political organization, 'created to expose and redress the abuses of crown colony government in Jamaica.'[76] Sandy Cox's newspaper *Our Own* challenged the concept of power existing in the hands of a governor.[77] The National Club also served as a training ground for Marcus Garvey.[78]

During the period from 1927 to 1935 Marcus Garvey worked in organizing Pan-African-based political change. Trevor Munroe and Arnold Bertram state, 'After the loss of the PPP candidates in the 1930 elections, Garvey understood the inevitable frustrations of leading a mass movement, whose members were denied the right to vote. Consequently, in the edition of the *Blackman* of August 23, 1930, he advocated full adult suffrage.'[79] The *Blackman* was published from March 1929 to February 1931 and thereafter Garvey published the *New Jamaican* from July 1932 to September 1933.[80] In 1936 the nationalist Jamaica Progressive League (JPL) was launched and in 1937 Kenneth George Hill founded the National Reform Association (NRA). Also in 1937 the Jamaican weekly nationalist newspaper *Public Opinion* was created.[81] Writers for *Public Opinion* included Amy Bailey, a black Jamaican feminist, writer and social worker, who, Veronica Marie Gregg states, wrote, 'at least seventy weekly columns in *Public Opinion* (1937–1942) and in *Jamaica Standard* (1938–1939); in the *Gleaner* there were dozens of public letters, commentaries, opinion pieces, essays of general reach, and articles from the 1940s until the year of her death, 1990'.[82]

Linked to the Labour protests (explored earlier in the book), the 1930s saw the development of the trade union movement and new political parties. In September 1938 the People's National Party (PNP) was launched by Norman Manley, O. T. Fairclough and Ken Hill. In May 1938 Bustamante organized the Bustamante Industrial Trade Union (BITU) and in 1940 established the Jamaica Labor Party (JLP). There was evidence given to the Moyne Commission regarding the Jamaican franchise. In June 1939 the Legislative Council adopted recommendations later known as the 'Smith Constitution'.[83] The Smith Constitution's recommendations consisted of a lower chamber (a House of Assembly) with fourteen members representing parishes each serving for five years; an upper chamber (Legislative Council) with ten governor-nominated members; and an Executive Council consisting of ten members, with five chosen by the House of Assembly and five chosen by the governor.[84] This proposal was vehemently opposed by the PNP and in September 1940 at their Party Conference they restarted the campaign for self-government (suspended for wartime) and declared their commitment to socialism in Jamaica.[85]

In 1941 discussions took place in London on the Jamaican constitution with the governor, Sir Arthur Richards. Meanwhile in Jamaica the campaign for political representation intensified.[86] In March 1941 the governor returned to Jamaica with Colonial Office proposals for constitutional change. In February 1942 the colonial secretary agreed to Universal Adult Suffrage and new constitutional boundaries. However, the governor would still have executive authority.[87] The Elected Members Association, the People's National Party and the Federation of Citizens' Associations agreed a joint memorandum on proposals for constitutional change, which was sent to the Colonial Office.[88] On 27 October 1944 an Order in Council on the new constitution was signed and elections under Universal Adult Suffrage took place in December 1944.[89] With the backing of the working-class population, the result of the election for the 1944–1949 government with the new constitution was a JLP victory, with twenty-two of the thirty-two elected members coming from that party, while the PNP secured five representatives and there were five who were independent.[90]

Patrick, Empire and Jamaican politics

Patrick did not write about his specific political affiliations or whether he had strong political views in relation to the new constitution, self-rule or the new political parties formed since his absence from Jamaica, but in many instances in the mid-1940s he referred to political developments and events in Jamaica. His references to particular individuals and politicians are sometimes vague and occur within the context of discussing other subjects, and so are difficult to fully explore. Before he returned to Jamaica he mentioned the Empire in a letter to Duncan in relation to the appointment of Archbishop Dtr Fisher, stating he believed he would be suitable to lead the Christian people and refers to rescuing the relics of 'our beautiful Empire'.[91] Patrick often expresses admiration and love of the British Royal family (which seems to go hand in hand with his faith) and this sentiment remains constant throughout his letter writing. For example, in 1950 he wrote 'I was unable to attend the Trooping of the Colours for my Beloved King George's Birthday but I again attended a Roman Catholic High Mass, and drank two quarts of Three Dagger Rum.'[92] In 1951 he wrote that he had been keenly listening to [the news] of the illness and recovery of the monarch.[93]

Patrick, however, developed a critique against the workings of colonialism based on his experiences of war and new understandings of Jamaica after being away for several years. Writing in a July 1945 letter, he stated that Britain had not done justice to Jamaica 'by allowing it to be in its present condition after quite five hundred years of hold upon the territory'.[94] Jamaicans who had experience of serving in the 'Mother Country', often on their return saw their home countries' political, economic and social conditions in relation to colonialism in a new light. As documented by Stephen Bourne, Ivor Cummings reflected in a 1974 BBC television series called *The Black Man in Britain, 1550-1950* on the changes in political outlook of Caribbean servicemen and servicewomen returning to countries including Jamaica after the war. Cummings stated,

> When they returned home after the war, they returned to the same government they had left. It was autocratic and people didn't want this. They resented this and the fact that the economic conditions in these places were absolutely awful. For the returning servicemen and women, the officials, the governors, and others were very tiresome people indeed and didn't know how to deal with those who had been away in the war. After the war I was sent out to the Caribbean and I

visited the three major islands, including Jamaica, and I was absolutely appalled. There were no opportunities for these people. The whole thing quite horrified me and I told everyone exactly what I felt about this. It was quite clear to me that this was a watershed. This whole war experience had been a watershed, that there were going to be changes.[95]

During the Second World War the United States extended its reach into the British Caribbean, building upon its history of expansionism in the region. After holding a conference in Havana, Cuba, in July 1940, the United States went on to form a number of military bases in British colonies. Charlie Whitham has explored US foreign policy in the Second World War in relation to the British Caribbean.[96] Whitham documented the background to the Destroyers-Bases Deal of 2 September 1940, where the British authorities granted permission to the United States to build air and naval military bases on eight countries in the British Caribbean in return for fifty American destroyers.[97] Munroe and Bertram stated, 'Without doubt, the exigencies of the war provided the United States with an opportunity to impose the Monroe Doctrine on a wider geographical area.'[98] In The National Archives' Colonial Office records that there is a sub-series concerning wartime lease proposals which took place in 1940 of Caribbean land, including Jamaican land, to be leased to the United States. In a cypher telegram sent on 6 September 1940 from the Colonial Office to the governors of various Caribbean colonies, it was stated that 'full facilities for preliminary examination and inspection should be given to United States representatives on arrival but actual negotiations or commitments should not repeat not be entered into. Meanwhile consideration has been given here to maximum concession which H.M.G. as at present advised consider could be offered in each Colony without detriment to our own interests within scope of agreement.'[99] Eventually in March 1941, after much controversy and negotiating over the terms of the agreements the land leases were formally agreed to and a US military base in Jamaica was established.[100]

After his return to Jamaica, Patrick expressed defiant criticism of Jamaican colonial rulers and strong opposition to British leases of Jamaican land to the United States. He wrote that as the land was populated leasing or selling the land meant a return to the slave trade. He first heard about land-leasing when he was a POW, writing to Duncan in 1945 'I am come back to hear that America, has a 99 year lease on Jamaica a fact that has staggered me as I did hear about it through the German propaganda in 1940 while a captive at Bordeaux.'[101] That he believed the land-leasing news was propaganda highlights the shock he must have felt when returning to Jamaica and hearing of the reality of the land leases. In late 1947 Patrick wrote to Duncan 'I am determined that the coloured people must have their liberty because "All Good things comes from God to the people,["] and we too are intitled to liberty. Next letter when I am stronger I hope to give you a better account of what is going on in West Indies.'[102] This call for liberty was based on the desire to see black people gain freedom based on an understanding of the racism inherent in colonial rule.

In the 1950s Patrick wrote of the political changes and leaders in Jamaica, though not often in detail. In 1950 Patrick refers to a *Times* newspaper Duncan had sent him, stating 'the cutting you enclosed from the Times is well appreciated and I was interested to have read that the present Labour Leader of Jamaica has 80 % Arawak Blood and 20 % Negro.'[103] By 1955 Patrick told Duncan, 'You may have heard by now of the serious conditions this Island is in with political rogues and criminals instigated by your own home administration and you will be surprise to know who is behind this deadly political set up.'[104]

Patrick's experiences as a POW also affected his post-war life in relation to finances, work, health and everyday life. In one of Patrick's earlier letters in August 1945 he referred to his status as a former POW, writing 'To think that after my long and faithful services to the Crown nobody has even been to see me' and he feared that his captivity was 'a very disgraceful thing to my name and I shall have to leave here perhaps for good'.[105] Perhaps after the 1945 *Gleaner* interview was published, military or government officials did not get in touch with him, or perhaps he had heard people talk about his captivity in a negative light. Patrick's fear that his being a POW was seen as disgraceful is a sentiment raised by other POWs. For example, in Hal LaCroix and Jorg Meyer 2007 *Journey Out of Darkness: The Real Story of American Heroes in Hitler's POW Camps* they documented an American POW imprisoned in the German Second World War camps who recalled that all POWs felt shame from 'just the fact that we were captured'.[106]

Patrick also had the great challenge in getting his army pension arranged and paid. He wrote in August 1945 that he had not yet received his pension.[107] In December 1945 he wrote of a rumour that POWs – 'we who was in Deutschland' – would receive £1,000 and as a result he would be able to build a house in Jamaica to receive Duncan when he came to stay.[108] By December 1945, perhaps because of this news, but also because he had been socializing a little, he seemed to have settled back into Jamaican life and reflected on his life story in the process of this experience of homecoming. He wrote that 'instead of being in Germany, England or Paris, I am at home and very happy to have returned for a little I will be sure to write a long story of my life one-day'.[109] Though it appears he never wrote this life story, researching, writing, learning and reading was of central importance to his emotional life experiences post-war. The next chapter focuses on some of these emotional experiences during his return to and settling in Jamaica.

Resuming Life: Identity, Community and Belonging

Patrick's experiences during his time away from Jamaica, specifically, the considerable trauma resulting from his wartime experiences served to profoundly shape his post-war life. His post-war experiences in Jamaica were challenging, particularly when trying to secure long-term work. In his letters to Duncan he documented a myriad of personal experiences, detailing his search for work but also his ideas, thoughts and viewpoints, ranging from religious belief and identity, sexuality and desire, to day-to-day activities such as attending the cinema, swimming and dancing to his long-term life plans, particularly his desire to remigrate to Britain. This chapter explores some of these experiences and thoughts, focusing primarily on the details included in the letters to Duncan.

Queer socializing and transatlantic friendship

Significant expressions of identity appear in Patrick's writings in relation to friendship, love and queer sexuality. These identities are sometimes alluded to and sometimes directly expressed. Queerness in the twentieth-century Caribbean, as documented earlier in the book, is increasingly being explored. However, there are many more stories to be uncovered on exploring queer desire, expression and identity in the earlier part of the century. Not only the contents but the existence of Patrick's correspondence is of key importance: he writes as a queer Caribbean man in 1940s and 1950s Jamaica, and through these letters we are able to gain details about his day-to-day life as well as his expressions of sexuality and identity. These letters are of immense significance. They not only enable us to understand and bring to the fore Patrick's life story, but they also expand our knowledge of the queer Caribbean in general. In Patrick's letters there were several instances where he mentions and alludes to his queer desire and identity. For example, in one letter he referred to the sexual encounter he had hoped for in New York and those he hopes for in Jamaica, stating that he 'did not see G.B. in New York and I'm obliged to go swimming often to see what I can get out of mankind.'[1] Is G.B. George Bergen? Perhaps Bergen, Duncan Grant's former lover, was one of Patrick's former lovers too. As explored previously, Patrick, Duncan, Edward Le Bas and possibly George Bergen were part of a pre-war queer network of male friends, lovers and companions. Just before he mentioned G.B. he stated 'Give my love to Edward and do not forget me when you see your other and any of my friends.'[2]

In addition to the reference about going swimming every day, Patrick also referred in other letters to his queer identity and experiences in Jamaica. During the early part of his post-war remigration he is open about his sexuality, even when writing in an elusive manner. For example, in June 1945, a few months after returning, he wrote to Duncan that 'I must see you again soon to tell you of the really beautiful men God have created out here.'[3] During his time in Jamaica, Patrick often thought about his queer London friends, reflecting and reminiscing on their lives and on London's geographical spaces of significance to his social group, such as the Café Royal. In his July 1945 letter he wrote 'I was pleased to hear news of you going to the Cafe Royal, with The Bells, it makes me happy to know that you still find enjoyment – do have the nicest times you can find round London.'[4] Patrick was also in touch (or wished to be in touch) with Edward Wolfe and in a 1950 letter to Duncan he enclosed a letter for Duncan to send on to Edward.[5]

Though it is difficult to arrive at a comprehensive understanding of the subject matter, emotional content or style of writing of Duncan's letters to Patrick, as already stated, there are clues within Patrick's letters as to their content. Duncan often wrote to Patrick about his friends and family. For example, in December 1945 Patrick wrote 'I am sorry to hear that your dear aunt had a stroke, but glad to know that your mother, Mrs Bell and Quentin are well.'[6] As well as passing on news of family and friends Duncan often mentioned his artwork, which Patrick responded to and referenced in his replies. For example, in a discussion about Christmas in a 1945 letter, Patrick mentioned a dramatic Christ figure which Duncan had just completed, using Edward as the model.[7] During the Second World War, Duncan Grant, along with Vanessa Bell and Quentin Bell, was commissioned to paint murals on the life of Christ in the Berwick Church and in these murals Edward Le Bas posed as the model for Christ.[8] In a later letter in 1950 Patrick referred to Duncan's studio which was destroyed during the war, writing 'if I were you I would take my Document, and walk straight into the House of Commons and so what is described as (Raize Hell)' until he got back Whistler's Fitzroy Street studio.[9]

There were sometimes gaps in correspondence between Patrick and Duncan. For example, Patrick wrote in May 1946 what a long time it had been since they had been in touch and that he thought it was Christmas time since he had last heard from him. By this time, Patrick reported to Duncan that he had not left Jamaica since but had moved away from Kingston to live in Montego Bay. In several letters Patrick mentioned the artwork he had created. In November 1945 Patrick mentioned drawing a picture and posting it to Duncan.[10] In May 1946 he wrote that he had been drawing and colouring portraits from inspiration of 'King George as Duke of York and the scene of the crucifixion also one of the nativity and many others', and he sent these portraits on to Duncan.[11] To my knowledge, these portraits are not currently located at the Tate Archive but perhaps they remain preserved elsewhere. Patrick did not mention other artists in Jamaica or whether or not he visited art exhibitions in, for example, Kingston. The Jamaican arts movement in the mid-twentieth century included artists such as Edna Manley and Albert Huie. Albert Huie was a Jamaican artist who was based in Kingston and exhibited his work at venues including the Institute of Jamaica. His artwork portrayed the landscape, daily life and people of the Jamaican countryside as well as downtown Kingston, in works such as the 1955 *Crop Time* and 1959 *Trench Town*.[12] Edna Manley was born in England to a Jamaican mother and English father. Moving to Jamaica in 1922 with her husband and future political leader, Norman Manley, she established herself as a key artist in Jamaica. Her most influential work was *Negro Aroused* (1935), a sculptural form representing the struggles and protest of people of African heritage.[13] In the late 1930s Manley arranged for the works of several London Group artists to be sent to the Institute of Jamaica for exhibition. Included in the works was a portrait by Duncan Grant, a drawing by Roger Fry, a landscape by Quentin Bell and a nude study by Vanessa Bell. Today, these works can be viewed at the National Gallery of Jamaica.[14] In December 1937 the *Gleaner* covered the official opening of an exhibition at the Institute of Jamaica organized by the Empire Art Loan Collections Society. The exhibition included watercolours, drawings, engravings, etchings, woodcuts, linocuts and lithographs. The *Gleaner* argued that the exhibition afforded 'a particularly notable survey to the many black and white artists working in Jamaica'. Included in the exhibition were works by Edmund X. Kapp and Laura Knight. Those pieces singled out as outstanding were the items 'presented to the Institute by various donors in England collected and brought out by Mrs Manley'. Duncan Grant's piece was a large portrait painting of his mother. The *Gleaner* described Duncan as 'one of the foremost of the younger British painters, whose great grand-father Sir John Peter Grant was former Governor of Jamaica'.[15] Was Duncan Grant's painting on view during the 1940s and 1950s? If so, undoubtedly Patrick would have visited the gallery as he spent so much time at the Institute of Jamaica.

In May 1946 Patrick wrote of how he went swimming every day, that home was a great place, and his health was now good, writing 'I tell you how much I fret about you and cannot think why you do not make up your mind and come out here for a little. This is how I enjoy myself I swim every day and my skin is so dark now that it would take you many day to find the shade suitable to my complexion.'[16] He also reported that he wanted to try his luck in Canada or the United States for about five or ten years and later return to England when conditions had improved and asked Duncan to send him a ticket. By this time, he was living in Montego Bay and had links with other people who had experienced war service as he had a job as secretary for the ex-servicemen's organization of the parish.[17] In late 1946 Patrick reported that he had received his army gratuity and would be receiving a life pension from the government.[18] He also told Duncan that he would be back in England the following month so would let him know the time of his arrival.[19]

London remigration

One of the two letters preserved in the archive from Duncan to Patrick because it was 'returned to sender', was sent in August 1947 to Patrick at 69 Woodberry Road, Manor Holme, London, N.4.[20] This short letter is thus important, giving a glimpse of the other side of the correspondence and is quoted in full:

> My Dear Pat,
>
> I have not heard anything of you for a long time Please let me know how you are getting on. I am very well and painting a good deal out of doors but I seldom can come to London, When I come we must meet & have a drink. Please write soon.
>
> It has really been a fine summer so far, for England & I think you are lucky to have come at this time of year.
>
> Let me know what sort of work you are doing & whether you have begun your legal studies.

Are you still at the same address? I have no news. My life is very simple here & I am enjoying my work.

Love

yours Duncan.[21]

This letter was sent during Patrick's short return to London. It appears from contents of the letter as well as a further letter that Patrick had enrolled at a London-based university for his legal studies. However, Patrick returned to Jamaica in November 1947. The address Patrick gave as his residence in London in the passenger return for the voyage back to Jamaica was 77 Wimpole Street and he described himself as a student. The Marylebone address of 77 Wimpole Street was, it appears, a building for student residences, probably medical students due to its location. In 1947 at the time of the electoral register there were fifteen people living there, including Nigerian student Alfred O. Ogedengbe.[22] Like many student residences throughout London, 77 Wimpole Street highlights the multi-ethnic and diverse character of student life in the 1930s and 1940s. Also residing there was someone called Leaford C. Williams, who it appears was Leaford Clemetson Williams, a black Jamaican man born in 1924 who lived in England until he migrated to the United States in August 1947.[23] Patrick was not listed on the 1947 electoral register but the register may have been taken before he moved there or he might have used the address for correspondence care of a friend.

Patrick's migration, even if temporary, was part of the initial post-war migration of Caribbean people immediately after the Second World War and part of a larger movement of peoples from Africa, Asia, the Caribbean and continental Europe. As Matthew Mead points out during the late 1940s up to 1951, migrants came to Britain not just from the Caribbean, Africa and Asia, but also Europe, particularly Polish migrants recruited under the European Voluntary Workers scheme.[24] Mead analysed the mythologies and memorialization surrounding the arrival of the *Empire Windrush*. In particular, he explored the reasons for and public memory processes in the memorialization of the figure of 492 Jamaican migrants on board the *Windrush*, when there appears to have been 531 Jamaicans on the ship, along with many more Caribbean and other migrants as passengers. In total there were 1027 listed passengers on the boat, including sixty-six migrants from Poland.[25] Additionally, as Mead points out, other boats arrived before the *Windrush* with Caribbean migrants in the post-war period. For example, on 21 December 1947 the *Almanzora* docked at Southampton with approximately 200 Caribbean migrants and in March 1947 the *Ormonde* docked in Liverpool with about 100 Jamaican migrants on board.[26]

In fact, the *Almanzora* was the ship that Patrick travelled on when making his return journey from Southampton to Jamaica in November 1947, before the ship returned back to Southampton disembarking migrants in December. Patrick wrote from Jamaica that he went back on a giant ship called *Almanzora*, which was as large as the liner *Queen Mary* and which had over a thousand passengers and troops on board.[27] Patrick sailed as a 'C' grade passenger. Ivor Cummings was travelling on this same voyage, though in 'A' grade. As explored previously in the book, Cummings was another queer black man of interwar London. Cummings was a civil servant and travelling to Jamaica for work. By this time Cummings worked for the Colonial Office. Did they know one another or meet one another on the ship? The ship was a space of homosocial bonding and socializing, which Patrick enjoyed. He wrote 'It was great fun for me going to the Ships Cinema, and dancing with Sailors and Soldiers, at nights for three weeks, as there were no women with us the voyage was rather pleasant and there was plenty of good food.'[28] On his return from London in 1947, he wrote that 'I am not leaving Kingston until after the end of the year when I hope to travel to Montego Bay for swimming and dancing'.[29]

Education and study in Jamaica

As highlighted in the reasons for his 1947 migration to London, Patrick maintained his ambitions to study law after his release from confinement. Although, it appears, he did not continue with his formal legal studies in Jamaica, he did continue to study from law books sent to him via the POW/ Bodleian educational service. In May 1946, when living in Montego Bay, Patrick wrote to Duncan that 'the two law books you kindly sent me while in captivity I brought them home with me and after re-studying them, I recently posted them back to the Bodlyan Library at Oxford University which I hope you agree with'.[30]

Patrick continued his education in Jamaica through self-taught study and in February 1948 Patrick first mentioned the Institute of Jamaica, an institution which was going to become of central importance to him (Figure 8.1).[31] He wrote to Duncan of the links between the Institute and Duncan's grandfather, writing that 'the Institute was founded by the late Sir Anthony Musgrave, in 1879 who was a personal friend of the late Sir John Peter Grant'.[32] Patrick started to go there regularly to read and study and made friends at the Institute. In a

Figure 8.1 The Institute of Jamaica, Photograph taken by author, 2014.

letter sent a year later in February 1949 Patrick detailed the extensive research he had carried out at the Institute of Jamaica on the Jamaican career of John Peter Grant. Patrick wrote,

> In 1866 Sir John Peter Grant arrived in Jamaica, Governor. He had been an Administrator in India. He was a very strong and able man and He at once set about to reorganize the Institution of the Colony. A Legislative Council of the Governor, six officials and three non official members were appointed by the Crown. A Privy Council was also appointed Parochial Boards were nominated by the Crown Government. The 22 Parishes into which the Island was then divided were reduced to fourteen. The Police Force was entirely reorganized, and District Courts were established. The judges of the Courts were officers of the Crown and it was felt that in the Peoples opinion that better justices than they had hitherto been able to get. Coolies immigration which had been stopped for some time was now resumed. The Church of England, in Jamaica, was disestablished. Communications with Europe was established (1889) and the Rail Way (then owned by a private Company) was extended to Old Harbour.[33]

He then referred to the reforms made by Governor Grant in higher education, irrigation and public service concluding 'he was one of the Greatest Governors' and 'was succeeded by Sir William Gray in (1874) followed by Sir Arthur Musgrave'.[34] He finished this letter with a p.s. 'I love history'.[35] Over a year later in June 1950 he told Duncan that he had 'now finished my study of Sir John Peter Grants, as Jamaica's greatest Administrator and after a search I was handed a picture of Him which used to hang in the Institute of Jamaica 12 East Street Kingston Jamaica'.[36] His heavily romanticized viewpoint of this governor was no doubt shaped by his feelings for Duncan, as well as his (developing) ideas on British imperial history and the records available in the Institute.

Faith, community, health and belonging

Patrick occasionally mentioned his family in letters to Duncan but not often. However, this absence does not mean that he did not keep in touch with family members as his letters to Duncan represent a partial view of his life. During much of the 1950s he was living on the north coast of the island working in the tourist industry (explored later in this chapter) and would not have been able to visit his mother to the same extent as when he lived in Kingston. However, he did keep in touch and visit his mother and had knowledge of family news. In relation to building a sense of family and community, a central theme of Patrick's Jamaican letters concerns the increasing significance of his Catholic faith, which provided him with spiritual comfort, friends and support. He often wrote about or referenced his faith in letters to Duncan. For example, in a 1945 letter sent to wish Duncan a Happy Christmas, he started the letter with 'While shepherds watch this flock by night, All seated on the ground, The angel of the Lord, came down, And glory shond around'.[37] In this same letter he reported that he was 'received by His Grace the Archbishop of the West Indies and have been entertained by a great many Jamaicans and old friends'.[38] When Patrick lived in St Mary, the Roman Catholic Church St Anthony was important to him. He attended High Mass on various occasions, for example, in 1950 he attended one mass wearing his Lord Baden-Powell of Gildwell Uniform and Ribbons.[39]

Patrick's health deteriorated throughout the years and he also experienced loneliness at many points in his life during his time in post-war Jamaica. One reason for the loneliness stemmed from having been away from Jamaica for so long in addition to his experiences of being a POW. The church, however, was a solace to him. In 1950 he wrote to Duncan that he had no friends in Jamaica and also that nobody believed he was Jamaican so he makes up himself to be French.[40] He intended to remigrate again to London in 1951 as he wrote to Duncan that he was meant to travel on the *Producer* and was packed to go but as the ship was not a government ship he was not allowed to travel on it.[41] He reported that he was still out of work and that was why he wanted to have another try at life in London, stating 'They still have my Cards at Stepney Labour Exchange and they have again promised to help me when I return.'[42] Perhaps he lived in Stepney during 1947 when he briefly returned to London. In a 1953 letter he mentioned how he used to live at a Rowton House in Whitechapel and this may have been his address for some of 1947.[43] During 1951 he mentioned receiving help from a kind doctor, from an Anglican reverend Jones and another person called Blare who was the superintendent of the PWD in the parish.[44] In April 1951 he was still based in Portland, spending most of his time assisting in a school.[45] He reported that various upsetting things had happened since he had left Kingston but he had been able to obtain enough work. He asked Duncan to send the Stepney Labour Exchange a note to say that he had been travelling and working in Jamaica since he had left the university.[46]

In August 1951 a massive hurricane, named Charlie, hit Jamaica, having disastrous effects on the island. The hurricane and its aftermath was one of the reasons many people migrated from Jamaica to Britain. David Longshore states 'Some 40,241 buildings were either damaged or destroyed, forcing the displacement of an estimated 50,000 people. One hundred sixty-two men, women, and children on the island were killed, while another 2,000 were injured, making Charlie the deadliest storm to have struck Jamaica since Black River Hurricane claimed 164 lives in mid-November 1912.'[47] Patrick wrote to Duncan to let him know he had survived. He described it as the most disastrous thing that he had experienced in Jamaica, with a loss of nearly two hundred lives. He described Port Royal as being completely destroyed and he had read that Kingston was just as bad. He again wrote of wanting to migrate to London and that the government was considering him for a passage. He wished to settle down to a practice in England and reported still keeping up as best as he could (presumably he is referring to his law studies) and being able to take out a book from the local library when he wanted one.[48] He reported being not as lonely as before as he now saw a lot of Americans.[49] There was also a doctor helping him who was also a soldier.[50]

Patrick had maintained a friendship with Captain Rutty at the Manor House Hotel, the hotel where he worked during the 1930s before migrating to Wales. He wrote in February 1952 that he was under the care of Rutty when he heard the bad news of the death of the king, and that he was wearing a mourning band and would be at the 'Parish Church for the occasion of the

Royal Funeral wearing my tropical Military Uniform, mourning band and decorations' and 'naturally will be at the Roman Catholic Church at 9 o'clock on Friday evening'.[51]

A letter sent in March 1953 indicates that Patrick and Duncan had not been in touch for about five months and Patrick wondered if a letter might have gone astray as he moved so much but he was expecting a 'purce' from him to help him out with finances. He then reported to Duncan the sad and distressing time they were having in Jamaica, which was no fault of their own. Patrick described important events which had taken place in Jamaica, stating 'you may not know but Sir H. Allan the only Negro Knight in Jamaica died here some weeks ago. His death has caused great allarm among the common peoples'.[52] He reported 'I was allowe[d] to go with the Kings House Party wearing my Pioneer Dress, and in all my born days I have never seen so many Glittering Uniforms. I was allowed to stand at the Tate of Holy Cross to watch Mr W. Churchill Pass in an Open Motor Car Proceeded, and followed by the Millet a might of Jamaica. I later left Kingston myself for here staying for one week in Annotto Bay'.[53] In April 1953 he wrote from Portland that he had been attending his church a great deal (Little Church of St Anthony and St Mary in Port Antonio) as Lent concluded with an all-night watch and the long three-hours devotion.[54]

At many points in the 1950s Patrick expressed the desire to remigrate. In 1952 he wrote to the British Government, addressing W. S. Churchill, for a passage to London. The colonial secretary's office replied in April 1953 that they were not able to do this.[55] In July 1954 Patrick wrote that he was still out of work and might have to return to England.[56] Patrick's health problems emanating from the war and his post-war experiences culminated with him suffering a heart attack in January 1955. He had previously experienced a heart attack in the middle of Mass in the Old Church in Port Antonio. Because of these life experiences he decided he wanted to leave Jamaica for one of the smaller islands.[57] He hoped Duncan was well and painting again but told Duncan he rarely left the countryside and 'worse than all' did not keep company.[58] By March 1955 Patrick was or had recently been living in Buff Bay. Duncan had sent him some funds, which were badly needed as he reported he was out of work and he was no longer assisted by the war department for a pension or allowance. He recollected the story of the good Shepherd and another story of no greater love than a man who lays down his life for his friend. It appears by this juxtaposition that Patrick was reflecting on his bond with Duncan.[59] Patrick also relayed other political and personal news. He reported that his doctor told him that his heart was normal again after the heart attack and that he had undergone an X-Ray showing the hole in his back from the May 1940 bullet wound. Patrick also reported the changing political situation in Jamaica, that 'since about a few weeks ago there has been a change of Government in Jamaica and the Peoples Nationel party is now into Power having at the head of Mr Norman W. Manley Q.C.'[60]

Patrick was in correspondence with military officials to try to get a pension again, applying to the Ministry of Pensions.[61] He wrote to Duncan in August 1955 informing him that he had visited Up Park Camp to see a military doctor who had been sent from England to examine soldiers who had served in the BEF in France. The medical board stated that he should be given a 100 per cent disability pension with back pay. Again Duncan acted as a close friend whom he would confide in and who would look after his personal medical letters as he sent Duncan the correspondence for his judgement.[62] Patrick had started to plan to travel or migrate from Jamaica during 1955, perhaps to Cuba. In August 1955 he wrote of getting vaccinations and trying to sort out his visa and of needing to first travel to Haiti.[63] Again he continued his studying, but it appears that his study of law was put on hold for his increasing interest and study in science, literature and his 'study of God and the Christian religion'.[64]

Queer identity and experience in the 1950s

It is difficult to know from Patrick's letters but perhaps Patrick's quiet life in the 1950s also involved not having any intimate sexual or romantic relationships or encounters. When exploring his 1950s correspondence, Patrick's queer identity and desire was in the main not explicitly articulated. A 1951 letter does, however, reference his relationship with Duncan. In this letter Patrick informed Duncan that at no time must anybody know their business and one day they would play in their studio again but that life 'out in these parts' was different to England so he needed to be careful, which was why he would not even write to his old girlfriend.[65] As his 1951 reference suggests, after being away from Britain he became more cautious about expressing his sexuality within letter writing, though his juxtaposition of life in Britain as opposed to Jamaica was perhaps written with his 1930s Bloomsbury experiences in mind – where he socialized with queer Bloomsbury group friends and lovers and met Duncan in the Fitzrovia studio for sex and companionship – and not with early 1950s Britain, with the occurrence of high-profile criminal prosecutions of gay men.

In relation to queer identity, Patrick's existence as a queer man in 1950s Jamaica is an important addition to the history and historiography of queer Jamaica. What were the experiences like for other queer people in Jamaica during this time? Evidence for queer lives in 1950s Jamaica include, as explored in Chapter 2, autobiographical and oral history reflections. Newspapers are another source for exploring how homosexuality was publically viewed, though press reporting does not reflect or document the everyday experiences and identities of queer Jamaicans living their lives or the complexities and multifaceted relationships and experiences within local communities. In 1957 the *Gleaner* reported on that year's report of the Wolfenden Committee (established by the British Government in 1954), which recommended that homosexual acts between consenting adults in private should no longer be deemed a crime.[66] In a *Gleaner* column entitled 'Face the Facts' the writer stated that the 'heat of the reaction' to the report and to the Archbishop of Canterbury's comments in the UK were not surprising but 'what is surprising is the heat of the reaction in Jamaica, and the efforts here and there to inject a sectarian religious flavour into the debate'. Of the report's conclusions the columnist wrote that 'the committee's purpose was not to aid the homosexual, but to aid the nation in dealing with homosexuality in the context of today' and that 'it should be borne in mind that the modern concept is more to regard sexual abnormality (in the same way as insanity) as a terrible misfortune to the individual rather than as a crime'.[67]

A few years earlier, in February 1954 Archdeacon Fox of St James Parish Church held a sermon on homosexuality in Jamaica. The *Gleaner* wrote of this sermon that 'Archdeacon Fox expressed his deep concern over the decline in moral standards and especially over the prevalence of homosexuality in a section of the community that usually merits our highest respect. Unpleasant, as it may be to some people it is rank folly to gloss over such social evils as this; neither tolerance nor ignorance of such vice merits any excuse.'[68] The *Gleaner* received various statements from other churches in response to Fox's sermon and the newspaper stated 'With few exceptions, churchmen, schoolmasters, and others in contact with the youth of Montego Bay, have warmly congratulated Archdeacon Fox for last Sunday's outspoken sermon disclosing the dangerous rise of homosexual vice here'.[69] Questions which arise after reading this article include: Who were the 'few exceptions' the *Gleaner* noted did not congratulate Fox on his sermon? Did the churches Patrick attended preach against homosexuality within their sermons and how did Patrick emotionally react to such homophobia? How did others in the community or congregation react?

No information is given in Patrick's letters to his feelings and emotions relating to this specific sermon or article, but as his 1951 letter highlights, he felt less able to express himself than before and thus was careful not to write anything too obvious on the subject of homosexuality or his personal queer desire within his letters.

Film and art

Patrick's emotional sustenance and joy was maintained through his love of film and cinema going. Attending the cinema and enjoying films was of central importance to Patrick throughout his life. He often wrote about his love of cinema describing the various films he had seen, films he wanted to see and films he believed the industry should be making. For example, in April 1945 when he was still based in Britain he described going to the cinema to see 'Scheoca' which he described as a 'jolly nice film, and I would like to see the film industry making more historical films than gangster ones'.[70] His love of cinema held an especially important place in his life during the 1950s as he did not socialize a great deal and referenced his loneliness in letters. During this time, he wrote that though he was still by character very quiet he went to the cinema very often. He wrote that 'I think that the old House Keeper was the best character in the Film "Limelight" Only last night I saw "The Son of Dr. Jakyll["], and the night before "Affairs in Trinidad["] ytty are all very lovely and I like them'.[71] In another letter, also written on 31 August 1955, he mentioned more films he had watched, 'I saw Casa Nova and yesterday afternoon I went to the matonee show specially to the Queen of England on horse back also the film Thunder Boy'.[72] In January 1955 he wrote that he found the 'morning pictures very entertaining' and that he had recently seen the films *Magic Face* and *Second Chance*.[73] He also read books during his spare time and in 1955 wrote that he had been inspired by *The Berlin Diary* by W. Shirer.[74] He did mention, however, not reading as much as he used to and this change seems to be linked to his health.[75]

Patrick and Duncan continued to write to one another about art. During the 1950s Duncan Grant was commissioned to paint murals in the Russell Chantry of Lincoln Cathedral, which he completed in 1958. Patrick asked about the murals in his letters. In March 1958 he wrote, 'Are you still Painting the Lincoln Cathedral? It must be interesting' and one year later in March 1959 he again asked 'Are you still Painting the Lincoln Cathedral?' Patrick would have been especially interested in this painting as his likeness was probably used to represent one of the porter figures in the Lincoln ship loading scene on the west wall mural. Additionally, as explored earlier in the book, Patrick had a love of cathedrals and visited many during his time in Britain.[76]

Employment, tourism and plans to remigrate

Although he experienced periods of unemployment Patrick found work in a variety of places during the mid-to-late 1950s, most notably in the hotel industry. He re-entered employment within the hotel industry at some point in the 1950s, probably in 1956 to 1957, after his health had improved and during this time he lived in a number of tourist areas in the north of the island including Montego Bay and Ocho Rios. During this time, he also experienced an improvement in his living situation. In April 1956 he reported that for the past six months he had been staying with the daughter of Mrs Hardy Barratt at Castle Gordon Hotel in Port Maria and that the arrangement was most simple but had been life saving.[77]

Jamaica's hotel industry post-war was much different to the industry Patrick worked in during the 1930s. The *Pan Am Clippers* taking tourists between Jamaica and Miami started in 1930 and revolutionized Jamaican tourism in facilitating travel to the island from the United States for tourists other than the wealthy. Post-war the Pan Am Company grew its operations and promotion in Jamaica substantially. As Frank Taylor has documented, 'When the company began operating in Jamaica at the end of 1930 it had four employees, but by 1955 its personnel at the Kingston office numbered sixty-two, and at Montego Bay the staff amounted to a dozen.'[78] Pan Am also began using the Palisadoes Peninsula airport, which was built in the Second World War for military purposes. In 1941 Royal Dutch Airlines (KLM) began using the airport, which was used by Dutch oil workers in Curaçao to travel there with their families for holidays in Jamaica.[79] In regard to British travel the British Overseas Airways Corporation (BOAC) promoted tourism in Jamaica, focusing on promoting Jamaica's summer tourist trade. Taylor states that by the mid-1950s eight international airlines were working in Jamaica and thereafter tourism's leading destinations changed due to airfield locations. Montego Bay became a increasingly popular destination.[80] For example, in late 1956 BOAC opened an air service between Jamaica and Montreal, Canada. To celebrate the service, the *Gleaner* reported, BOAC planned to make 'two inaugural flights on November 29 and December 4 bringing down two groups of press, public relations, and travel industry representatives from Canada on a courtesy trip to the island'.[81] Jamaica's North Coast was central to the post-war tourist boom and this is the area Patrick moved to and worked in during the late 1950s. The industry gradually opened its hotels for longer periods of the year and by 1962 hotels remained open throughout the year.[82]

Initiatives were established by the government to aid tourism, including the Hotels Aid Law of 1944 which significantly facilitated the construction of hotels.[83] Though tourism fostered income for the island, it also had many problems including labour exploitation and exclusionary practices against the local population. For example, one of the key problems with these North Coast resorts was the exclusion of Jamaicans in using beaches. Many beaches were private property under colonial law but this was not heavily enforced until the advent of tourism where several beaches were shut off to the local population.[84]

In relation to his hotel work, Patrick worked at a number of hotels for short periods of time, generally finding temporary employment over specific tourist seasons. He wrote to Duncan about the various hotels where he found employment but did not generally provide further detail on the nature of the work, the conditions of employment or any friends he might have met through this work. He worked at the 'House Hotel' (probably the Manor House Hotel where he worked in the 1930s) during the tourist season of 1956 to 1957 and thereafter had another job for a few months at the Jamaica Inn in Ocho Rios. In 1957 he wrote to Duncan that he would stay in Ocho Rios as there was better prospect of getting work there suitable to his disability.[85] Though he continued working in the tourist trade it was also difficult to find steady employment in this line of work. During Christmas 1957 he worked as the head waiter at the Balcony Inn and then worked at the Jamaica Arms but by March 1958 he had no work and so went to Montego Bay to search for employment.[86] During the tourist season of Christmas 1958 he worked back at the Jamaica Inn in Ocho Rios as a valet (the profession in which he worked during the 1930s) and stayed there until at least March 1959.[87] In April 1960 he wrote to Duncan that although the last tourist season was a failure he had a job as a chef for about two months.[88]

Susan Lewis, the *Gleaner's* North Coast correspondent, published various articles on the tourist industry of 1950s Ocho Rios. Ocho Rios was a destination popular with Europeans and Americans, including celebrities and politicians. In 1957 Susan Lewis wrote, 'for a day spent at this season in the small village of Ocho Rios has the cosmopolitan tang, a feeling of celebrities, the arts, excitement of music, dancing and important events. For in a tourist resort like Ocho Rios with its major industry, personalities and people, you are apt to meet any of the world's great on any day.[89] The Jamaica Inn in Ocho Rios, where Patrick worked during two separate tourist seasons, was one of the premier hotels in 1950s Jamaica (and is still open today). Those staying at the Jamaica Inn during the 1950s included actor Richard Burton.[90] In the 1957 *Gleaner* article Lewis described the characteristics of the Jamaica Inn as follows:

> There the Elkins have created their own atmosphere of a large luxurious country home, with guests following a leisurely routine of a swim before breakfast, sunbathing until 1 pm, cocktails from 1 to sometimes 2 o'clock, late high lunch and then utter silence for the afternoon while almost everyone takes a long nap. Dinner from 8 until 10 and then some dancing and 11 o'clock bedtime more often than not.[91]

This description, while not providing information on the experiences and lives of the workers at the Jamaica Inn, such as Patrick, gives some indication of their daily routine.

There were problems related to the rapid development of Ocho Rios as a tourist destination. In September 1956 Susan Lewis published the results of a brief survey undertaken in Ocho Rios on the costs involved in living in the town. Lewis interviewed Mitzi Luke who owned a small drygoods store called Luke's Magnet. Luke stated that it was 'all well and good' if you worked at one of the big hotels as 'the hotel takes care of your housing and food. But if you work in a shop, or as a secretary away from the hotels, or as a teacher, you are just out of luck. Housing is acute for all classes. And you cannot live in Ocho Rios on £5 per week which is an average middle class wage.'[92] Another interviewee, Ed Helwig, who was head gardener at the Jamaica Inn, spoke of his difficulty in finding accommodation in Ocho Rios and stated that 'when I was a single man, I was glad to live in hotel quarters, but now that I am married and have a child, we would like a little place of our own to rent'.[93] Luke also spoke of the facilities available for locals, including the lack of beach facilities open to the public, stating 'also there's nothing for any middle class person to do after work. The closest public beach is Dunn's River, four miles away. How are you going to get there with no bus service?'[94] At the same time as this tourism development, the area was also being developed for bauxite mining. In August 1956, Lewis wrote an article in the *Gleaner* entitled 'a prison without bars', quoting W. H. Edwards 'long time public servant and resident of Ocho Rios' who stated that the 'middle class in Ocho Rios are in a prison without bars'.[95] Explaining this point he continued, 'Squeezed between the luxury resort life of the hotels and seaside residences on the east, and what I call the red zone of bauxite docks on the West, the middle class not only has no place to live, they have no recreation, no cultural facilities, no park, no library, no place to take a safe walk even.'[96]

Remigration

In June 1956 Patrick mentioned travelling again and that the funds he had last year were not enough to take him off the island. He hoped to go to New York and reported he had big opportunities waiting for him there. Interestingly in this context he mentioned Lady Stanley again, passing on to Duncan her Kensington and Penrhos addresses (not knowing that by this time Penrhos had been sold by Lyulph). He had composed a letter to Lady Stanley which he wanted Duncan to forward, stating 'I so much want her to get my letter and feel sure that she will help me to get to New York.'[97] He received his new passport in 1957 and so could start planning his travels, but it would be a few years before he remigrated.[98] Instead of New York, Patrick eventually returned to London at some point in 1960 or 1961. The next chapter explores some of his London experiences, including his search for work in 1960s London, his queer friendships and his remembrance of the war.

The Lonely Londoners: Patrick in Early 1960s London

This concluding chapter explores Patrick's brief return to London before his death in July 1963, contextualizing Patrick's experiences of life in London with the large post-war migration of Caribbean people to Britain. It explores his attempts to find employment and the importance of continuing his friendship with Duncan. It focuses on Patrick's remembrance of the war, its long-term effect and the memorial activities he took part in during this time. It also focuses attention on the painting Duncan created of Patrick during this time (entitled *Portrait of Pat Nelson*), most recently sold in 2012 at a Christie's London auction.

Caribbean post-war migration

After spending much of the 1940s and the 1950s wanting to migrate to either one of the smaller Caribbean islands, to New York or to England, Patrick eventually migrated back to London at some point during the period 1960–1961. Patrick's name does not appear on passenger returns so perhaps he arrived after 1960 (the passenger returns within The National Archives' record series BT26 do not continue after that year). Therefore, I do not know the precise date he arrived and what his first address was after remigrating to London. Patrick was one of many Caribbean migrants who decided to migrate and make their home in post-war Britain. As Mary Chamberlain states, 'Between 1948 and 1973 approximately 550,000 people of Caribbean birth arrived in Britain.'[1]

The Lonely Londoners is the classic novel of post-war Caribbean migration which represents many, though by no means all, aspects of this early experience of Caribbean migrants coming to Britain in the 1950s. Published in 1956 by Trinidadian writer Sam Selvon, who migrated to Britain in 1950, the novel centres around a group of Caribbean men moving to 1950s London, who socialize with one another in their new home of the imperial metropole, poetically exploring their hopes, worries, desires, struggles to find employment, their socializing, romantic and sexual experiences with women, and the minutiae of daily life. It centres on a particular characterization of black working-class men's migratory and settlement experiences, with black women's experiences generally not focused upon. Patrick's story is in many ways different to the central characters of *The Lonely Londoners* as he was remigrating and was older than the male characters in the novel. With regard to being a return migrant, Patrick's experiences can be compared more readily to other Caribbean migrants who travelled to Britain in the 1930s and then remigrated to Britain post-war, often after having served in the war. His story is not unique in this respect as many other immediate post-war Caribbean migrants, including those on the *Empire Windrush*, had previously spent time living in Britain, usually serving in the military in the Second World War.

This migration of Caribbean people to Britain in the late 1940s continued and increased in the 1950s and early 1960s due to a range of factors, many described in Patrick's letters to Duncan such as the growing economic crisis in the Caribbean and environmental disasters such as the 1951 hurricane in Jamaica. In addition to these factors, migration was influenced by the labour shortages in post-war Britain, the restrictive 1952 US immigration legislation targeting Caribbean migrants and a major traditional destination route for short- and long-term migration, the influence of family and friends who had already migrated, the British recruitment schemes in the Caribbean and also, to a certain extent, the influence of the mythology of the 'mother country' which was propagated in the colonial Caribbean education system. During the late 1950s and early 1960s, there was an added pressure to migrate to Britain before the restrictive immigration legislation of 1962 was implemented. As Tracy Skelton states 'The flow of Caribbean migrants to Britain during the mid-1950s numbered 25,000 annually, however the rush to beat the new immigration restrictions resulted in 107,000 arrivals from the region in 1961 and 1962.'[2] A number of historians including Bob Carter, Clive Harris and Shirley Joshi have documented that from the early 1950s the state was involved in exploring attempts to control migration, specifically the migration of black people, stating

> While the government was systematically collecting information about black people to support a draft immigration bill prepared in 1954 it was also opposing measures such as Fenner Brockway's bill prohibiting racist discrimination, despite growing evidence that discrimination was widespread. Successive

governments not only constructed an ideological framework in which black people were to be seen as threatening, alien and unassimilable but also developed policies to discourage and control black immigration.[3]

Though the main characters were Caribbean men in *The Lonely Londoners* novel and in many other fictional and historical explorations of post-war migration, many Caribbean women and children also migrated to Britain. As Mary Chamberlain argues 'The emphasis on labour as the principal propeller of migration has necessarily led to a male bias in migration studies. Men, it is assumed, are the pioneer migrants, sending later for their wives and children.'[4] Margaret Byron has explored the gendered perspectives of employment relating to the Caribbean migration movement to Britain, highlighting that 'studies of transitions in occupational patterns occurring during the migration process have often lacked reference to gender dynamics'.[5] Many women were part of the early 1950s migrations, including those recruited from the Caribbean to work in the National Health Service. The experiences of Caribbean and African nurses in the early NHS are the subject of a BBC television programme *Black Nurses: The Women Who Saved The NHS*, broadcast as part of the 2016 BBC season Black and British.[6] The life experiences of Caribbean people living in 1950s and 1960s Britain has been documented, remembered and reflected upon in a vast array of oral histories, memoirs, autobiographies, television programmes and other testimonies. Additionally, historians have explored the complex experiences of Caribbean migrants, including everyday interactions between individuals, the experiences of state and 'everyday' racism, the experiences of family life, religion, social life, activism, education, employment and community life, as well as how Caribbean people have remembered their experiences of migration and settlement reflecting back in time.[7]

Mpalive-Hangson Msiska argues about *The Lonely Londoners*, 'The novel elaborates Black metropolitan identity as a dialectical tension between the utopic and diastopic view of the metropolis. The resolution of that tension is not straightforward and reveals the complexity of the formation of Black subjectivity in the metropolis.'[8] Like these complex dreams, hopes and realities – both utopian and dystopian – within the *Lonely Londoners*, Patrick had imaginations and ambitions of what life could be like back in England which were in part based on his 1930s experiences, but also influenced by the exhaustion of his war and post-war years in Jamaica. He believed that employment would be easier to find in London and that by migrating his life might take a future different direction.

Homosociality, queer identity and friendship

The Lonely Londoners highlights the potential isolation that can befall migrants without a support network and the benefits of being able to rely on networks of friends. The novel starts, for example, with the main protagonist Moses Aloetta travelling to Waterloo Station to meet Henry Oliver, a fellow migrant from Trinidad, his home country. Moses did not know this Henry Oliver personally but he was a friend of a friend in Trinidad who asked him to help Henry.[9] Though Patrick had pre-existing London friends he had made in the 1930s, it appears he had not kept in touch with many of these individuals as the years progressed and importantly he led and had always led a very different life to those friends with race and class privilege such as Duncan. Unlike the *Lonely Londoners* protagonists, Patrick did not seem to rely on a large Caribbean-based support network for accommodation and work. However, just because Patrick did not focus on these possible connections in his letters to Duncan it does not mean that they did not exist. As mentioned previously, there was at least one Caribbean man who supported Patrick in the latter years of his life, the queer Jamaican man Richie Riley whose life is explored later in the chapter. It appears that the support of friends such as Richie was a key factor in Patrick eventually finding secure housing.

Nadia Ellis' work has provided an important examination of the work of anthropologists, social commentators in academia and public discourse with regard to the parallel, but separate, public policy discourses concerning post-war sexuality and race relations, highlighting how wartime and post-war ethnographers, sociologists and social workers such as Edith Ramsay interacted with the black community of the East End, focusing on perceived morality with regard to hostels such as the Colonial House on Leman Street where Ramsay wrote about what she considered grave moral issues which 'need not be described'. Ellis has argued that Ramsay expressed the 'particular inflection of the language of sexual indecency here, (the moral problem that dare not speak its name)' and expressed a presumption that black migrants could be steered away from 'vice' with different accommodation provisions but did not attempt to explore or acknowledge the existence of queer sexualities among black migrants.[10] Ellis states, 'In the postwar era, black men became migrant spectacles, visible for their racial difference but separable from the ever-accreting images around male homosexuality. Separable, that is, except for when they were figured as potentially vulnerable to the compromising desire of queer white men.'[11] Ellis' research is particularly illuminating and useful when thinking about Patrick's life, especially in relation to how contemporary commentators, historians and sociologists were often concerned with black migrants' sexuality with regard to heterosexuality and mixed-race relationships, often pathologizing both black lives and mixed relationships in the process, but black queer lives and expressions of identity such as Patrick's were never documented or acknowledged.

A key migratory motivation for Patrick would have undoubtedly been his feelings of love, friendship and connection to Duncan even if he knew he probably would not see Duncan greatly after returning. Duncan had been Patrick's main, constant friend in a life that had often been lonely. Returning to London and being able to meet up with Duncan from time to time would have been a joyful and important hope for Patrick. Nicola Mai and Russell King have advocated 'for an "emotional turn" in migration and mobility studies which explicitly places emotions, especially love and affection, at the heart of migration decision making and behaviour'. In their special issue of *Mobilities*, published in 2009, they sought not to ignore economic and structural forces of migration but 'to shift the interplay between sexuality, affectivity and migration to the centre of the analysis, rather than situating it at the margin or in the background'.[12]

An important aspect of the turn towards analysing emotion in mobility and migration studies has been the importance of queer studies within this new body of research, with work published by Eithne Luibhéid, Martin Manalansan and Anne-Marie Fortier.[13] Martin Manalansan states, 'The queer perspective suggests that sexuality is not an all encompassing reality but one that intersects with and through other social, economic, and cultural practices and identities. At the same time, a queer notion of sexuality enables migration research to go beyond normative and universalized family patterns and biological rationales'.[14] It is particularly interesting when exploring emotional theories of mobility and migration to understand how migrations in the past were partly shaped by emotions and desires, including non-heteronormative and queer desires – for example, by looking at the individual personal histories of queer black migrants to document stories that are often ignored or marginalized. These desires do not exist in isolation; they interact and intersect with other hopes, plans and experiences – in the case of Patrick, his experiences of being a black former POW, with long-term health problems, a Jamaican man seeking work and a man living in post-war colonial Jamaica all combined with these emotional reasons to lead him to migrate. Patrick Nelson's life story highlights economic considerations often merged with other motives such as loneliness, friendship, love, desire and hopes and dreams for his future.

Employment and the East End of London

Patrick had to contend with seeking work and housing in a city in which racism was prevalent in both sectors. Additionally, he also undoubtedly experienced prejudice relating to disability, due to his physical health. As explored in Chapter 4, the East End was geographically important for black settlement and employment. Patrick's life in early 1960s London centred to a great deal around the East End and he resided in many of the lodging houses set up in the area populated by men from across the world, including the African diaspora. The first 1960s letter within the archive was postmarked April 1961. In this letter Patrick referenced that he was residing at Queen Victoria Hostel in East India Dock Road, Poplar. As in Jamaica, Patrick continued working in the hotel industry and was employed at the Berners Hotel in Berners Street.[15] In a short note written in early May 1961 Patrick again referenced residing at the Queen Victoria Seamen's Rest on East India Dock.[16] The Queen Victoria Seamen's Rest in East India Dock was established in 1843 as a Seamen's Mission of the Methodist Church.[17]

Some of Patrick's 1960s letters in the archive are undated and one letter, which it appears was composed in late 1961 to early 1962, was sent from Paris. In this letter Patrick wrote that finding employment was again difficult in London and so he decided to try his luck in Paris. He reported that it was not like the old times. (Patrick and Duncan probably visited Paris together at some point in the 1930s, where they would have socialized among the artistic and queer Parisian avant-garde.) This letter was written from Hotel du Départ.[18] In this letter he mentioned that he had moved from 177 Whitechapel Road to Tower House.[19]

The next short piece of correspondence in the archive is dated 5 May 1962 where Patrick could be contacted care of Tower House, 57 Fieldgate Street in the East End. He also reported in this letter that he had a cubicle for another five nights.[20] During this period of time he was unemployed and was trying to find employment. He stated that the Ministry of Labour in Denmark Street and Settle Street in Stepney were seeking to help him with either employment or housing.[21] Tower House was a Rowton House property (Rowton Houses are described in the next section of this chapter). Another undated letter which appears to be from this period was written when Patrick was living at 747 Commercial Road, where he had booked a room for three weeks. This was another property which provided temporary accommodation in the East End. He told Duncan that his travelling days were over and he would never again leave the British Isles. Duncan was due to visit this address, so there is some written evidence that they saw one another in 1962.[22] Patrick also saw Lady Stanley during this time. He wrote that he went to visit the House of Lords, visited Lady Stanley of Alderley and on the day of writing his letter he had just returned from Buckingham Palace.[23] In July 1962 Patrick wrote that he was well, was working, and that he may have secured a bedroom at the 'same' address (possibly Tower House or 747 Commercial Street). In London he continued to visit the cinema and in one piece of correspondence he wrote that he had to hurry the letter as he was off to see the film *Ben Hur*.[24]

Arlington House

In November 1962 Patrick found a temporary job at a factory. He wrote to Duncan on 12 November that 'after a hard search this morning' he had found another temporary job. It was at a 'wharm Factory' and he was due to start the day afterwards on 13 November.[25] He wrote this letter card from Arlington House, where he was temporarily living.[26] Arlington House's full name was Rowton House, 220 Arlington Road and it was established in 1905 as one of a series of large accommodations for men. The first Rowton House was established in 1892 in Vauxhall. Founded by Lord Rowton as a response to the lack (and bad conditions) of temporary accommodation around Britain, Rowton Houses were large lodging houses for working men. As Jane Hamlett and Rebecca Preston document, 'This enterprise was not solely charitable but was designed to be self-supporting; it was one of a range of semi-philanthropic initiatives that emerged in response to the 1880s' housing crisis in London.'[27] After Vauxhall, Rowton Houses Limited established four more houses including Camden Town's Arlington Road's House and the Whitechapel Rowton House. As explored, Patrick had in fact stayed at the Whitechapel Rowton House previously, probably in 1947 and also in 1961. Arlington House today is preserved as a Grade II listed building.

Rowton Houses could accommodate many people and were set at a cheap rate of 6 pence a night. Arlington Road's House accommodated over 1000 men and the houses also included facilities such as day rooms, rooms with cubicles and laundry facilities, and were designed to provide a sense of domesticity with, for example, the inclusion of reading rooms.[28] George Orwell described Arlington House in the 1933 *Down and Out in Paris and London*. Describing the type of places where homeless people might sleep, he wrote of the common lodging houses:

> The best are the Rowton Houses, where the charge is a shilling, for which you get a cubicle to yourself, and the use of excellent bathrooms. You can also pay half a crown for a 'special', which is practically hotel accommodation. The Rowton Houses are splendid buildings, and the only objection to them is the strict discipline, with rules against cooking, card-playing, etc. Perhaps the best advertisement for the Rowton Houses is the fact that they are always full to overflowing.[29]

The Arlington Rowton House also appears in other literature, referenced in stories and in songs, such as Madness' 1984 song *One Better Day* which has the opening lyric 'Arlington House, address: no fixed abode'.[30] Historically the houses had been a home for men of various backgrounds, including many of Irish heritage, in need of temporary accommodation. Many individuals stayed for short periods of time, but others made their home at Arlington House for longer periods, including several years. For example, Thomas Addison lived as a resident at Rowton House, Arlington Road during 1925, 1929 and 1930; Francis Atholl Ball resided at Rowton House, Arlington Road in 1930, 1932, 1933 and 1934; and Thomas Aylott resided at Rowton House, Arlington Road from the mid-1920s, the 1930s, 1940s, the 1950s, up to 1961 (when it was named Arlington House on the registers) though perhaps as Aylott lived there for so long he was a staff member instead of a resident.[31] Though the houses had been seen as an improvement from the lodging conditions of the late nineteenth and early twentieth centuries and the space felt like home for many residents, the residents often lacked privacy due to the strictness of the porters and superintendents and the thin cubicle partitions.[32]

In 1961 there were listed 1046 men residing at Arlington House. The electoral register for that year provides clues as to what Arlington House might have been like during Patrick's stay a year later.[33] By the 1960s conditions had deteriorated and Rowton House entered public discourse as an example of a bad place to reside. For example, in research carried out by Terrance Morris and Pauline Morris in Pentonville Prison around the early 1960s, a man who was serving a prison sentence there conveyed his experiences of conditions in the cells, by writing a poem for the research with the opening lines 'Three in a cell is the general Order/This might be O.K. for a Rowton House Border'.[34]

Perhaps Patrick knew about Arlington House through the Labour Exchange. What were Patrick's experiences living there as a black and queer man? Were there other men of colour living in Arlington House? In one memoir of the 1920s, Rowton House was recalled as a place which carried out racial discrimination. Ismaa'il, a Somali seaman and poet recorded his experiences of a visit to London in an autobiography later published by Richard Pankhurst. Ismaa'il recalled visiting the 1924 Empire exhibition in Wembley, writing

> After the first afternoon at Wembley, we went to Bloomsbury to get a lodging as we had decided to stay a week. Most lodging places were full, but, to my friend's amazement, even those house-keepers who had a spare room would not take me in. Tired and disheartened, we thought we would try Rowton House, where we thought anybody would be given a night's lodging; but here also we were politely told: «The establishment does not accept coloured gentlemen». We dragged ourselves on, until, at last, we were given hospitality by an old Russian Jew who had tramped through Siberia to China.[35]

After a period of further maritime employment, he decided to stay in Whiteway, a place he felt was home but the memory of this experience haunted him. He recalled

> A new bus service, running between Stroud and Cheltenham now passed through the Colony. As I was fond of going to the Cinema I used it frequently to go to Stroud and back. One evening I missed the return bus and had to come back on foot. The night was as black as ink, a cold wind was raging, and soon the rain began to fall in torrents. I was but an outcast, an African. To the physical discomfort was added but Rowton House came to my mind, and other similar experiences in this very neighbourghood [sic], and I felt I could not ask for shelter, because I was but an outcast, an African. To the physical discomfort was added a feeling of misery and isolation, a hundred times more unbearable, and my mind began to wander strangely.[36]

As shown previously in this book, and in Ismaa'il's recollections, racism in interwar Bloomsbury accommodation was well known, but that it extended to a homeless shelter was devastating to Ismaa'il. Did this racism at Rowton House continue into the post-war period? How ethnically diverse were the houses' residents? It is difficult to explore the backgrounds of those staying at Arlington House from electoral registers, though there were, as it appears, occasionally men of colour staying. At least one man of colour resided at Arlington House in the interwar period. In his 1938 autobiography *The Green Fool*, Patrick

Kavanagh recalled staying at Arlington House and remembered the many Irish migrants who stayed there. He also recalled 'Among the inhabitants of Rowton House was a Ceylonese cook. He sat apart from us on the bench, as indeed he sat apart from all white men. I moved in his direction because he looked so down in the mouth, and my self-pity was taking the form of pity for others. He was suspicious of my advances and not inclined to be communicative. The warmth of my address eventually thawed the frost of his silence. I didn't blame him for his bitter aloofness after I had heard his story. He had been getting the dirty end of the stick of life for a long time.'[37] This Ceylonese cook was, it is likely, called Leslie. As explored previously in this book, often cooks and domestics would advertise for work in appointments and situations vacant sections of local and national newspapers and Leslie was one of these individuals who put an advert in the newspaper. In December 1937 Leslie advertised for work in *The Times*, giving the Arlington House address of 220 Arlington Road. He wrote 'Ceylonese, refined, 36, single, experienced secretary, masseur-infirmier and caterer (Paris diplomas), drives car, plays bridge, travelled, fluent French, Dutch, German, Flemish, Malay.'[38] During the period Patrick stayed at Arlington, Onnik Vosguerchian was also a resident. Onnik was born in 1897 in Tottenham. His father was an Armenian carpet buyer from Constantinople who migrated to Britain. Onnik served in the First World War in the Royal Scots Fusiliers and resided at Rowton House, Arlington Road during 1959 and 1962.[39]

In the 1950s and 1960s Rowton House residents were often subject to class prejudice. By this time the houses and their inhabitants were stereotyped in popular culture. In a 1950s study, psychiatric social worker Margaret Eden (who worked in an observation ward in a local authority hospital) expressed,

> I had never realised before how many people had no fixed home and no roots. For some there is little I can do except to fix them up at hostels or refer them to the National Assistance Board. For others who are more employable we can arrange a visit to the local D.R.O., with whom we have a very good contact, while they are still with us, so that the hopeless gap between leaving the shelter of the hospital and facing the great problems of finding work, lodging and money can be bridged. They feel that to give an address such as Rowton House prejudices their chances of getting a job. Until they can pay a deposit they cannot get lodgings, until they have a fixed address they cannot get a regular allowance from the National Assistance Board. They inevitably get caught in a vicious circle of frustrations. One of our great needs is for a hostel to which they could be discharged while re-establishing themselves in life.[40]

Perhaps, in addition to racism and disability prejudice, Patrick had the additional struggle of finding work because of his Arlington House and other lodging house addresses. Homelessness and issues surrounding hostels such as Arlington House were discussed on 13 June 1961 within the House of Lords debate on the Criminal Justice Bill, with testimony from men who had left prison and were given vouchers by the National Assistance Board for Rowton House. The testimony shows how Patrick might have heard of Arlington – perhaps being recommended by the National Assistance Board. It also highlights the reputation and stereotyping of those living at Arlington. In the debate, Lord Stonham moved an amendment for after-care for ex-prisoners. In talking about the amendment he spoke about some of the letters he had received from ex-prisoners. One man aged twenty-four wrote that he was released from Wakefield Prison in October 1959 and

> when leaving the prison I was given a train warrant to London, a letter for the National Assistance Board and 2s. 9d. Arriving at London I went straight to the N.A.B. and produced the letter to confirm I had just been released from prison. They kept me waiting for six hours before finally telling me that … the only thing they could do for me was to give me one week's voucher for the Rowton House. I refused it. I am not a tramp, a dosser, a meth drinker, a pimp, or a general layabout, but a young man of 24 … who challenged the law, did not succeed, took the punishment, and was released with every intention of not crossing the path of the law again. If I had been given an opportunity to make good, I would not have abused it … . I have nearly finished my sentence of two-and-a-half years now.[41]

Duncan in the 1960s London

Duncan was seventy-five years old when Patrick remigrated to London. He and Vanessa continued living and painting at Charleston in Sussex and travelling abroad for long periods where they would paint. In 1961 Vanessa prepared for a show at the Adams Gallery due to open in October 1961, but in Spring she fell ill with bronchitis and died after a short illness.[42] Duncan, Spalding described, 'wept unconsolably, grief mingling with guilt over the hurt he had caused the person who had shared his life for some forty years'.[43] Though he continued to go about daily activities, the loss of someone he had shared his life with was profound. He had other friends and companions he spent time with after Vanessa's death, including presumably Patrick. Duncan and Edward Le Bas had also remained friends and during 1961 Le Bas, 'seeing how miserable Duncan was' when he had dinner at Edward's home, organized a holiday for the two of them in France where they travelled around sites including the Chantilly Forest, Beauvais and Allery.[44] One of the key people in Duncan's life at this time was Paul Roche. They had kept in contact with one another writing letters twice a week for many years after Roche moved away for work. Roche came back to visit Duncan after hearing the news of Vanessa's death and Duncan arranged for him to stay at 28 Percy Street.[45] During this period he spent much time with a new friend Lindy Guinness. They developed a strong friendship and she became a regular visitor to Charleston.[46]

Duncan and Patrick continued their friendship when Patrick returned to London. It appears that they met occasionally but it is difficult to know how often they saw one another. During this time Patrick posed at least once more as an artist model for Duncan. The resulting painting is entitled *Portrait of Pat*

Figure 9.1 Duncan Grant, *Portrait of Pat Nelson*, oil on canvas, approx. 1960–1963.

Nelson (Figure 9.1), and measures 63.5 → 38.1 cm in size painted with oil on board. It was recently sold at the Christie's Interiors sale on 29 May 2012 in South Kensington.[47] This painting is undated so it could have been created during Patrick's 1947 trip but by looking at Patrick's age in the portrait it seems more likely that it was created shortly before his death in the early 1960s. By this time Patrick and Duncan had been lovers then friends for at least two decades and Duncan was the main constant in Patrick's life. The painting indicates their close connection and comfort in each other's company. This painting is unlike the previous portraits both Duncan and Edward Wolfe created during the 1930s. The picture conveys an impression of an artist who knows the sitter well. Additionally, some of the weariness and trauma of Patrick's life experience is evident in his pose, but a sense of ease and comfort at being portrayed by Duncan at this time and place is also apparent. Patrick is posing less (or being represented less) as a professional artist model and more as a friend.

War remembrance, 1962

Patrick's memories and emotions of war time were an intrinsic part of his post-war life and identity. He was one of many people who took part in commemorative rituals marking the war. Along with wearing his uniform and medals at services in Jamaica, he also importantly attended the Whitehall Cenotaph service on 11 November 1962. In a letter on 12 November 1962 he wrote to Duncan, 'Yesterday I went to the Memorial Service in Whitehall I honestly will never forget the War.'[48] This sentence though short is evocative and emotive, touching not only on his remembrance but also on how the war had irrevocably shaped his life.

The details of the Cenotaph service were not described in Patrick's letter. The short sentence in this letter about the service and war reveals not only Patrick's emotion and intent but also the importance he placed on attending the service. In *Trauma and the Memory of Politics*, Jenny Edkins has explored the London Cenotaph in comparison with the Vietnam Wall in a discussion on war memorials and remembrance. Edkins states, 'Memorials and memorialisation are among the ways people confront the challenge of responding to trauma and the contending temporalities it invokes,' and that both the Whitehall Cenotaph and the Vietnam Veterans Memorial in Washington are 'exceptional in that they seem to encircle trauma rather than absorbing it in a national myth of glory and sacrifice'.[49] Here Edkins means that both show '*trauma time*, as opposed to linear narrative time'.[50] Patrick was very much traumatized by the war and attending the Cenotaph and other memorials in his uniform was an important way not only to commemorate, but also to mentally cope with his experiences.

The Cenotaph was created in 1919 by the War Cabinet Committee on Peace Celebrations. Inspired by the ceremony in Paris it was decided that a 'pylon' be created.[51] As Edkins explains, for the first service in 1919 wreaths were laid by the monument, a two-minute silence was introduced and a march of 5,000 was planned. From the beginning the service attracted an unexpectedly large crowd that wanted to commemorate and lay flowers. Although police recommended moving the monument as a result of its popularity, the government opposed any move and from that 1919 service onwards the location was seen as a sacred site and it was decided that a permanent monument would be built there.[52] The previous simplistic design of the monument was kept, which, as Edkins argues, 'provides a monument that succeeds because it does not conceal the trauma of war but yet provides a means of marking it. It attempts no narrative of interpretation.'[53] Over one million people visited the monument and grave of the Unknown Soldier in the week after the 1920 Armistice day.[54] The ceremony has transformed over the decades and is much more formally timed and organized.[55]

Significantly, as noted in Chapter 4, 1919 – the year of the first ceremony – saw violent racism carried out against black people in Britain. The Victory Parade to the Cenotaph is a further painful example of this post-war anti-black racism as African and Caribbean troops were excluded from the parade. David Olusoga states of the Victory Parade, 'No troops from the West Indies were present, a final insult to the people of the British Caribbean who had been among the most supportive of the war effort in 1914.'[56]

What was the ceremony like in 1962? Details of the service can be found in newspaper and archival sources. For example, *The Hartford Courant* on 12 November 1962 reported,

> Queen Elizabeth II led the homage of the nation and the Commonwealth to the dead of two world wars in a solemn remembrance ceremony before the Cenotaph in Whitehall on Sunday. The queen, dressed in black, appeared beside the Cenotaph just before nearby Big Ben began striking 11. She was followed by the Duke of Edinburgh, her husband wearing the uniform of an admiral of the fleet, and the Duke of Gloucester, her uncle, wearing a gray greatcoat over his field marshal's uniform. Massed bands of the Brigade of Guards hushed their play of solemn melodies when the queen appeared. The firing of a gun in the

Horse Guards parade ground signaled the start of two minutes of silence. Royal Air Force trumpeters then sounded the last post and the queen stepped forward to lay a wreath by the side of the Cenotaph and bowed her head. Then wreaths were placed by Prince Philip, Duke of Gloucester, Prime Minister Harold Macmillan, Lord Attlee, former party prime minister; Hugh Gaitskill, head of the Labor [*sic*] party; Jo Grimond, head of the Liberal party, and representatives of all members of the Commonwealth.[57]

It is not known whether Patrick attended the ceremony on his own or with friends – perhaps he attended it with other former members of the 76 Company (if he had stayed in touch with anyone from the Company) or fellow Caribbean ex-servicemen and ex-servicewomen.

Patrick and Richie: Queer black Jamaica in London

Importantly, queer black Jamaican friendship was a significant aspect of Patrick's life in 1960s London. By May 1963 Patrick was living in North London at 32 Ferme Park Road, Finsbury. This was his last residence in London before his death. He either shared his residence with or rented from someone he described as his old friend Mrs Williamson, whose name had not previously appeared in Patrick's letters. Another name first mentioned in this letter was Richie. Patrick wrote that both Richie and Mrs Williamson were old friends of his.[58] In letters from Richie in the Tate Archive his postal address is given as 132 Seymour Place. It is clear that Richie's last name was Riley as Seymour Place was also given as an address by performer Richie Riley in a letter published in *The Stage*. Additionally, in the electoral register a Richard Riley is listed as living at 132 Seymour Place. These sources highlight, as discussed previously, that Patrick's friend was queer black Jamaican performer and artist Richie Riley.[59]

In the oral history interview with the Black Cultural Archives, previously explored in Chapters 2 and 4, Riley reflected on his post-war migration to Britain though he did not explicitly comment on his queer identity.[60] After *Les Ballets Nègres*, Riley became involved in the West Indian Standing Conference, established in 1958 as an umbrella organization representing African Caribbean communities in Britain. Riley remembered the Conference forming from various other smaller organizations an 'executive from which anything that was relevant to black people was discussed and worked on from the executive point of view' such as sending a delegation to the police in response to the police in Ladbroke Grove targeting black people and meeting with the home secretary 'on various points of police harassment, etc', campaigning for black inspectors to be employed on London Transport and interviewing teachers in relation to black children being designated 'Educationally Subnormal'. Riley was the education and cultural officer for the Conference and recalled meeting with black parents about their children's experiences of racism in the British school system. Through the Conference Riley was involved with setting up supplementary summer schools within various boroughs in London.[61] Riley also spoke of black activism that he took part in before the establishment of the West Indian Standing Conference around the time of the Notting Hill racist riots. He recalled that Amy Garvey lived in the Notting Hill area and 'we were all meeting at Mrs Garvey's house at the time. And the question of racialism and problems affecting black people were discussed there. The person who really organised it was Richard Hauser, a man from, from Australia, who was an expert in, in racial problems and we used to meet at – this was before Standing Conference, we used to meet at Mrs Garvey's house in Oxford Gardens, that's where it was all discussed.'[62]

In this interview, Riley also recalled his social life from the time he first came to Britain in 1946. After being asked if he had any white friends and how he related to them, he recalled that his 'friends were drawn from what one would call a[n] intellectual group – artists and writers' and 'my friends were mostly people of intellectual quality, who have no racial prejudice as such'. When pressed further on this point, he did reflect that some 'had a superiority complex' but that 'quite a lot that I know haven't got it [meaning racism]'.[63] The interviewer did not ask anything more on this group of friends, so further details, including their names or any potential romantic partners, were not given in the interview.

In 1994 Riley was interviewed for a project exploring homosexual history in Britain carried out by the Hall Carpenter Archive. Nadia Ellis has provided an excellent and fascinating exploration of this interview, where though Riley had agreed to be part of a history project documenting gay and lesbian life in Britain he did not directly mention being a queer man in the interview. Ellis states,

> Riley's testimony indicates his keen awareness of the disciplining force of the archive and the multiple exclusions to which he is subject as a black, Caribbean-born man in Britain. The way he steers the conversation, employing a poetics of delicacy in refusing to label or pin down his sexuality, empowers him and provides valuable lessons to the researcher of queer Caribbean lives decades later.[64]

Similar to his BCA interview, Riley mentioned aspects of his social life in mid-twentieth-century London, including his involvement in the artworld. Riley, like Pasuka, was to go on to train as an artist. He described meeting Quentin Crisp when he went to do modelling at the British Art Society and 'then afterwards, sometime after, I met him in Soho, and then discovered that he used to frequent this café in Soho where a group of us used to meet because it was a sort of theatrical café'.[65]

During the time Patrick and Richie definitely knew each other. Berto Pasuka also died, in fact just a few months before Patrick. Richie's name appears in Patrick's last few letters. Patrick wrote to Duncan on 7 June 1963 answering Duncan's request that they meet. He let Duncan know that he would come on Monday at 8.30 pm and he hoped that Richie would make it possible to go. Perhaps Richie, with Patrick's declining health, was someone who supported him physically or financially.[66] This note to Duncan was very short, as were all of his post-war correspondences. Patrick wrote in the last sentence of this card that he had 'a very severe pain on my chest', did not know how to stop it and would have to see a doctor the next week.[67] This appears to be the last letter Patrick ever sent to Duncan. The next letter in the archive written ten days later on 17 June 1963 was sent by Richie Riley, who wanted to let Duncan know that Patrick was a patient at St Pancras Hospital, Ward 4. Patrick's landlady had phoned Richie the previous Saturday worried as Patrick had not returned home Friday night. They telephoned a few hospitals in the area and on Sunday a nurse phoned the landlady to let them know that Patrick had been admitted after taking ill at work that Friday. Richie reported that it was not too good and was a problem with his heart.[68] After decades of ill health and personal struggle, Patrick died of a heart attack a month later in July 1963. From his death certificate we can see at the time of his death he was living at 32 Ferme Park Road, where he had been living from at least May 1963 and was working as a packer. He died at St Pancras Hospital on 24 July 1963.[69] Richie Riley wrote again to Duncan Grant the day after the funeral, which took place on 3 August 1963 at Southgate Cemetery. Richie wrote that 'the funeral was attended by 4 from the House where he lived and myself I took a beautiful cross of flowers and the whole thing was quiet and very sad'.[70] Though not many people attended his funeral, the letter from Richie shows that Patrick was loved and cared for at the end of his life and honoured at his funeral by his close friends and neighbours.

Patrick's life story as documented through these letters is a crucial, profound and personal record of a man traversing many significant histories of the twentieth century. His life experiences included living in Jamaica under colonial rule, working in an aristocratic Welsh estate, serving in the British forces in the Second World War and being imprisoned as a POW. His letters spanning a period of twenty-five years give new insight into a number of histories, including Caribbean history, black British history, queer history and histories of the Second World War. The epilogue briefly explores some of these themes.

Epilogue: Patrick's Life Story and its Historical and Contemporary Context

Patrick's life intersected with several key moments within British and Jamaican history. This epilogue briefly touches on some of the key themes that arise within the book, reflecting on how an examination of Patrick's life provides rich detail and greater clarity to historical reflections of a range of topics and themes. Marginalized or under-explored voices and memories, as found in sources such as private letters, can provide historians with more complex, multifaceted and nuanced understandings of broader historical phenomena. Through an examination of Patrick's life story – his experiences of life in the hotel industry of 1930s Jamaica, of being a black migrant in both rural Wales and cosmopolitan London, interacting with members of the Bloomsbury Group and Queer and Black 1930s and 1940s Britain in addition to his life in post-war Jamaica viewing the political processes of decolonization – we learn much about interwar, wartime and post-war Britain and Jamaica.

A key period of Patrick's life. which also provides a deeper understanding of the Second World War, is Patrick's time in the Auxiliary Military Pioneer Corps and the British Expeditionary Force, where his letters detail his being wounded and captured near Dunkirk and then being made a POW in various Frontstalags and Stalags for over four years. A particular episode of public re-remembering of the German invasion of France and the Dunkirk evacuations provides one reason that Patrick's story and many other similar stories need to be remembered. In 2013 BBC Radio 4 broadcast the programme 'Presenting the Past – How the Media Changes History' in which the host Juliet Gardiner, who worked as a historical consultant to the 2007 film *Atonement*, stated their unease that the film portrayed a wounded black soldier at Dunkirk, arguing that it would have been 'almost impossible' for a black soldier to have served in the British Expeditionary Force in France. Gardiner suspected that *Atonement*'s inclusion of a black soldier was about grafting today's multicultural present onto the past, which they argued 'gave a misleading impression of how Britain was at the time'. This programme was most recently repeated on 9 October 2016 on

Radio 4 Extra.[1] Patrick's life story directly challenges this problematic statement, illustrating the importance of acknowledging and reading the work that has been undertaken by historians of black Britain.

I first spoke about Patrick's letters and life in a series of events organized under the umbrella *Queer Black Spaces*, an event series co-organized by myself and Caroline Bressey which brought together historians, geographers, artists, poets, writers and others to share work and experiences on diverse black queer voices.[2] The first *Queer Black Spaces* took place in February 2013, where I presented a brief exploration of Patrick's life and I have continued to present on his life at other events in the series. Thus this book and the period of time discovering Patrick's life has been intimately connected with presenting research on his life to queer black audiences and queer people of colour communities. Curating *Queer Black Spaces* and writing this work on Patrick Nelson were both inspired by understanding that black queer lives within a historical perspective have been neglected in much history writing. This book has been inspired by a number of initiatives within Britain, the United States and Jamaica seeking to redress these historical omissions, in particular the work of Ajamu and the rukus! archive project in researching and documenting queer black history in Britain and depositing this history within the London Metropolitan Archives.[3] Patrick's life is a testament and a document for queer black history in Jamaica and Britain and shows the multiple experiences of a queer black man living under colonial rule, migrating to Britain and serving in the Second World War, with the profound personal, emotional costs that military service entailed for him.

Notes

Introduction

1 Patrick Nelson to Duncan Grant, 6 December 1945, Tate Archives.
2 Though various official military records state that he was born in 1916, in a letter to Duncan Grant in March 1945 he tells Duncan that yesterday was his birthday and he was twenty-eight years old. Patrick Nelson to Duncan Grant, 18 March 1945, Tate Archives.
3 AHRC - Award Reference AH/I027371/1. For more information, see the UCL Equiano Centre website, http://www.ucl.ac.uk/equianocentre/projects/docl.
4 Emery, Mary L. *Modernism, the Visual, and Caribbean Literature.* Cambridge: Cambridge University Press, 2007.
5 For studies on interwar black Britain, see the work of Hakim Adi. Examples of his work are: Adi, Hakim. *Pan-africanism and Communism: The Communist International, Africa and the Diaspora, 1919-1939.* Trenton, NJ: Africa World Press, 2013; Adi, Hakim. 'The Comintern and Black Workers in Britain and France 1919-37'. *Immigrants & Minorities,* Vol. 28 No. 2–3 (2010), pp. 224–45 and Adi, Hakim. *West Africans in Britain, 1900-1960: Nationalism, Pan-Africanism, and Communism.* London: Lawrence & Wishart, 1998. See also: Matera, Marc. *Black London: The Imperial Metropolis and Decolonization in the Twentieth Century.* University of California Press, 2015; Pennybacker, Susan D. *From Scottsboro to Munich: Race and Political Culture in 1930s Britain.* Princeton, N.J: Princeton University Press, 2009 and Makalani, Minkah. *In the Cause of Freedom: Radical Black Internationalism from Harlem to London, 1917-1939.* Chapel Hill: University of North Carolina Press, 2011.
6 Spalding, Frances. *Duncan Grant: A Biography.* First published, London: Chatto & Windus, 1997.
7 Tate Archive catalogue http://archive.tate.org.uk.
8 Spalding, *Duncan Grant,* p. 192.
9 https://janus.lib.cam.ac.uk/db/node.xsp?id=EAD/GBR/0272/PP/CHA.
10 Sotheby's, *Catalogue of Valuable Autograph Letters, Literary Manuscripts and Historical Documents: Including the Most Complete Autograph Manuscript of 'in Memoriam' with Other Letters and Poetical Manuscripts by Alfred Lord Tennyson* (auction, London, Sotheby's, 21–22 July 1980). Illustrated Catalogue 9341, London: Sotheby Parke Bernet, 1980.

11 Jamaican Archives and Records Department, http://www.jard.gov.jm/.

12 Digitized genealogical records utilized are from ancestry.co.uk and familysearch.org.

13 See http://www.archiveswales.org.uk/anw/get_collection.php?inst_id=39&coll_id=10886&expand= In October 1939 Lyulph Stanley wrote to Dr Thomas Richards, of the Bangor University Library, stating that 'I have had a letter from my mother telling me of your visit to Penrhos, and that you have kindly undertaken to catalogue all the documents and letters of the 17th & 18th centuries now at Penrhos, on condition they be deposited in your library for that purpose, and on condition that any paper, letter or document be returned within 24 hours if called for: also all Farm accounts of the 19th century. I am most happy to agree to this arrangement and am very grateful to you for the trouble and interest you have taken in the matter.' Letter from Lyulph Stanley, 4, Honiton Mansions, Kings Road, Chelsea to Dr Richards 29 October 1939, Penrhos Archives, Bangor University, Archives and Special Collections.

14 Stoler, Ann Laura, 'Colonial Archives and the Arts of Governance', *Archival Science*, Vol. 2 (2002), pp. 87–109, abstract.

15 Stanley, Liz. 'The Epistolarium: On Theorizing Letters and Correspondences', *Auto/ Biography*, Vol. 12 (2004), pp. 201–35, 209.

16 Das, Santanu. 'Indian Sepoy Experience in Europe, 1914–18: Archive, Language, and Feeling', *Twentieth Century British History*, Vol. 25, No. 3 (2014), pp. 391–417, 397.

17 Ibid., p. 393.

18 Ibid., pp. 398–9.

Chapter 1

1 'A Lucky Young Man', *Gleaner*, 9 April 1937.

2 Ibid.

3 Ibid.

4 Watson, Roxanne S. 'Freedom of the Press under Attack during the 1938 Labor Uprisings in Jamaica: The Prosecution of the Publishers of the Jamaica Labour Weekly', *American Journalism*, Vol. 29, No. 3 (2012), pp. 84–112, p. 87.

5 The *Gleaner*, 13 September 1934, p. 5.

6 Ibid. For information on Herbert DeLisser's response to the political activities of Marcus Garvey, see footnote 2 on p. 115 of Hill, Robert A., editor in chief. The Marcus Garvey and Universal Negro Improvement Association Papers. Volume IX Africa for the Africans, 1921–1922, Berkeley: University of California Press, 1995.

7 Watson, 'Freedom of the Press under Attack during the 1938 Labor Uprisings in Jamaica', p. 87.

8 Robertson, James. 'Late Seventeenth-Century Spanish Town, Jamaica: Building an English City on Spanish Foundations', *Early American Studies*, Vol. 6, No. 2 (Fall 2008), pp. 346–90, p. 348.

9 Ibid.

10 Howard, David. *Kingston: A Cultural and Literary History*. Kingston, Jamaica: Randle Publ; Oxford: Signal Books, 2005, p. 20.

11 Dodman, David. 'Post-independence optimism and the legacy of waterfront redevelopment in Kingston, Jamaica', *Cities*, Vol. 24, No. 4 (2007), pp. 273–84, p. 273.

12 Howard. *Kingston*, p. 22.

13 Ibid., p. 63.

14 Ibid.

15 Clarke, Colin and David Howard. 'Colour, race and space: residential segregation in Kingston, Jamaica, in the late colonial period', *Caribbean Geography*, Vol. 10, No. 1 (Mar 1999), p. 4.

16 Ibid., p. 5.

17 Howard. *Kingston*, p. 63.

18 Moore, Brian L. and Michele A. Johnson (eds). 'Introduction', *"Squalid Kingston", 1890-1920: How the Poor Lived, Moved and Had Their Being*. Mona: Social History Project, Dept. of History, University of the West Indies, 2000, p. 3.

19 Howard. *Kingston*, p. 63.

20 Cundall, Frank. *Historic Jamaica*. London: Pub. for the Institute of Jamaica by the West India Committee, 1915, p. 154.

21 Howard. *Kingston*, p. 22.

22 Cooper, Wayne F. *Claude Mckay: Rebel Sojourner in the Harlem Renaissance: a Biography*. Baton Rouge: Louisiana State University Press, 1987, paperback 1996, pp. 22–4.

23 Howard. *Kingston*, p. 96.

24 Moore, Brian L. and Michele A. Johnson. *"They Do As They Please": The Jamaican Struggle for Cultural Freedom After Morant Bay*. Kingston: University of the West Indies Press, 2011, p. 225.

25 'Carib Theatre Starts To-day with Four Shows', the *Gleaner*, 13 April 1938

26 Moore and Johnson (eds). *'Squalid Kingston', 1890-1920*.

27 Moore and Johnson (eds). 'Introduction', *"Squalid Kingston"*, p. 4.

28 Clarke and Howard. 'Colour, race and space', p. 6.

29 Ibid.

30 Ibid., p. 8.

31 Johnson, Howard. 'Cuban Immigrants in Jamaica, 1868–1898', *Immigrants & Minorities*, Vol. 29, No. 1 (March 2011), pp. 1–32, p. 10.

32 Pringle, Kenneth. *Waters of the West*. London: G. Allen and Unwin, 1938 cited in Howard. *Kingston*, p. 65.

33 'The Brilliant Record of a Jamaica Cricketer – Mr Leopold Nelson's Career with the Lucas Club', the *Gleaner*, 12 January 1922, p. 8

34 'Asylum C.C. vs Gleaner C.C.', the *Gleaner*, 16 September 1899.

35 Jamaica, Civil Registration, 1880–1999, database with images, FamilySearch (https://familysearch.org/ark:/61903/1:1:QVS5-FGCH: 13 April 2015), Leopold Nelson, 01 Mar 1945, Death; citing Kingston, Kingston, Jamaica, Registrar General's Department, Spanish Town; FHL microfilm 1,872,985.

36 Up to at least the late 1930s, however, Leopold Nelson's career was still remembered; the 1937 article about Patrick describes him as the 'son of Mr Leopold Nelson, well known Jamaica cricketer and once star island wicket-keeper'. 'A Lucky Young Man', the *Gleaner*, 9 April 1937.

37 'The Brilliant Record of a Jamaica Cricketer – Mr Leopold Nelson's Career with the Lucas Club', the *Gleaner*, 12 January 1922, p. 8.

38 Cresser, Julian. 'Lucas Cricket Club: A Pioneering Jamaican Cricket Club', *Jamaica Journal*, Vol. 30, No. 3 (March/April 2007), pp. 24–7, p. 24.

39 Ibid., p. 25.

40 Ibid., p. 24.

41 Ibid., p. 25.

42 Ibid.

43 'The Brilliant Record of a Jamaica Cricketer – Mr Leopold Nelson's Career with the Lucas Club', the *Gleaner*, 12 January 1922, p. 8.

44 'Lucas founder dead', the *Gleaner*, 22 July 1933.

45 Cresser. Lucas Cricket Club, *Jamaica Journal*, p. 26.

46 Cresser, Julian. 'Sport and Integration: Cricket in Jamaica, 1880-1910', *The Jamaica Historical Review*, Vol. XXIV (2009), p. 28.

47 The *Gleaner*, 13 March 1929.

48 The *Gleaner*, 3 November 1904, p. 10.

49 Ibid, p. 10.

50 Cresser, 'Lucas Cricket Club', p. 26.

51 Ibid.

52 Ibid.

53 Moore and Johnson. '*They Do As They Please*', p. 264.

54 Cresser. 'Sport and Integration: Cricket in Jamaica, 1880-1910', p. 30.

55 T. A. Aikman, 'Coming visit of the English Cricket Team – Our Representatives – Who will wicket keep?', the *Gleaner*, 29 December 1928.

56 'Cricket in Old Capital', the *Gleaner*, 7 October 1919, p. 13.

57 The *Gleaner*, 25 March 1922, p. 6.

58 Leo Nelson, 'Views of Readers – Our Cricket Team in Barbados', the *Gleaner*, 20 April, 1925, p. 18.

59 The *Gleaner*, 13 March 1929.

60 The team he suggested was 'Nunes, (Captain); Martin, Barrow, Headley, DaCosta, Riley, Passailaigue, Hylton, Groves, Scott, Weeks, Lewin, and Beckford (W.G.)'. Leo Nelson, letter to the editor 'Cricket Team Suggested', the *Gleaner*, 2 October 1934.

61 Leopold Nelson to Pioneer Record Office, Bournemouth, 24 September 1940, Army Personnel Records.

62 Ibid.

63 'Miscellaneous', the *Gleaner*, 8 February 1916, p. 12.

64 'Posted as Missing. Mr Leo St Patrick Nelson Was With British Expedition in France'. The *Gleaner*, 30 September 1940.

65 Smith, Richard. *Jamaican Volunteers in the First World War: Race, Masculinity and the Development of National Consciousness*. Manchester: Manchester Univ. Press, 2004, pp. 48–9.

66 Ibid., p. 49.

67 Ibid., p. 50.

68 Ibid., p. 55–7.

69 Bourne, Stephen. *Black Poppies: Britain's Black Community and the Great War*. Stroud: History Press, 2014, p. 65.

70 Ibid.

71 Smith. *Jamaican Volunteers in the First World War*, p. 63.

72 Cited in Brown, Wayne. *Edna Manley: The Private Years, 1900-1938*. London: Deutsch, 1976, p. 67.

73 'A Local Force is Disbanded', the *Gleaner*,17 December 1918, p. 3.

74 Ibid.

75 The *Gleaner*, 6 August 1918, p. 2.

76 The *Gleaner*, 2 March 1945.

77 Jamaica, Civil Registration, 1880–1999, database with images, FamilySearch (https://familysearch.org/ark:/61903/1:1:QVSP-R2WF: 13 April 2015), Gertrude Nelson, 23 Jul 1978, Death; citing Cockburn Pen, Saint Andrew, Jamaica, Registrar General's Department, Spanish Town; FHL microfilm 1,768,930.

78 The *Gleaner*, 2 March 1945.

79 Letter from Leopold Nelson to Duncan Grant, 23.[4?] 1942, Tate Archives.

80 Letter from Leopold Nelson to Duncan Grant, 23.8.1944, Tate Archives.

81 Clarke, Colin and David Howard, 'Race and Religious Pluralism in Kingston, Jamaica', *Population, Space and Place*, Vol. 11 (2005), pp. 119–36.

82 Ibid., p. 120.

83 The *Gleaner*, 20 January 1937, p. 27.

84 All genealogical information is sourced from the website https://familysearch.org.

85 Jamaica, Civil Registration, 1880–1999, database with images, FamilySearch (https://familysearch.org/ark:/61903/1:1:QVSP-7WQQ: 13 April 2015), Leopold Nathaniel

Nelson and Gertrude Lucille Coles, 22 Jun 1921, Marriage; citing Kingston, Jamaica, Registrar General's Department, Spanish Town; FHL microfilm 1,667,255.

86 Brown-Glaude, Winnifred R. *Higglers in Kingston: Women's Informal Work in Jamaica*. Nashville, Tenn: Vanderbilt University Press, 2011, p. 2.

87 The *Gleaner*, 28 April 1908.

88 The *Gleaner*, 1 October 1908.

89 The *Gleaner*, 30 August 1911.

90 Thompson, Krista A. *An Eye for the Tropics: Tourism, Photography, and Framing the Caribbean Picturesque*. Durham: Duke University Press, 2006, pp. 5–6.

91 Michele A. Johnson, '"Decent and Fair": Aspects of Domestic Service in Jamaica, 1920-1970', *The Journal of Caribbean History*, Vol. 30, No. 1 (1996), p. 83.

92 The *Gleaner*, 3 July 1923.

93 Cundall. *Historic Jamaica*, p. 155.

94 De Lisser H. G. *Jane: A Story of Jamaica*. Kingston, Jamaica: *Gleaner*, 1913, cited in Howard. *Kingston*, pp. 96–7.

95 The *Gleaner*, 27 April 1935.

96 The *Gleaner*, 22 April 1939.

97 Watson, Roxanne. 'Marcus Garvey's Trial for Seditious Libel in Jamaica', *Journalism History*, Vol. 33, No. 3 (Fall 2007), pp. 173–6.

98 Ibid., p. 176.

99 Ibid, p. 177.

100 Ibid.

101 Ibid.

Chapter 2

1 'A Lucky Young Man', the *Gleaner*, 9 April 1937.

2 MacDonald, Robert H. *Sons of the Empire: The Frontier and the Boy Scout Movement, 1890-1918*. Toronto: University of Toronto Press, 1993, p. 3.

3 Ibid., p. 10.

4 Ibid., p. 11.

5 Ibid., p. 7.

6 Ibid. p. 10.

7 The *Gleaner*, 29 May 1912.

8 The *Gleaner*, 13 November 1909.

9 The *Gleaner*, 14 July 1911.

10 The *Gleaner*, 9 October 1911.

11 The *Gleaner*, 26 January 1912.

12 The *Gleaner*, 12 November 1914 and 29 March 1915.

13 The *Gleaner*, 31 December 1915 and 11 August 1917.

14 The *Gleaner*, 11 August 1917.

15 'Boy Scouts Association of Jamaica, Report of a meeting of the Committee of the Council held on December 13th, 1923', Pamphlet, National Library of Jamaica, Pam 369.43.

16 'The Imperial Jamboree of Boy Scouts', the *Gleaner*, 26 August 1924, p.11.

17 'Jamaica Boy Scouts Going to Jamboree', the *Gleaner*, 18 June 1924, p. 6 and UK Incoming Passenger Lists, 1878–1960, *Oriana*, 31 Jul 1924, via ancestry.co.uk

18 'The Great Imperial Scout Jamboree', the *Gleaner*, 19 November 1924.

19 UK Incoming Passenger Lists, 1878–1960, *Oriana*, 31 Jul 1924, via ancestry.co.uk

20 Patrick Nelson to Duncan Grant, 2 July 1954, Tate Archives.

21 The *Gleaner*, 5 October 1932.

22 Ibid.

23 Wu, Jialin Christina. 'A Life of Make-Belief: Being Boy Scouts and 'Playing Indian' in *British Malaya (1910–42)*' in Miescher, Stephan, Michele Mitchell and Naoko Shibusawa (eds) *Gender, Imperialism and Global Exchanges*. Chichester: Wiley Blackwell, 2015, p. 225.

24 Ibid.

25 Paton, Diana. *The Cultural Politics of Obeah: Religion, Colonialism and Modernity in the Caribbean World*. Cambridge; New York: Cambridge University Press, 2015, p. 242.

26 S.P. Sheet 200A – Qualification Form, Patrick Nelson, Army Personnel Records.

27 Ibid.

28 'Elocution Championships in St. James Great Success', the *Gleaner*, 14 December 1935, p. 24.

29 'First Jamaican to be Captured by the Germans Returns Home', the *Gleaner*, 10 June 1945.

30 Damousi, Joy. *Colonial Voices: A Cultural History of English in Australia, 1840-1940*. Cambridge: Cambridge University Press, 2010.

31 Ibid., p. 17.

32 Advertised in editions of the *Gleaner*, including the *Gleaner*, 18 July 1871.

33 The *Gleaner*, 3 April 1888.

34 The *Gleaner*, 17 July 1899.

35 'Local News', the *Gleaner*, 21 April 1887.

36 'Elocution Contests', the *Gleaner*, 28 May 1913.

37 The *Gleaner*, 26 August 1931.

38 The *Gleaner*, 18 July 1932.

39 'Annual All-Island Elocution Contest', the *Gleaner*, 22 February 1940, p. 7.

40 'A Lucky Young Man', the *Gleaner*, 9 April 1937.

41 Taylor, Frank F. 'The Tourist Industry in Jamaica, 1919 to 1939', *Social and Economic Studies*, Vol. 22, No. 2 (June 1973), pp. 205–28, p. 206.

42 Cocks, Catherine. *Tropical Whites: The Rise of the Tourist South in the Americas*. Philadelphia: University of Pennsylvania Press, 2013, p. 51.

43 *Illustrated London News*, West Indies Supplement, 3 October 1936, p. 560.

44 Taylor. 'The Tourist Industry in Jamaica, 1919 to 1939', pp. 207–8.

45 Ibid., p. 208.

46 Geoghegan, Joseph. 'Jamaica as a Health-Resort', *The Lancet*, 15 November 1924, p. 1046.

47 Thursfield, Thomas W. 'A Visit to Jamaica in March and April, 1905', *The Lancet*, 5 August 1905, pp. 395–7.

48 *The Handbook of Jamaica*, 1910, The Jamaica Archives, Spanish Town, Jamaica, 1B/65/9/27.

49 *The Handbook of Jamaica*, various years, The Jamaica Archives, Spanish Town, Jamaica.

50 Sibley, Inez K. 'History of Manor House', the *Gleaner*, 29 May 1960.

51 Legacies of British Slave-ownership database, https://www.ucl.ac.uk/lbs/claim/view/24643.

52 Sibley, Inez K. 'History of Manor House', the *Gleaner*, 29 May 1960.

53 See Bressey, Caroline. 'The Politics of Plantations. Laura and Oak Alley Plantation on the Great River Road', The Equiano Centre Black Presence blog, April 2012 https://www.ucl.ac.uk/equianocentre/blackpresenceblog/previous-posts/apr-2012. For a summary of research noting this phenomenon, see Dann, Graham M. S. and Robert B. Potter. 'Supplanting the Planters: Hawking Heritage in Barbados' in Dann, Graham, and A V. Seaton (eds). *Slavery, Contested Heritage and Thanatourism*, New York: Haworth Hospitality Press, 2001, p. 52.

54 *The Rutty Family*, by Frank Rutty, The Jamaica Archives, Spanish Town, Jamaica, 7/266.

55 Ibid.

56 Ibid.

57 The *Gleaner*, 21 October 1932.

58 Sibley, Inez K. 'History of Manor House', the *Gleaner*, 29 May 1960.

59 Ibid.

60 *Illustrated London News*, West Indies Supplement, 3 October 1936, p. 555.

61 The *Gleaner*, 4 November 1929, p. 20.

62 The *Gleaner*, 24 October 1938.

63 Curt Teich Collection, Lake County Discovery Museum http://www.lcfpd.org/museum/teich/collections/.

64 Thompson, Krista A. *An Eye for the Tropics: Tourism, Photography, and Framing the Caribbean Picturesque*. Durham: Duke University Press, 2006, p. 6.

65 The *Gleaner*, 26 May 1928, p. 17.

66 The *Gleaner*, 10 August 1926, p. 7.

67 The *Gleaner*, 27 December 1933, p. 12.

68 The *Gleaner*, 15 September 1923, p. 2.

69 The *Gleaner*, 23 December 1936, p. 9.

70 The *Gleaner*, 27 October 1926 and 'The World and his Wife', the *Gleaner* magazine, the *Gleaner*, 24 October 1931.

71 Constant Spring Hotel, Strike of employees, 1939, The Jamaica Archives, Spanish Town, Jamaica, 1B/5/77/130.

72 Palmer, Colin A. *Freedom's Children: The 1938 Labor Rebellion and the Birth of Modern Jamaica*. Chapel Hill: University of North Carolina Press, 2014, p. 9.

73 Ibid.

74 Watson. 'Freedom of the Press under Attack during the 1938 Labor Uprisings in Jamaica—', p. 92.

75 Ibid.

76 Palmer. Freedom's Children, pp. 16–17.

77 Claus F. – Stolberg (ed.). 'Introduction', in Jamaica 1938: *The Living Conditions of the Urban and Rural Poor: Two Social Surveys*, The Social History Project, Department of History, University of the West Indies, Mona, 1990, p. 1.

78 Ibid., p. 1.

79 Moyne, Walter E. G. *West India Royal Commission Report*. London: H.M.S.O, 1945, p. 16.

80 The *Gleaner*, 15 January 1938.

81 The *Gleaner*, 4 February 1938.

82 The *Gleaner*, 9 February 1938.

83 Ibid.

84 Pattullo, Polly. *Last Resorts: The Cost of Tourism in the Caribbean*. London: Latin America Bureau, 2005, p. 64.

85 Hilary Beckles cited in Ibid., p. 65.

86 Taylor, Frank F. *To Hell with Paradise: A History of the Jamaican Tourist Industry*. Pittsburgh, Pa: University of Pittsburgh Press, 1993, p. 112.

87 Ibid., p. 147.

88 Thompson. *An Eye for the Tropics*, p. 205.

89 Howard. *Kingston*, p. 52.

90 Thompson. *An Eye for the Tropics*, p. 236.

91 'Hotel Employees Want Higher Wages – Express Grievances at Meeting and Move to Submit Scheme to Board', the *Gleaner*, 6 June 1938.

92 The *Gleaner*, 25 October 1935.

93 Sir Archibald Hunter, the *Gleaner*, 30 June 1936.

94 'Cases Tried in the Halfway Tree Court', the *Gleaner*, 19 October 1934.

95 Silvera, Makeda. 'Man Royals and Sodomites: Some Thoughts on the Invisibility of Afro-Caribbean Lesbians' in Silvera, Makeda (anthologized by). *Piece of My Heart: A Lesbian of Colour Anthology*. Toronto: Sister Vision, 1991.

96 Elwin, Rosamund, ed. *Tongues on Fire: Caribbean Lesbian Lives and Stories*. Toronto: Women's Press, 1997.

97 Kempadoo, Kamala. *Sexing the Caribbean: Gender, Race, and Sexual Labor*. New York: Routledge, 2008.

98 Campbell, Kofi Omoniyi Sylvanus. *The Queer Caribbean Speaks: Interviews with Writers, Artists, and Activists*. New York, NY: Palgrave Macmillan, 2014.

99 Glave, Thomas. *Our Caribbean: A Gathering of Lesbian and Gay Writing from the Antilles*. Durham, N.C: Duke University Press, 2008.

100 Ellis, Nadia. *Territories of the Soul: Queered Belonging in the Black Diaspora*. Durham: Duke University Press, 2015.

101 Gay Freedom Movement in Jamaica Archives, Digital Library of the Caribbean, dloc.com/icirngfm.

102 See Oram, Alison, "'A sudden orgy of decadence": Writing about sex between women in the interwar popular press' in Doan, Laura L. and Jane Garrity (eds), *Sapphic Modernities: Sexuality, Women, and National Culture*. New York: Palgrave Macmillan, 2006.

103 See 'Committed for Trial at Home Circuit Ct', the *Gleaner*, 22 June 1933 and the *Gleaner*, 6 October 1933, p. 10.

104 The *Gleaner*, 24 October 1938, p. 8.

105 See Romain, Gemma and Caroline Bressey. 'Claude McKay: queer interwar London and spaces of black radicalism', in Katherine M. Graham and Simon Avery (eds). *Sex, Time and Place: Queer Histories of London, c.1850 to the Present*. Bloomsbury Academic, 2016.

106 'They were Britain's first black dance company. How come no one's ever heard of them? Keith Watson on Les Ballets Negres', *The Guardian*, 5 August 1999.

107 Richie Riley interviewed, Black Cultural Archives, digitized as part of the Moving Here project, Catalogue Reference: AMBH/BCA RROT/BCA

108 Ibid.

109 'The Philospher Views the Passing Show', *Public Opinion*, 28 May 1938, p. 4. Article referenced in: Matthew Parker, *Goldeneye: Where Bond Was Born: Ian Fleming's Jamaica* (London: Windmill Books, 2015), p. 87; p. 337n.

110 The *Gleaner*, 4 January 1929, p. 22.

111 The *Gleaner*, 10 August 1929.

112 'Not for the Squeamish', the *Gleaner*, 16 October, 1937.

113 The *Gleaner*, 8 November 1937.

114 'Interesting Lecture by Dr Ken. Royes', the *Gleaner*, 2 December 1937.

115 Hickling, Frederick W. *Psychohistoriography: A Post-Colonial Psychoanalytic and Psychotherapeutic Model*. London: Jessica Kingsley Publishers, 2012, p. 11.

Chapter 3

1 UK Incoming Passenger Lists 1878–1960 For Lyulph Stanley – arrival of 13 January 1937, via ancestry.co.uk.

2 The National Archives UK Incoming Passenger Lists, 1878–1960 Record for Mr L St P Nelson April 1937; accessed via ancestry.co.uk.

3 Lyulph's sister Mary Katherine Adelaide Stanley recalled in an unpublished short account of the Owen and Stanley families, 'My father died in 1931 and my mother came to live at Penrhos with Lyulph, aged fifteen, who was to inherit the place when he was twenty-one, my sister Pamela, and my youngest sister, Victoria.' Adelaide Lubbock, The Owens and the Stanleys of Penrhos – An Account of its Owners from 1513 to 1948, Bangor Archives, Penrhos collection, Penrhos VIII 272.

4 'Alderley Estate sold by Lord Stanley: Purchaser to Resell in Lots', *The Manchester Guardian,* 8 July 1938, p. 11.

5 Ibid.

6 Bangor University, Penrhos Manuscripts, Administrative and biographical history, http://www.archiveswales.org.uk/anw/get_collection.php?inst_id=39&coll_id=10886&expand= (accessed 13 August 2014).

7 UK Incoming Passenger Lists 1878–1960 For Lyulph Stanley, 1937, via ancestry.co.uk

8 Though known as Lyulph he is cited here as E. Lyulph to differentiate him from the Lyulph who knew Patrick Nelson.

9 Jones, Alan W. *Lyulph Stanley: A Study in Educational Politics.* Waterloo, Ont: Wilfrid Laurier University Press, 1979, p. 2.

10 Ibid., p. 2.

11 Ibid., pp. 8–9.

12 Griffin, Nicholas (ed.). *The Selected Letters of Bertrand Russell: Vol. 1.* London: Allen Lane, The Penguin Press, 1992, p. 19.

13 Stanley, Thomas H. O. *The Stanleys of Alderley: 1927-2001.* S.l.: AMCD, 2004, pp. 7–8; and Russell, Bertrand (edited by Richard A. Rempel, Andrew Brink and Margaret Moran). *Contemplation and Action, 1902-14.* London and New York: Routledge, 1993. First published 1985, Annotation note to paper 1,16:26, p. 545.

14 The 1881 England Census for Mary K. Stanley, ancestry.co.uk

15 'Obituary: Lord Stanley of Alderley Former Governor of Victoria', *The Manchester Guardian,* 24 August 1931.

16 See Holmes, Colin. *Anti-semitism in British Society, 1876-1939.* London: Edward Arnold, 1979, Routledge, 2016 p. 27 and Kushner, Tony. *Remembering Refugees: Then and Now.* Manchester: Manchester University Press, 2006, p. 27.

17 'Looking Back. The Year Reviewed'. *Holyhead and Anglesey Mail,* 1 January 1937.

18 Index to Alien Arrivals by Airplane at Miami, Florida, 1930–1942 for Lyulph Stanley, accessed via ancestry.co.uk on 16 November 2013.

19 Stanley, Peter E. *The House of Stanley: The History of an English Family from the 12th Century*. Edinburgh: Pentland Press, 1998, p. 409.

20 'Arrivals on "Costa Rica" Yesterday', the *Gleaner*, 16 March 1937.

21 Index to Alien Arrivals by Airplane at Miami, Florida, 1930–1942 for Lyulph Stanley, accessed via ancestry.co.uk.

22 UK Incoming Passenger Lists 1878–1960 For Honourable Henry Stanley – April 1937, accessed via ancestry.co.uk.

23 'Arrivals on "Costa Rica" Yesterday', the *Gleaner*, 16 March 1937.

24 'Change in Social Customs Here noted by visitor', the *Gleaner*, 9 April 1948.

25 Patrick Nelson to Duncan Grant, 19 March 1945, Tate Archives.

26 Cook, Matt. *Queer Domesticities: Homosexuality and Home Life in Twentieth-Century London*. Basingstoke and New York: Palgrave Macmillan, 2014, p. 27.

27 Sarti, Raffaella. 'Introduction', *Gender & History*, Vol.18, No.2 (August 2006), pp. 187–98, p. 189.

28 As Lucy Delap states, 'Throughout the twentieth century, domestic service had a compelling presence in British economic, social, and cultural life.' Delap, Lucy. *Knowing Their Place: Domestic Service in Twentieth-Century Britain*. Oxford: Oxford University Press, 2011, p. 1.

29 Ibid., p. 2. Other writers and historians have explored domestic service and its centrality to British history and experience, including Carolyn Steedman who has explored domestic service in the making of modern England and Lucy Lethbridge who has explored domestic service in twentieth-century Britain. See Steedman, Carolyn. *Labours Lost: Domestic Service and the Making of Modern England*. Cambridge, UK: Cambridge University Press, 2009 and Lethbridge, Lucy. *Servants: A Downstairs View of Twentieth-Century Britain*. London: Bloomsbury, 2013.

30 Lethbridge. *Servants*, p. 9.

31 Delap. *Knowing Their Place*, p. 12.

32 Ibid., p. 11.

33 Ibid., p. 12.

34 Ibid., p. 13.

35 Ibid.

36 See Kushner, Tony. 'An Alien Occupation – Jewish Refugees and Domestic Service in Britain, 1933-1948' in Mosse, Werner E., and Julius Carlebach (eds). *Second Chance: Two Centuries of German-Speaking Jews in the United Kingdom*. Tübingen: Mohr, 1991 and Kushner, Tony and Katharine Knox. *Refugees in an Age of Genocide: Global, National and Local Perspectives During the Twentieth Century*. London: F. Cass, 1999.

37 See Bressey, Caroline. 'Looking for Work: The Black Presence in Britain 1860-1920' in Caroline Bressey and Hakim Adi (eds). *Belonging in Europe: The African Diaspora and Work*. London: Routledge, 2011.

38 Delap. *Knowing Their Place*, p. 5, fn14.

39 Ibid., p. 14.

40 Ibid.

41 Ibid., p. 15.

42 Ibid., p. 15.

43 Ibid.

44 'The Man-Servant: Fifteen-Shilling Tax', *The Manchester Guardian*, 4 April 1934, p. 6.

45 Lethbridge. *Servants*, p. 154–5.

46 'Situations Wanted', the *Evening News* (Portsmouth) 1 December 1931, p. 10.

47 *Surrey Mirror and County Post*, 16 July 1937.

48 *Buckingham Advertiser and North Bucks Free Press*, 14 May 1932.

49 The *Western Morning News and Daily Gazette*, 16 April 1934, p. 2.

50 Waldemar-Leverton, Edith. *Servants and Their Duties: A Helpful Manual for Mistress and Servant*. London: C. Arthur Pearson, 1912, pp. 36–7.

51 Lethbridge. *Servants*, p. 209.

52 Ibid. p. 209.

53 Ibid., p. 212.

54 Ibid., p. 212.

55 'The Stage Stanleys', *The Evening Telegraph* (Dundee), 16 October 1937.

56 Lethbridge. *Servants*, p. 216.

57 S.P. Sheet 200A – Qualification Form, Patrick Nelson, Army Personnel Records.

58 *Derby Daily Telegraph*, Thursday 2 September 1937.

59 Geoffrey Butterworth, *The Story of Penrhos*, 4 November 1968, Bangor Archives, MS 20014.

60 1881 Wales Census, RG11/5595 via ancestry.co.uk.

61 An Inventory of the Contents of Penrhos, Holyhead, the Property of the late Lord Stanley of Alderley, K.C.M.G., taken for the purposes of Estate Duty, September, 1931, Bangor Archives, Penrhos VIII 139.

62 Schedule of real and/or leasehold property, Penrhos estate, Holyhead, Anglesey, Bangor Archives, Penrhos collection, Penrhos VIII, 13C.

63 WM/T/22 – Mr Hugh Jones talks about his employers on the Penrhos estate, Transcript of Interview, Anglesey Archives.

64 Ibid.

65 Ibid.

66 Ibid. Lyulph Stanley became Lord Stanley in 1971 after his brother died. He too died a few months afterwards in June 1971. Thus, Hugh Jones kept up to date with news about the Stanleys decades after they had left Penrhos.

67 Ibid.

68 Ibid.

69 'The Blizzard: Trail of Destruction. Anglesey Cut Off. Roads Blocked and Electricity Breakdown. Holyhead's Plight', *Holyhead and Anglesey Mail*, 5 March 1937, p. 10.

70 Advertisement: 'Stanley Hospital Holyhead, Annual Fete at Penrhos, Tuesday, July 27, 1937.' *Holyhead and Anglesey Mail*, 23 April 1937; 'Fete at Penrhos', *North Wales Chronicle*, 31 July 1869, p. 8.

71 Penrhos Almhouses Accts., Bangor Archives, Penrhos collection, Penrhos VII 532.

72 'Anglesey Council Elections: Recount in Holyhead Rural: Retiring Member Defeated', *Holyhead and Anglesey Mail*, 12 March 1937, p. 10.

73 WM/T/36/39 – Mr Cyril Parry, Transcript of Interview, Anglesey Archives.

74 Ibid.

75 Ibid.

76 'Anglesey County Council. Four Contests at Holyhead', *Holyhead and Anglesey Mail*, 26 February 1937, p. 8.

77 WM/T/36/39 – Mr Cyril Parry, Transcript of Interview, Anglesey Archives.

78 Alan Llwyd, *Black Wales: A History of Black Welsh People*. Gwasg Dinefwr Press, 2005, p. 25.

79 Ibid., p. 80.

80 *Holyhead and Anglesey Mail*, 29 January 1937, p. 4.

81 Tobin, Beth Fowkes. *Picturing Imperial Power: Colonial Subjects in Eighteenth-Century British Painting*. Durham, N.C: Duke University Press, 1999, p. 27.

82 See Bressey 'Looking for Work: The Black Presence in Britain 1860-1920'.

83 Lethbridge. *Servants*, pp. 216–17.

84 Cook. *Queer Domesticities*, p. 26.

85 Cook. *Queer Domesticities*, p. 122.

Chapter 4

1 UK Incoming Passenger Lists, 1878–1960 Record for Mr Leopold Nelson March 1938 via ancestry.co.uk.

2 Patrick Nelson to Duncan Grant, 19 July 1953, Tate Archives.

3 UK, Outward Passenger Lists, 1890–1960 Record for Leopold St Patrick Nelson, November 1937 via ancestry.co.uk.

4 UK Incoming Passenger Lists, 1878–1960 Record for Mr Leopold Nelson March 1938, via ancestry.co.uk.

5 1911 England Census for Henry Walter James, via ancestry.co.uk.

6 For an examination of Bristol's ethnically diverse and migrant history, see Dresser, Madge and Peter Fleming. *Bristol: Ethnic Minorities and the City, 1000-2001*. Chichester: Phillimore, 2007.

7 Joannou, Maroula. 'Nancy Cunard's English Journey.' *Feminist Review* Vol. 78 (2004), pp. 141–163, p. 151.

8 Jenkinson, Jacqueline. *Black 1919: Riots, Racism and Resistance in Imperial Britain.* Liverpool: Liverpool University Press, 2009, p. 14.

9 See Romain, Gemma and Caroline Bressey. 'Claude McKay: queer interwar London and spaces of black radicalism', in Katherine M. Graham and Simon Avery (eds) *Sex, Time and Place: Queer Histories of London, c.1850 to the Present.* Bloomsbury Academic, 2016.

10 See Jenkinson. *Black 1919.*

11 *The Melody Maker,* 7 March 1936, p. 2.

12 Ibid.

13 Walkowitz, Judith R. *Nights Out: Life in Cosmopolitan London.* New Haven: Yale University Press, 2012, p. 230.

14 Ibid., p. 232.

15 The *Gleaner,* 6 April 1932, p. 10 and the *Gleaner,* 14 September 1933, p. 7.

16 Registration form; Territorial army. Recruiting centre No. 6, Holloway N7, 11 January 1940, Army Personnel Records.

17 Egan, Bill. *Florence Mills: Harlem Jazz Queen.* Lanham, Md: Scarecrow Press, 2004, p. 170.

18 The Shim Sham Club and Bottle Parties; unregistered clubs and sale of liquor out of hours, The National Archives, MEPO 2/4494.

19 Claude McKay, 3 Provence Street, Islington N, to the director, British Museum, 2 April 1920 and Ruth Anna Fisher, 26 Tavistock Square, London, W.C.1. to The Librarian, The British Museum, London, WC1, 22 October 1920, British Museum Central Archive.

20 *The Crisis: A Record of the Darker Races,* November 1933, p. 257.

21 Anand, Mulk R. *Conversations in Bloomsbury.* Second edition, Delhi: Oxford University Press, 1995.

22 Ibid., preface to Second edition, p. 33.

23 Ibid., p. 34. The book *Negro,* published in 1934, included writers and works by African American and African diaspora writers and activists such as George Padmore, W. E. B. Du Bois, Alain Locke, Langston Hughes and Zora Neale Hurston and also included pieces by white queer writers and artists based in London such as John Banting.

24 Hale, Kathleen. *A Slender Reputation: An Autobiography.* London: Frederick Warne, 1994, p. 111.

25 London, England, Electoral Registers, 1832–1965 for Eric Derwent Walrond, via ancestry.co.uk

26 Walrond, Eric. 'The Negro in London', *The Black Man,* 1936, reprinted in Louis J. Parascandola (ed.). *Winds Can Wake Up the Dead: An Eric Walrond Reader.* Detroit, Mich: Wayne State University Press, 1998.

27 Cited in Egan. *Florence Mills,* p. 170.

28 McKay, Claude, *A Long Way from Home*. First published 1937 (2007 edition: edited and introduction by Gene A. Jarrett). New Brunswick, N.J: Rutgers University Press, 2007. p. 233.

29 Anand. *Conversations in Bloomsbury*, preface to Second edition, p. 35.

30 *The Keys: The Official Organ of the League of Coloured Peoples*. London: League, 1933–9.

31 Committee Records, Colour Bar Committee, 1929–1931, Friends' House Library.

32 The Indian Students' Union and Hostel, London – Sixteenth Annual Report, 1935, pp. 8–9.

33 Whittall, Daniel. 'Creating Black Places in Imperial London: The League of Coloured Peoples and Aggrey House, 1931–1943', *The London Journal*, Vol. 36, No. 3 (November, 2011), pp. 225–46.

34 'Obituary: Ivor Cummings' by Val Wilmer, *The Independent*, 4 December 1992 http://www.independent.co.uk/news/people/obituary-ivor-cummings-1561396. html.

35 Ibid.

36 London, England, Electoral Registers, 1832–1965 for Stella Jane Thomas, via ancestry.co.uk. Mark Matera comments on the lack of accommodation for African women and difficulties in securing accommodation, compared to men, and that 'unlike her brother, Stephen Thomas, however, Stella could not stay at the LCP's "Aggrey House" or the WASU hostel, so she lived at the YWCA during her time in London. Likewise, when she arrived in London in 1935 for training to become a teacher, the Sierra Leonean Constance Horton (later Cummings-John) had no choice but to stay there while her college was closed for a holiday break.' Matera, Marc. *Black Internationalism and African and Caribbean Intellectuals in London, 1919–1950*. Dissertation submitted in partial fulfilment of the requirements for the degree of Doctor of Philosophy, New Brunswick, New Jersey, 2008, p. 170.

37 UK, Incoming Passenger Lists, 1878–1960 for Olive Pearl Allen Baxter, 1930 and UK, Outward Passenger Lists, 1890–1960 for Edith F Allen Baxter, 1932, via ancestry.co.uk.

38 Matera, Marc. *Black Internationalism and African and Caribbean Intellectual in London, 1919-1950*, p. 11.

39 London, England Electoral Registers 1847–1965, via ancestry.co.uk.

40 Extract from Nicholas Laughlin. *Letters from London: Seven Essays by C.L.R. James*. Oxford, UK: Signal Books, 2003, pp. 19–21.The Bloomsbury Atmosphere originally published in the Port of Spain Gazette, 21 June 1932.

41 Matera, Marc. *Black London: The Imperial Metropolis and Decolonization in the Twentieth Century*. Oakland, California: University of California Press, 2015, p. 27.

42 Garnett, David. *Never be a Book Seller*, with a postscript by Richard Garnett and engraving by Howard Phipps. The Fleece Press, Denby Dale, 1995.

43 Ibid.

44 Spalding, Frances. *Duncan Grant*. London: Pimlico, 1998 (first published 1997), p. 1.

45 Ibid., p. 11.

46 Ibid., pp. 13–14.

47 Ibid., p. 27.

48 Ibid., p.41.

49 Ibid., p.45.

50 Ibid., p.68.

51 Ibid., p. 75.

52 Ibid., p. 83.

53 Ibid., pp. 83–4.

54 Shone, Richard. 'The Friday Club', *The Burlington Magazine*, Vol. 117, No. 866 (May 1975), pp. 279–84, p. 279.

55 Ibid.

56 Shone, Richard. *Bloomsbury Portraits: Vanessa Bell, Duncan Grant and Their Circle*. London: Phaidon Press, 1993, first published 1976, p. 93.

57 Spalding, *Duncan Grant*, p. 107.

58 Ibid., pp. 157–8.

59 Ibid., p. 159.

60 Ibid., p. 163.

61 Ibid., p. 165.

62 Ibid., p. 183.

63 Ibid., p. 189.

64 Rosner, Victoria (ed.). 'Introduction' in *The Cambridge Companion to the Bloomsbury Group*. New York: Cambridge University Press, 2014, p. 8.

65 Taylor, John R. *Edward Wolfe*. London: Trefoil Books for Odette Gilbert Gallery, 1986, p. 7.

66 Ibid., pp. 11–12.

67 Ibid., pp. 12–15.

68 Ibid., p. 15.

69 Spalding. *Duncan Grant*, p. 210.

70 Ibid., p. 208.

71 Ibid., p. 213.

72 Ibid., p. 216.

73 Ibid., p. 216.

74 Ibid., p. 224.

75 Shone. *Bloomsbury Portraits*, p. 206.

76 'The Independent Gallery', *The Observer*, 24 June 1923.

77 Spalding. *Duncan Grant*, pp. 292–3.

78 Ibid., p. 294.

79 Ibid., p. 299.

80 Ibid., p. 325. For example, in July 1931, Duncan, along with Vanessa Bell, exhibited still-life compositions at the Cooling Galleries' exhibition of watercolours and drawings by members of the London Artists' Association; in July 1932 he exhibited work in the summer exhibition of paintings and drawings by eminent British artists at the Beaux Arts Gallery. During 1934 he exhibited work alongside artists including Vanessa Bell at the Wednesday–Thursday Gallery in Brompton Road, and the Graves Art Gallery in Sheffield included Duncan Grant's work in the 661 works at its opening in July 1934. These represent just a few of the many exhibitions in which he took part. 'Cooling Galleries', *The Times*, 13 July 1931, p. 10; 'Beaux Arts Gallery', *The Times*, 20 July 1932, p. 10; 'Art Exhibitions', *The Times*, 18 April 1934, p. 14; 'The Graves Art Gallery', *The Times*, 5 July 1934, p. 12.

81 Helen McCloy, 'London Art: the Rising Tide of Modernism Here and There', *New York Times*, 12 July 1931.

82 Spalding. *Duncan Grant*, p. 355.

83 Shone. *Bloomsbury Portraits*, p. 237.

84 Spalding. *Duncan Grant*, p. 357.

85 James, C L. R. *The Case for West-Indian Self Government*. London: L. and Virginia Woolf at the Hogarth Press, 1933.

86 Snaith, Anna. 'Conversations in Bloomsbury: Colonial Writers and the Hogarth Press' in Potts, Gina, and Lisa Shahriari (eds). *Virginia Woolf's Bloomsbury: Volume 2*. Basingstoke: Palgrave Macmillan, 2010, p. 141.

87 Anand. *Conversations in Bloomsbury*, p. vii.

88 Snaith, 'Conversations in Bloomsbury', p. 138.

89 Anand. *Conversations in Bloomsbury*, p. viii.

90 Ibid., pp. viii–ix.

91 Spalding. *Duncan Grant*, p. 358.

92 Ibid., p. 371.

93 Faulkner, S. 'Homoexoticism: John Minton in London and Jamaica, 1950-1951', in Tim Barringer, Douglas Fordham and Geoff Quilley (eds). *Art and the British Empire*, Manchester: Manchester University Press, 2006, p. 171.

94 Houlbrook, Matt. *Queer London: Perils and Pleasures in the Sexual Metropolis, 1918-1957*. Chicago: University of Chicago Press, 2005, pp. 118–19.

95 PRO MEPO 3 990: 'Use of Plainclothes Officers in Detecting Indecency Offences in Urinals' Wontners Solicitors to Supt. (5 August 1933), referenced in Houlbrook. *Queer London*, p. 119.

96 Ellis, Nadia. *Territories of the Soul: Queered Belonging in the Black Diaspora*. Durham: Duke University Press, 2015.

97 McKay, *A Long Way From Home*, p. 68.

98 For information on these networks, see Stevenson, Jane. *Edward Burra: Twentieth-century Eye*. London: Jonathan Cape, 2007.

99 Bourne, Stephen. *Elisabeth Welch: Soft Lights and Sweet Music*. Lanham, Md: Scarecrow Press, 2005, p. 34.

100 UK, Outward Passenger Lists, 1890–1960 for Kenneth Macpherson, via ancestry. co.uk.

101 Walkowitz, Judith R. *Nights Out: Life in Cosmopolitan London*. New Haven: Yale University Press, 2012, p. 240.

102 Rye, Howard, 'Visiting Fireman – Garland Wilson', *Storyville*, Vol. 119 (1985), p. 184.

103 Ibid., p. 186.

104 Ibid., p. 187.

105 Ibid.

106 Ibid., p. 188.

107 Ibid.

108 Metropolitan Police, Vine Street station, 'C' Division, 14 October 1935, Superintendent, Shim Sham Club, Ltd, 35/37 Wardour Street, W.1., Jack Isow – Notice of Appeal in MEPO 2/4494, The National Archives, UK.

109 Houlbrook. *Queer London*, p. 71.

110 Ibid., pp. 71–2.

111 Ibid., pp. 74–5.

112 CRIM 1/903, The National Archives, UK.

113 Ibid.

114 'Two Years for Club Owner', *Hartlepool Mail*, 27 January 1937, p. 6.

115 Rex v Billie Joyce and others in CRIM 1/903, The National Archives, UK.

116 CRIM 1/903, The National Archives, UK.

117 Patrick Nelson to Duncan Grant, 7 August 1945, Tate Archives.

118 Houlbrook. *Queer London*, p. 86.

119 Patrick Nelson to Duncan Grant, no date, approx 1938, Tate Archives.

120 Ibid.

121 Patrick Nelson to Duncan Grant, no date, approx 1939, Tate Archives.

122 Daley, Harry. *This Small Cloud: A Personal Memoir*. London: Weidenfeld and Nicolson, 1986, p. 147.

123 Ibid.

124 Ibid., pp. 156–7.

125 Ibid., pp. 157–8.

126 Wilmer, Val. 'Obituary Letter: Richie Riley', *The Guardian*, 22 May 1997.

127 National Library of Wales, Angus McBean Manuscripts, https://archiveswales. llgc.org.uk/anw/get_collection.php?coll_id=414&inst_id=1&term=angus%20 mcbean

128 Interview with Richie Riley, Black Cultural Archives, as part of the Oral History Project The Myth of the Motherland – Arrival and Settlement, digitized as part of the *Moving Here* project, Catalogue Reference:AMBH/BCA RROT/BCA.

129 Ibid.

130 Ibid.

131 Wilmer, Val. 'Obituary Letter: Richie Riley', *The Guardian*, 22 May 1997.

132 Glyn Kelsall, 'Negro Ballet: Berto Pasuka on Coming London Season', *The Stage*, 7 February 1946.

133 Wiggins, Edgar A. 'France Sees, Likes First All-Negro Ballet', *The Chicago Defender* 19 October 1946.

134 Patrick Nelson to Duncan Grant, no date, approx 1938, Tate Archives.

135 Ibid.

136 1938 photographic portrait of Patrick Nelson, Private Collection.

137 Patrick Nelson to Duncan Grant, no date, approx 1939, Tate Archives.

138 Ibid.

139 Ibid.

140 Ibid.

141 Ibid.

142 Ibid.

143 Ibid.

144 Patrick Nelson to Duncan Grant, from No. 5 Group HQ, AMPC, BEF, France,12 May 1940, Tate Archives.

145 Patrick Nelson to Duncan Grant, no date, approx 1939, Tate Archives.

146 Ibid.

147 Patrick Nelson to Duncan Grant, 20.11.1939, Tate Archives.

148 Patrick Nelson to Duncan Grant, 9 February 1948, Tate Archives.

149 Ibid.

150 Ibid.

151 Patrick Nelson to Duncan Grant, 13 or 15 February 1949, Tate Archives.

152 Patrick Nelson to Duncan Grant, 4 April 1956, Tate Archives.

153 Duncan Grant to Patrick Nelson, 12 May 1940, Tate Archives.

154 *Portraits by Duncan Grant: an Arts Council Exhibition*. London: Arts Council, 1969.

155 Deghy, Guy and Keith Waterhouse. *Café Royal. Ninety Years of Bohemia, Etc.* [with Plates.]. Hutchinson: London, 1955, p. 157.

156 For example, see Dabydeen, David. *Hogarth's Blacks: Images of Blacks in Eighteenth Century English Art*. Athens: University of Georgia Press, 1987; Bindman, David, Henry L. Gates, and Karen C. C. Dalton (eds). *The Image of the Black in Western Art*. Cambridge, Mass: Belknap Press of Harvard University Press, 2010 and *Picturing Imperial Power*; Tobin, Beth Fowkes *Colonizing Nature: The Tropics in British Arts and Letters, 1760–1820*.

157 See Gilroy, Paul and Tate Gallery. Picturing Blackness in British Art, 1700s–1990s: 28 November 1995–10 March, 1996, Tate Gallery. London: Tate Pub, 1995; Marsh, Jan. 'Pictured at Work: Employment in Art (1800–1900)', Immigrants & Minorities, Vol. 28, No.2 (2010), pp. 154–63; 'Black Victorians: Black People in British Art 1800–1900' organized jointly by the Manchester Art Gallery and Birmingham City Museum and Art Gallery, 2005–2006. Marsh, Jan (ed.). *Black Victorians: Black People in British Art, 1800-1900*. Aldershot, Hampshire: Lund Humphries, 2005; and *Black Chronicles II*, http://autograph-abp.co.uk/exhibitions/black-chronicles-ii.

158 See 'The Image of the Black in Western Art', http://www.imageoftheblack.com/.

159 Bindman, David and Henry L. Gates (eds) *The Image of the Black in Western Art: The Twentieth Century*. Cambridge, Massachusetts: Harvard University Press, 2014.

160 Spaces of Black Modernism, curated by Gemma Romain and Caroline Bressey with Tate Britain curators Emma Chambers and Inga Fraser. Tate Britain, 2014–2015, http://www.tate.org.uk/whats-on/tate-britain/display/bp-spotlight-spaces-black-modernism-london-1919-39.

161 See, Phillips, Sarah R. *Modeling Life: Art Models Speak About Nudity, Sexuality, and the Creative Process*. Albany: State University of New York Press, 2006 and Desmarais, Jane, Martin Postle and William Vaughan (eds). *Model and supermodel: the artist's model in British art and culture*. Manchester University Press, 2006.

162 Spalding. *Duncan Grant*, p. 302.

163 Ibid.

164 Faulkner, 'Homoexoticism: John Minton in London and Jamaica, 1950-1951', p. 171.

Chapter 5

1 Patrick Nelson to Duncan Grant, 1939, Tate Archives.

2 Ibid.

3 Patrick Nelson to Duncan Grant, 20 November 1939, Tate Archives.

4 Patrick Nelson to Duncan Grant, undated, approx late 1939, on RAF letter headed paper, Tate Archives.

5 Patrick Nelson to Colonel i/c Pioneer Records Dunholme Manor Bournemouth Hants, sent from 40 Norfolk Street, 30 November 1944, Army Personnel Records.

6 Army Form B200B Statement of Service, Patrick Nelson, Army Personnel Records.

7 Letter from Leopold Nelson, Lucas Cricket Club, to Auxiliary Military Pioneer Corps, Bournemouth, 24 September 1940, Army Personnel Records.

8 Lambo, Roger. 'Achtung! The black prince: West Africans in the Royal Air Force, 1939–46', *Immigrants & Minorities*, Vol. 12, No.3 (1993), pp. 145–63, p. 145.

9 'Recruiting Regulations for the Royal Air Force', 1923, TNA AIR 10/965, cited in Kushner, 'Without intending any of the most undesirable features of a colour bar': race, science, Europeanness and the British armed forces during the twentieth century', in Schaffer, Gavin (ed.). *Racializing the Soldier*. London: Routledge, 2013, p. 153.

10 Lambo, 'Achtung! The black prince: West Africans in the Royal Air Force, 1939–46', p. 149.

11 For information on Cy Grant, see the Cy Grant Trust project and website http://cygrant.com.

12 Kushner. 'Without intending any of the most undesirable features of a colour bar', pp. 151–2.

13 See Bourne, Stephen. *The Motherland Calls: Britain's Black Servicemen & Women, 1939–45*. Stroud, Gloucestershire: The History Press, 2012; Sherwood, Marika. *Many Struggles: West Indian Workers and Service Personnel in Britain, (1939–45)*. London: Karia Press, 1985 and Olusoga, David. *The World's War*. Head of Zeus, 2014.

14 Bourne. *The Motherland Calls*, pp. 35–6 and George Padmore, 'British MP's Flay Color Ban In Parliament Debate' Defender London Correspondent, *The Chicago Defender*, 30 October 1943.

15 George Padmore, 'British MP's Flay Color Ban In Parliament Debate' Defender London Correspondent, *The Chicago Defender*, 30 October 1943.

16 BT 350, Merchant Seamen, 1918–1941 Records, via findmypast.co.uk, record for Henry King, Identity certificate number 442605.

17 George Padmore, 'British MP's Flay Color Ban In Parliament Debate'.

18 The King Household, 111 John Scurr House on the 1939 Register, via findmypast.co.uk.

19 *Portsmouth Evening News*, 29 October 1943.

20 Bourne. *The Motherland Calls*, p. 24.

21 Killingray, David. 'Race and rank in the British army in the twentieth century', *Ethnic and Racial Studies*, Vol. 10, No. 3 (1987), pp. 276–90, p. 281.

22 Rush, Anne S. *Bonds of Empire: West Indians and Britishness from Victoria to Decolonization*. Oxford: Oxford University Press, 2011, pp. 129–30.

23 Thompson, Dudley with Margaret C. Thompson. *From Kingston to Kenya: The Making of a Pan-Africanist Lawyer*. Dover, Mass: Majority Press, 1993, p. 1.

24 Ibid., p. 17.

25 Ibid., p. 1.

26 Ibid., p. 17.

27 Ibid., p. 17.

28 Ibid., p. 17.

29 Ibid., p. 19. For information on the Frome Sugar Estate labour protests, see Palmer, Colin A. *Freedom's Children: The 1938 Labor Rebellion and the Birth of Modern Jamaica*. Chapel Hill: The University of North Carolina Press, 2014.

30 Thompson. *From Kingston to Kenya*, p. 21.

31 Ibid., p. 22.

32 Ibid., p. 23.

33 Ibid.

34 Ibid., pp. 26–7.

35 Ibid., p. 29.

36 Ibid., p. 30.

37 Ibid., p. 31.

38 Rhodes-Wood, Major E. H. *A War History of the Royal Pioneer Corps, 1939-1945*. Aldershot, Gale & Polden Ltd, 1960, p. 1.

39 Ibid., pp. 1–2.

40 Ibid., p. 2.

41 Ibid., p. 4.

42 Ibid., p. 8.

43 Ibid., pp. 8–9.

44 'A New Corps. Military Pioneers to Ensure Supplies'. *The Times*, 26 October 1939, p. 5.

45 Part II – description of Nelson Patrick on enlistment, Patrick Nelson, Army Personnel Records.

46 'A New Corps. Military Pioneers to Ensure Supplies.' *The Times*, 26 October 1939, p. 5.

47 'Military Pioneer Corps: Rush of Recruits', *The Manchester Guardian*, 27 October 1939, p. 8.

48 'Rush to Join the Army: Ready Response of Volunteers. Queues in London'. *The Times*, Saturday, 28 October 1939, p. 3.

49 'Pioneers Needed For The Forces. Recruiting Rally in London'. *The Times*, 16 April 1940, p. 8.

50 Rhodes-Wood. *A War History of the Royal Pioneer Corps, 1939-1945*, pp. 10–11.

51 Ibid., p. 21.

52 Patrick Nelson to Colonel i/c Pioneer Records Dunholme Manor Bournemouth Hants, sent from 40 Norfolk Street, 30 November 1944, Army Personnel Records and Army Form B200B Statement of Service, Patrick Nelson, Army Personnel Records.

53 Army Form B200B Statement of Service, Patrick Nelson, Army Personnel Records.

54 Rhodes-Wood. *A War History of the Royal Pioneer Corps, 1939-1945*, pp. 9–10.

55 Ibid., p. 12.

56 Ibid., p. 17.

57 Ibid., p. 18.

58 Ibid., p. 18.

59 Ibid., p. 19.

60 Ibid., p. 25.

61 Ibid., pp. 21–3.

62 Rhodes-Wood. *A War History of the Royal Pioneer Corps, 1939-1945*, p. 22.

63 'Aliens Policy', *The Manchester Guardian*, 27 November 1940, p. 4.

64 Jackson, Ashley. 'Supplying War: The High Commission Territories' Military-Logistical Contribution in the Second World War'. *The Journal of Military History*, Vol. 66, No. 3 (Jul., 2002), pp. 719–60, pp. 719–20.

65 Rhodes-Wood. *A War History of the Royal Pioneer Corps, 1939-1945*, p. 24.

66 Smalley, Edward. *The British Expeditionary Force, 1939-40*. New York, NY: Palgrave Macmillan, 2015, pp. 15–17.

67 Ibid., p. 19.

68 Ibid., p. 19.

69 Ibid., pp. 10–11. Smalley cites Mark Connelly's work exploring this subject.

70 Ibid., p. 1.

71 Army Form B200B Statement of Service, Patrick Nelson, Army Personnel Records

72 Duncan Grant to Patrick Nelson, 12 May 1940, Tate Archives.

73 Patrick Nelson to Duncan Grant, No. 5 Group HQ, B.E.F., France, 11 May 1940, Tate Archives.

74 Ibid.

75 War diary for 29 March 1940 to May 1940 and Field Returns of officers and other ranks, The National Archives, WO 167/1311, No. 76 Coy, A.M.P.C.

76 Ibid.

77 Ibid.

78 Rhodes-Wood. *A War History of the Royal Pioneer Corps, 1939-1945*, p. 33.

79 Ibid., pp. 33–4.

80 Ibid., p. 34.

81 Ibid., p. 34.

82 Ibid., p. 35.

83 Ibid.

84 Ibid.

85 Ibid.

86 Ibid.

87 Ibid., p. 36.

88 Ibid., p. 37.

89 Ibid., pp. 37–40.

90 War diary for 29 March 1940 to May 1940 and Field Returns of officers and other ranks, The National Archives, WO 167/1311, No. 76 Coy, A.M.P.C.

91 Ibid.

92 Ibid.

93 Ibid.

94 'Two Tanks Captured by Pioneers', *The Times*, 24 May 1940.

95 War diary for 29 March 1940 to May 1940 and Field Returns of officers and other ranks, The National Archives, WO 167/1311, No. 76 Coy, A.M.P.C.

96 Raffael Scheck, 'French African Soldiers in German POW Camps, 1940–1945' in Byfield, Judith A, Carolyn A. Brown, Timothy Parsons and Ahmad A. Sikainga (eds). *Africa and World War II*. New York: Cambridge University Press, 2015, p. 446.

97 War diary for 29 March 1940 to May 1940 and Field Returns of officers and other ranks, The National Archives, WO 167/1311, No. 76 Coy, A.M.P.C.

98 Ibid.

99 Ibid.

100 Folly, Martin H. *The Palgrave Concise Historical Atlas of the Second World War*. New York: Palgrave Macmillan, 2004, Map 7: The Fall of the Low Countries and France 1940.

101 Wylie, Neville. *Barbed Wire Diplomacy: Britain, Germany, and the Politics of Prisoners of War, 1939-1945*. Oxford: Oxford University Press, 2010, p. 68.

Chapter 6

1 'First Jamaican to be Captured by the Germans Returns Home. Patrick Nelson tells of his experiences in the notorious "Stalag 8B", Silesian Prison Camp'. The *Gleaner*, 10 June 1945.

2 Ibid.

3 Ibid.

4 Letter from Gertrude Nelson, Kingston, Jamaica, to A.M.P.C. Records Office, Bournemouth to Duncan Grant, 3.2.1941, Army Personnel Records.

5 Patrick Nelson to Colonel i/c Pioneer Records Dunholme Manor Bournemouth Hants, sent from 40 Norfolk Street, 30 November 1944, Army Personnel Records.

6 'Mr Patrick Nelson War Prisoner in Germany', the *Gleaner*, 21 February 1941.

7 The *Gleaner*, 17 July 1941.

8 In June 1941 the War Office in Liverpool sent a request to Pioneer Corps Record Office in Bournemouth to send the list of names of personnel missing from Pioneer Corps in BEF companies to be circulated to all companies of Pioneer corps to help throw light on the circumstances in which officers and men on the list were last seen. Pioneer Corps Record Office sent the requests and received some replies but in many cases they also had no more information on missing personnel's location. Seven men were included in this list from 76 Company, Patrick was not included on this list as by this time he was listed as a POW and not as missing. Correspondence between the War Office and the Pioneer Record Office, June 1941 in file PD 96, WO

361/34, TNA. In 1942, a year after Patrick's name had been taken off the missing list, more information on Pioneer Corps members who were missing was sent to the Record Office and then the War Office.

9 Letter from Leopold Nelson, Lucas Cricket Club, to Auxiliary Military Pioneer Corps, Bournemouth, 24 September 1940, Army Personnel Records.

10 Letter from Gertrude Nelson, 12 Hart Street, Kingston, Jamaica, to Duncan Grant, 17 December 1940, Army Personnel Records. Duncan forwarded a copy of the letters from Gertrude and the Belgian Red Cross to the Pioneer Corps on 8 February 1941.

11 Leopold Nelson to Duncan Grant, 24 September 1940, Tate Archives.

12 Letter from Duncan Grant, Charleston, Firle, Sussex to Colonel Dean, 27 January 1941, Army Personnel Records.

13 Letter sent on behalf of Lieutenant Colonel, R.A., Officer in Charge, A.M.P.C. Records Office, Bournemouth to Duncan Grant, 3 February 1941, Army Personnel Records.

14 Letter from Duncan Grant, to Pioneer Corps Record Office, Bournemouth, 8 February 1941, Army Personnel Records.

15 Letter from Pioneer Corps Record Office, Bournemouth to Duncan Grant, 12 February 1941, Army Personnel Records.

16 Letter from Pioneer Corps Record Office, Bournemouth to Gertrude Nelson, 13 February 1941, Army Personnel Records.

17 Letter from Leopold Nelson, Kingston, Jamaica to Lt. Col. D.J. Dean, 11 February 1941, Army Personnel Records.

18 Ibid.

19 Letter from Pioneer Corps Record Office, Bournemouth to Colonel Dean, 5 May 1941, and letter from Pioneer Corps Record Office, Bournemouth to Leopold Nelson and Gertrude Nelson, 5 May 1941, Army Personnel Records.

20 Letter from Mary Lucie-Smith, Jamaica Central War Assistance Committee to Pioneer Corps Record Office, Bournemouth, 8 May 1941, Army Personnel Records.

21 Letter from Mary Lucie-Smith, Jamaica Central War Assistance Committee to Duncan Grant, 20 or 28 April 1941, Duncan Grant/Patrick Nelson letters, Tate Archives.

22 Note referring to Leopold Nelson and Patrick Nelson, Prisoners of War (Jamaicans), The Jamaica Archives.

23 Letter from Leopold Nelson, Kingston, Jamaica to Duncan Grant, 27 October 1942, Tate Archives.

24 Wylie, Neville. *Barbed Wire Diplomacy: Britain, Germany, and the Politics of Prisoners of War, 1939-1945*. Oxford: Oxford University Press, 2010, p. 66.

25 Kochavi, Arieh J. *Confronting Captivity: Britain and the United States and Their POWs in Nazi Germany*. Chapel Hill: University of North Carolina Press, 2005, pp. 9–10.

26 Letter from Pioneer Corps Record Office, Bournemouth to Major T. H. Woodland, 7D, 9 January 1943, Army Personnel Records.

27 Referred to in letter from Pioneer Corps Record Office, Bournemouth to Duncan Grant, 12 February 1941, Army Personnel Records.

28 Letter from Duncan Grant, to Pioneer Corps Record Office, Bournemouth, 22 June 1941, Army Personnel Records.

29 Letter from Gertrude Nelson and Leopold Nelson, Jamaica to Pioneer Corps Record Office, Bournemouth, 23 June 1941, Army Personnel Records.

30 Letter from Pioneer Corps Record Office to Duncan Grant, Bournemouth, 2 July 1941, Army Personnel Records.

31 POW letter from Patrick Nelson to Duncan Grant, opened by Censor 2785; postmarked 16 October 1940, Tate Archives.

32 Letter from Duncan Grant, to Pioneer Corps Record Office, Bournemouth, letter received 3 February 1942, Army Personnel Records.

33 Letter from Pioneer Corps Record Office, Bournemouth to Duncan Grant, 4 February 1942, Army Personnel Records.

34 'Convention relative to the Treatment of Prisoners of War. Geneva, 27 July 1929', https://www.icrc.org/ihl/INTRO/305?OpenDocument

35 Kochavi, Arieh J., 'Why None of Britain's Long-Term POWs in Nazi GermanyWere Repatriated During World War II', *Canadian Journal of History/Annales canadiennes d'histoire*, Vol. XXXIX, (April/avril 2004), pp. 63–85, p. 65.

36 Letter from Duncan Grant to Pioneer Corps Record Office, Bournemouth, 4 June 1942, Army Personnel Records.

37 Letter from Leopold Nelson, Kingston Jamaica to Duncan Grant, 23 [April?] 1942, Tate Archives.

38 Letter from The War Office (CAS P.W.) to Pioneer Corps Record Office, Bournemouth, 20 August 1942, Army Personnel Records.

39 Hester Bourne for director, War Organisation of the British Red Cross Society and Order of St John of Jerusalem. Prisoners of War department, to Duncan Grant, 28 July 1942, Tate Archives.

40 'Mr Patrick Nelson Alive and Well', the *Gleaner*, 6 November 1940.

41 Scheck, Raffael. French Colonial Soldiers in German Captivity During the Second World War. New York, NY: Cambridge University Press, 2014.

42 Ibid., p. 3.

43 Ibid.

44 Ibid., pp. 3–4.

45 Scheck, Raffael. 'The Killing of Black Soldiers from the French Army by the "Wehrmacht" in 1940: The Question of Authorization', *German Studies Review*, Vol. 28, No. 3 (Oct., 2005), pp. 595–606, p. 595.

46 Adler., K. H. 'Indigènes after Indigènes: post-war France and its North African troops', *European Review of History: Revue européenne d'histoire*, Vol. 20, No. 3 (2013), pp. 463–78.

47 POW letter from Patrick Nelson to Duncan Grant, opened by examiner 3511; postmarked 30.10.42, Tate Archives.

48 Adler. ' Indigènes after Indigènes: post-war France and its North African troops', pp. 463–78.

49 Scheck. *French Colonial Soldiers in German Captivity During World War II*, p. 6.

50 Lusane, Clarence. *Hitler's Black Victims: The Historical Experiences of Afro-Germans, European Blacks, Africans, and African Americans in the Nazi Era*. New York: Routledge, 2003.

51 Ibid., p. 151.

52 POW letter from Patrick Nelson to Duncan Grant, opened by examiner 1095; postmarked 16.7.42, Tate Archives.

53 POW letter from Patrick Nelson to Duncan Grant, opened by examiner 3511; postmarked 30.10.42, Tate Archives.

54 Ibid.

55 Wylie. *Barbed Wire Diplomacy*, p. 4.

56 Typed leaflet entitled 'Communication with Prisoners of War Interned Abroad', n.d., Tate Archives. BOLD wording is in original.

57 Copy of letter from Patrick Nelson to Lady Davson, 28 Februay 1943, enclosed in Margot Davson, West India Committee to Duncan Grant, 26 March 1943, Tate Archives.

58 Leopold Nelson to Duncan Grant, 4 February 1943, Tate Archives.

59 POW letter from Patrick Nelson to Duncan Grant, opened by examiner 7555; postmarked 15.12.42, Tate Archives.

60 POW postcard from Patrick Nelson to Duncan Grant, dated 24 January 1943.

61 POW letter from Patrick Nelson to Duncan Grant, opened by examiner 1095; postmarked 16.7.42, Tate Archives.

62 West India Committee notes to Duncan Grant, no date, Tate Archives.

63 'Seek Information about Jamaican Prisoners of War', the *Gleaner*, 9 June 1942.

64 R. D. R. Hill, acting colonial secretary, Jamaica to Mrs E. Herrick, 26 August 1943, Prisoners of War (Jamaicans) – List of, The Jamaica Archives, IB/5/77/3.

65 Kochavi. *Confronting Captivity*, p. 301, footnote 103,

66 Ibid., p. 10.

67 Ibid., p. 10.

68 Ibid., pp. 10–11.

69 MacKenzie, S. P. 'The Treatment of Prisoners of War in World War II', *The Journal of Modern History*, Vol. 66, No. 3 (Sep., 1994), pp. 487–520, p. 489.

70 'Services' News Column. Life in German Prison Camp: Boston Airman relates his Experiences'. *The Lincolnshire Standard*, 30 September 1944.

71 'First Jamaican to be Captured by the Germans Returns Home. Patrick Nelson tells of his experiences in the notorious "Stalag 8B", Silesian Prison Camp'. The *Gleaner*, 10 June 1945.

72 Jay, John. *Facing Fearful Odds: My Father's Story of Captivity, Escape and Resistance 1940-1945*. South Yorkshire: Pen & Sword Books Ltd, 2014.

73 Ibid., pp. 2–3.

74 Ibid., p. 110.

75 Ibid., p. 103.

76 Ibid., Introduction and Acknowledgements.

77 Makepeace, Clare. 'Living beyond the barbed wire: the familial ties of British prisoners of war held in Europe during the Second World War', *Historical Research*, vol. 86, no. 231, February 2013.

78 POW postcard from Patrick Nelson to Duncan Grant, dated 19 October 1942, Tate Archives.

79 POW letter from Patrick Nelson to Duncan Grant, opened by examiner 7555; postmarked 15.12.42, Tate Archives.

80 POW postcard from Patrick Nelson to Duncan Grant, dated 30 April 1944, Tate Archives.

81 POW letter from Patrick Nelson to Duncan Grant, opened by examiner 3263; dated 17 March 1943, Tate Archives.

82 POW postcard from Patrick Nelson to Duncan Grant, dated 11 March 1944, Tate Archives.

83 POW letter from Patrick Nelson to Duncan Grant, opened by examiner 1095; postmarked 16.7.42, Tate Archives.

84 POW letter from Patrick Nelson to Duncan Grant, opened by examiner 3511; postmarked 30.10.42, Tate Archives.

85 *The Evening Telegraph* (Dundee), 5 July 1944, p. 5.

86 POW letter from Patrick Nelson to Duncan Grant, opened by examiner 1095; postmarked 16.7.42, Tate Archives.

87 POW letter from Patrick Nelson to Duncan Grant, opened by examiner 7555; postmarked 15.12.42, Tate Archives.

88 'First Jamaican to be Captured by the Germans Returns Home. Patrick Nelson tells of his experiences in the notorious "Stalag 8B", Silesian Prison Camp'. The Gleaner, 10 June 1945.

89 Postcard from Educational Books Section, Prisoners of War Department of the Red Cross and St John War Organisation, New Bodleian Library, Oxford to Duncan Grant, sent approximately February 1943, Tate Archives.

90 Margot Davson, West India Committee to Duncan Grant, 26 March 1943, Tate Archives.

91 Letter from Educational Books Section, Prisoners of War Department of the Red
    Cross and St John War Organisation, New Bodleian Library, Oxford to Duncan
    Grant, dated 15 March 1943, Tate Archives.

92 Postcard from Educational Books Section, Prisoners of War Department of the Red
    Cross and St John War Organisation, New Bodleian Library, Oxford to Duncan
    Grant, dated 31 March 1943, Tate Archives.

93 POW letter from Patrick Nelson to Duncan Grant, opened by examiner 3511;
    postmarked 30.10.42, Tate Archives.

94 POW letter from Patrick Nelson to Duncan Grant, opened by examiner 687,
    21 November 1942, Tate Archives.

95 POW postcard from Patrick Nelson to Duncan Grant, Passed P.W. 6345, dated
    27.8.43, Postmarked 02.10.43, Tate Archives.

96 POW letter from Patrick Nelson to Duncan Grant, opened by examiner 3263;
    dated 17 March 1943, Tate Archives.

97 POW letter from Patrick Nelson to Duncan Grant, dated 10 December 1943, Tate
    Archives.

98 POW letter from Patrick Nelson to Duncan Grant, Passed P.W. 9612, Postmarked
    25.11.43, Tate Archives.

99 Jackson, Paul. *One of the Boys: Homosexuality in the Military During World War II.*
    Montréal: McGill-Queen's Univ. Press, 2004.

100 Ibid., p. 261.

101 Ibid., p. 264.

102 Ibid., p. 262.

103 Laugesen, Amanda. *'Boredom Is the Enemy': The Intellectual and Imaginative Lives
    of Australian Soldiers in the Great War and Beyond.* Farnham: Ashgate, 2012,
    p. 222.

104 Ian Sabey, *Stalag Scrap Book*, Melbourne, 1947, cited in Laugesen, Amanda.
    *'Boredom Is the Enemy': The Intellectual and Imaginative Lives of Australian Soldiers
    in the Great War and Beyond.* Farnham: Ashgate, 2012, p. 222.

105 Laugesen. *'Boredom Is the Enemy'*, p. 222.

106 *The Clarion* is sourced from the website http://www.lamsdorf.com/the-clarion.html

107 *The Clarion*, Stalag VIIIB, Number 5, May 1943, p. 2.

108 Ibid.

109 'Services' News Column. Life in German Prison Camp: Boston Airman relates his
    Experiences'. *The Lincolnshire Standard*, 30 September 1944.

110 Copy of letter from Patrick Nelson to Lady Davson, 28 February 1943, enclosed
    in Margot Davson, West India Committee to Duncan Grant, 26 March 1943, Tate
    Archives.

111 'First Jamaican to be Captured by the Germans Returns Home. Patrick Nelson tells of his experiences in the notorious "Stalag 8B", Silesian Prison Camp'. The *Gleaner*, 10 June 1945.

112 *The Clarion*, Stalag VIIIB, Number 6, June–July 1943, p. 12

113 *The Clarion*, Stalag VIIIB, Number 7, p. 4.

114 Jay, John. *Facing Fearful Odds*, p. 196.

115 Grant, Cy. *A Member of the Royal Air Force of Indeterminate Race: Wartime Memoirs of a Former RAF Navigator & POW*. Bognor Regis: Woodfield, 2006, revised edition 2012, p. 56.

116 Ibid., p. 57.

117 'First Jamaican to be Captured by the Germans Returns Home. Patrick Nelson tells of his experiences in the notorious "Stalag 8B", Silesian Prison Camp'. The *Gleaner*, 10 June 1945.

118 'Services' News Column. Life in German Prison Camp: Boston Airman relates his Experiences'. *The Lincolnshire Standard*, 30 September 1944.

119 'First Jamaican to be Captured by the Germans Returns Home. Patrick Nelson tells of his experiences in the notorious "Stalag 8B", Silesian Prison Camp'. The *Gleaner*, 10 June 1945.

120 Kochavi, Arieh J. *Confronting Captivity: Britain and the United States and Their POWs in Nazi Germany*. Chapel Hill: University of North Carolina Press, 2005

121 Letter from War Organisation of the British Red Cross Society and Order of St John of Jerusalem. Prisoners of War Department to Duncan Grant, 8 June 1944, Tate Archives.

122 Ibid.

123 Letter from the Prisoner of War Department, West India Committee, to Duncan Grant, dated 27 June 1944, Tate Archives.

124 Copy of letter from Patrick Nelson to Lady Davson, 5 March 1944, enclosed in Margot Davson, West India Committee to Duncan Grant, approximately April 1944, Tate Archives.

125 Robertson, Graham, 'Pioneers in forensic psychiatry. Professor T. C. N. Gibbens (1912–83): Academic and teacher'. *The Journal of Forensic Psychiatry*, Vol. 5, No. 3 (1994), pp. 551–68.

126 Ibid., p. 553.

127 Ibid., p. 554–5.

128 Moss, Pamela, 'Shifting from nervous to normal through love machines: Battle exhaustion, military psychiatrists and emotionally traumatized soldiers in World War II', *Emotion, Space and Society* Vol. 10 (2014), pp. 63–70, pp. 63–4.

129 Robertson, 'Pioneers in forensic psychiatry. Professor T. C. N. Gibbens (1912–83)', p. 556. See Worldcat reference http://www.worldcat.org/title/psychology-of-the-prisoner-of-war/oclc/54335765. Gibbens also published an article on the

psychological effects of captivity. Gibbens, T. C. N. 'The Prisoner's View of Time—By a Former Prisoner of War.' *The Prison Journal*, 41.2, 1961, pp. 46–9.

130 Robertson. 'Pioneers in forensic psychiatry. Professor T. C. N. Gibbens (1912–83)', p. 555.

131 E. T. Perry, The War Office (Cas. P.W.) to Duncan Grant, September 1944, Army Personnel Records.

Chapter 7

1 'First Jamaican to be Captured by the Germans Returns Home. Patrick Nelson tells of his experiences in the notorious "Stalag 8B", Silesian Prison Camp.' The *Gleaner*, 10 June 1945.

2 Ibid.

3 E. C. Gepp, director of Prisoners of war, War Office, to Duncan Grant, September 1944, Tate Archives.

4 'British Prisoners On Way Home. From our Special Correspondent.' *The Times*, 12 September 1944, p. 4; 'More Repatriates Home. From our Correspondent.' *The Times*, 18 September 1944, p. 2.

5 'Repatriates Due To-Day.' *The Times*, 15 September 1944, p. 4.

6 E. C. Gepp, director of Prisoners of war, War Office, to Duncan Grant, September 1944, Tate Archives.

7 Ibid.

8 Army Form B200B Statement of Service, Patrick Nelson, Army Personnel Records.

9 Evelyn Butterfield, personal assistant for Prisoners of war, West India Committee, 16 October 1944, Tate Archives.

10 Bell, Amy H. *London Was Ours: Diaries and Memoirs of the London Blitz*. London: I.B. Tauris, 2008

11 Patrick Nelson to Paymaster, Pioneer Records Office, Bournemouth, Army Personnel Records, 30 November 1944.

12 Patrick Nelson to Duncan Grant, late 1944, Tate Archives.

13 Patrick Nelson to Duncan Grant, 12 November 1944, Tate Archives.

14 Surrey, England, Electoral Registers, 1832–1945, ancestry.co.uk.

15 Ibid.

16 Patrick Nelson to Duncan Grant, 8 November 1944, Tate Archives.

17 Patrick Nelson to Duncan Grant, 12 November 1944, Tate Archives.

18 Leopold Nelson to Duncan Grant, 15 January 1945, Tate Archives.

19 Patrick Nelson to Duncan Grant, 12 November 1944, Tate Archives.

20 Patrick Nelson to Duncan Grant, 8 November 1944, Tate Archives.

21 Ibid.

22 Patrick Nelson to Duncan Grant, 12 November 1944, Tate Archives.

23 Ibid.

24 Patrick Nelson to Duncan Grant, 21 November 1944, Tate Archives.

25 'First Jamaican to be Captured by the Germans Returns Home. Patrick Nelson tells of his experiences in the notorious "Stalag 8B", Silesian Prison Camp'. The *Gleaner*, 10 June 1945.

26 Patrick Nelson to Duncan Grant, 10 December 1944, Tate Archives.

27 'First Jamaican to be Captured by the Germans Returns Home. Patrick Nelson tells of his experiences in the notorious "Stalag 8B", Silesian Prison Camp'. The *Gleaner*, 10 June 1945.

28 Patrick Nelson to Duncan Grant, 12 November 1944, Tate Archives.

29 Patrick Nelson to Duncan Grant, 8 November 1944, Tate Archives.

30 Patrick Nelson to Duncan Grant, 21 November 1944, Tate Archives.

31 Ibid.

32 Patrick Nelson to Duncan Grant, 21 November 1944, Tate Archives.

33 Patrick Nelson to Duncan Grant, 10 December 1944, Tate Archives.

34 Patrick Nelson to Duncan Grant, 7 January 1945, Tate Archives.

35 Patrick Nelson to Duncan Grant, 8 November 1944, Tate Archives.

36 Patrick Nelson to (military officials, probably the Pioneer Corps Record Office), 14 November 1944, Army Personnel Records.

37 Patrick Nelson to Pioneer Records Office, Bournemouth, Army Personnel Records, 30 November 1944.

38 Patrick Nelson to Duncan Grant, 10 December 1944, Tate Archives.

39 Memo from P. C. Field, Lieut. Col. RAMC, Queen Alexandra's Military Hospital to Officer i/c Records, Pioneer Corps, Bournemouth, 9 December 1944, Army Personnel Records.

40 'Editorial notes', *The Journal of the Royal Institute of Public Health and Hygiene*, Vol. 8 (1945), p. 139.

41 Moss, Pamela. 'Shifting from nervous to normal through love machines: Battle exhaustion, military psychiatrists and emotionally traumatized soldiers in World War II', *Emotion, Space and Society* Vol. 10 (2014), pp. 63–70, p. 67.

42 Patrick Nelson to Duncan Grant, 9 May 1946, Tate Archives.

43 Patrick Nelson to Duncan Grant, 31 December 1944, Tate Archives.

44 Patrick Nelson to Duncan Grant, 22 February 1945, Tate Archives.

45 Patrick Nelson to Duncan Grant, 4 March 1945, Tate Archives.

46 Patrick Nelson to Duncan Grant, 18 March 1945, Tate Archives.

47 Patrick Nelson to Duncan Grant, 19 March 1945, Tate Archives.

48 Ibid.

49 UK, Navy Lists, 1888–1970 for Lyulph Henry Victor Owen Stanley, via ancestry. com.

50 Patrick Nelson to Duncan Grant, 19 March 1945, Tate Archives.

51 Ibid.

52 Patrick Nelson to Duncan Grant, 26 March 1945, Tate Archives.

53 Ibid.

54 Ibid.

55 Ibid.

56 Patrick Nelson to Duncan Grant, 8 April 1945, Tate Archives.

57 Vickers, Emma. 'Queer sex in the metropolis? Place, subjectivity and the Second World War'. *Feminist Review*, Vol. 96, urban spaces (2010), pp. 58–73.

58 Ibid., p. 59.

59 Ibid., p. 62.

60 Ibid., p. 64.

61 Patrick Nelson to Duncan Grant, 11 April 1945, Tate Archives.

62 A. M. Khachadourian, Colonial Office, to Patrick Nelson, 5 April 1945, Tate Archives.

63 Patrick Nelson to Duncan Grant, 7 August 1945, Tate Archives.

64 Patrick Nelson to Duncan Grant, 30 February 1945, Tate Archives.

65 Army Form B200B Statement of Service, Patrick Nelson, Army Personnel Records.

66 Card with information on Patrick Nelson, Army Personnel Records.

67 New York Passenger Lists, 1820–1957, Record for Leopold St Patrick Nelson, 26 April 1945, via ancestry.co.uk.

68 Patrick Nelson to Duncan Grant, sent from Kingston, Jamaica, 20 June 1945, Tate Archives.

69 Patrick Nelson to Duncan Grant, 24 July 1945 and 7 August 1945, Tate Archives.

70 Patrick Nelson to Duncan Grant, sent from Kingston, Jamaica, 20 June 1945, Tate Archives.

71 Ibid.

72 Patrick Nelson to Duncan Grant, 7 August 1945, Tate Archives.

73 Ibid.

74 Patrick Nelson to Duncan Grant, 22 October 1945, Tate Archives.

75 Munroe, Trevor and Arnold Bertram. *Adult Suffrage and Political Administrations in Jamaica, 1944-2002: A Compendium and Commentary*. Kingston, Jamaica: Ian Randle, 2006, p. 58.

76 Hill, Robert A and Marcus Garvey. *The Marcus Garvey and Universal Negro Improvement Association Papers: Vol. 1*. Berkeley: University of California Press, 1983, p. 21, footnote1.

77 Munroe and Bertram. *Adult Suffrage and Political Administrations in Jamaica*, pp. 58–9.

78 Ibid., p. 58.

79 Ibid., p. 59.

80 Patsides, Nicholas. 'Marcus Garvey, Race Idealism and His Vision of Jamaican Self-government'. *Caribbean Quarterly*, 51.1 (2005): 37–52, p. 37.

81 Munroe and Bertram. *Adult Suffrage and Political Administrations in Jamaica*, p. 61.

82 Gregg, V. M. '"How with this rage shall beauty hold a plea": The Writings of Miss Amy Beckford Bailey as Moral Education in the Era of Jamaican Nation Building'. *Small Axe*, vol. 11 no. 2, 2007, pp. 16–33, p. 17.

83 Munroe and Bertram. *Adult Suffrage and Political Administrations in Jamaica*, pp. 67–8.

84 Ibid., p. 68.

85 Ibid., p. 69.

86 Ibid., p. 69.

87 Ibid., p. 70.

88 Ibid., p. 71.

89 Ibid., p. 71.

90 Ibid., p. 97.

91 Patrick Nelson to Duncan Grant, 7 January 1945, Tate Archives.

92 Patrick Nelson to Duncan Grant, 26 June 1950, Tate Archives.

93 Patrick Nelson to Duncan Grant, no date, approx August 1951, Tate Archives.

94 Patrick Nelson to Duncan Grant, 24 July 1945, Tate Archives.

95 Ivor Cummings took part in the episode 'Soldiers of the Crown'. Quoted in Bourne, Stephen. *The Motherland Calls: Britain's Black Servicemen & Women, 1939-45*. Stroud, Gloucestershire: The History Press, 2012, p. 16.

96 See Charlie Whitham. 'The thin end of the wedge: the British Foreign Office, the West Indies and avoiding the Destroyers-Bases Deal, 1938–1940', *Journal of Transatlantic Studies*, 2013, 11:3, 234–48.

97 Ibid.

98 Munroe and Bertram. *Adult Suffrage and Political Administrations in Jamaica, 1944-2002: A Compendium and Commentary*, p. 79.

99 13140/40, Cypher Telegram, governor – Jamaica (Jamaica is underlined, chosen from list of: Jamaica, Trinidad, Leewards, Windwards, Bahamas and British Guiana), sent6 September 1940, 16.15 hrs, document number 1 in CO323/1808/17, Leases to the USA, TNA

100 For more information on the US land leases, see Baptiste, Fitzroy A. War, *Cooperation, and Conflict: The European Possessions in the Caribbean, 1939-1945*. New York: Greenwood Press, 1988.

101 Patrick Nelson to Duncan Grant, 24 July 1945, Tate Archives.

102 Patrick Nelson to Duncan Grant, 4 December 1947, Tate Archives.

103 Patrick Nelson to Duncan Grant, 26 June 1950, Tate Archives.

104 Patrick Nelson to Duncan Grant, 30 January 1055, Tate Archives.

105 Patrick Nelson to Duncan Grant, 7 August 1945, Tate Archives.

106 LaCroix, Hal and Jorg Meyer. *Journey Out of Darkness: The Real Story of American Heroes in Hitler's POW Camps: an Oral History.* Westport, Conn: Praeger Security International, 2007, p. 20.

107 Patrick Nelson to Duncan Grant, 7 August 1945, Tate Archives.

108 Patrick Nelson to Duncan Grant, 6 December 1945, Tate Archives.

109 Ibid.

Chapter 8

1 Patrick Nelson to Duncan Grant, 24 July 1945, Tate Archives.

2 Ibid.

3 Patrick Nelson to Duncan Grant, 20 June 1945, Tate Archives.

4 Patrick Nelson to Duncan Grant, 24 July 1945, Tate Archives.

5 Patrick Nelson to Duncan Grant, 9 March 1950, Tate Archives.

6 Patrick Nelson to Duncan Grant, 6 December 1945, Tate Archives.

7 Ibid.

8 For more information on the murals, see the Berwick Church website http://www.berwickchurch.org.uk.

9 Patrick Nelson to Duncan Grant, 26 June 1950, Tate Archives.

10 Patrick Nelson to Duncan Grant, 21 November 1945, Tate Archives.

11 Patrick Nelson to Duncan Grant, 9 May 1946, Tate Archives.

12 Howard, *Kingston: A Cultural and Literary History*, p. 199.

13 Earl McKenzie calls the work prophetic as 'three years after its completion the island was plunged into a series of riots which protested against the exploitation of the black working class. These riots led to the establishment of the main political parties, the trade unions, and eventually self-government.' Earl McKenzie, 'The Cultural Importance of Edna Manley's Art', *Caribbean Quarterly*, Vol. 52, No. 4 (December 2006), pp. 49–56.

14 'List of pictures, etc, presented to the Institute by Mrs Edna Manley and others in 1937', National Library of Jamaica, List of exhibitions, 1939–1944, NLJ, MST 156b, Vol 1. For more information, see the National Gallery of Jamaica website https://nationalgalleryofjamaica.wordpress.com/tag/london-group/.

15 'Governor Sees Prints and Drawings at the Institute', the *Gleaner*, 17 December 1937.

16 Patrick Nelson to Duncan Grant, 9 May 1946, Tate Archives.

17 Ibid.

18 Patrick Nelson to Duncan Grant, no date, approx late 1946, Tate Archives.

19 Ibid.

20 Duncan Grant to Patrick Nelson, 12 August 1947, Tate Archives.

21 Ibid.

22 London, England, Electoral Registers, 1832–1965; 1947; 77 Wimpole Street, via ancestry.co.uk.

23 Leaford Williams in the New York, Passenger Lists, 1820–1957, via ancestry.co.uk

24 Mead, Matthew. 'Empire Windrush: The cultural memory of an imaginary arrival', *Journal of Postcolonial Writing*, Vol. 45, No. 2 (2009), pp. 137–49, p. 143.

25 Ibid., pp. 142–4.

26 Ibid., p. 144.

27 Patrick Nelson to Duncan Grant, 4 December 1947, Tate Archives.

28 Ibid.

29 Patrick Nelson to Duncan Grant, 4 December 1947, Tate Archives.

30 Patrick Nelson to Duncan Grant, 9 May 1946, Tate Archives.

31 Patrick Nelson to Duncan Grant, 9 February 1948, Tate Archives.

32 Ibid.

33 Patrick Nelson to Duncan Grant, 13 or 15 February 1949, Tate Archives.

34 Ibid.

35 Ibid.

36 Patrick Nelson to Duncan Grant, 26 June 1950, Tate Archives.

37 Patrick Nelson to Duncan Grant, 6 December 1945, Tate Archives.

38 Ibid.

39 Patrick Nelson to Duncan Grant, 26 June 1950, Tate Archives.

40 Ibid.

41 Patrick Nelson to Duncan Grant, 20 March 1951, Tate Archives.

42 Ibid.

43 Patrick Nelson to Duncan Grant, 17 April 1953, Tate Archives.

44 Patrick Nelson to Duncan Grant, 20 March 1951, Tate Archives.

45 Patrick Nelson to Duncan Grant, 4 April 1951, Tate Archives.

46 Ibid.

47 Longshore, David. *Encyclopedia of Hurricanes, Typhoons, and Cyclones*. New edition. New York: Facts on File, 2008, p. 92.

48 Patrick Nelson to Duncan Grant, no date, approx August 1951, Tate Archives.

49 Ibid.

50 Ibid.

51 Patrick Nelson to Duncan Grant, 12 February 1952, Tate Archives.

52 Patrick Nelson to Duncan Grant, 17 March 1953, Tate Archives.

53 Ibid.

54 Patrick Nelson to Duncan Grant, 17 April 1953, Tate Archives.

55 Letter from colonial secretary's office to Patrick Nelson, 15 April 1953, enclosed in letter from Patrick Nelson to Duncan Grant, approximately 1953, Tate Archives.

56 Patrick Nelson to Duncan Grant, 2 July 1954, Tate Archives.

57 Patrick Nelson to Duncan Grant, 30 January 1955, Tate Archives.

58 Ibid.

59 Patrick Nelson to Duncan Grant, 24 March 1955, Tate Archives.

60 Ibid.

61 W. G. Bowe, Capt. For Command Paymaster, Caribbean Area to Patrick Nelson, enclosed in Patrick Nelson to Duncan Grant, 31 August 1955, Tate Archives.

62 Patrick Nelson to Duncan Grant, 31 August 1955, Tate Archives.

63 Ibid.

64 Ibid.

65 Patrick Nelson to Duncan Grant, no date, approx August 1951, Tate Archives.

66 For information on the Wolfenden Committee and Report, see Lewis, Brian. *Wolfenden's Witnesses: Homosexuality in Postwar Britain*. Basingstoke, Hampshire: Palgrave Macmillan, 2016.

67 'Face the Facts', the *Gleaner*, 12 December 1957.

68 The *Gleaner*, 22 February 1954.

69 The *Gleaner*, 18 February 1954.

70 Patrick Nelson to Duncan Grant, 8 April 1945, Tate Archives.

71 Patrick Nelson to Duncan Grant, 31 August 1955, Tate Archives.

72 Ibid.

73 Patrick Nelson to Duncan Grant, 30 January 1955, Tate Archives.

74 Patrick Nelson to Duncan Grant, 6 January 1955, Tate Archives.

75 Patrick Nelson to Duncan Grant, 30 January 1955, Tate Archives.

76 Patrick Nelson to Duncan Grant, 10 March 1958 and 8 March 1959, Tate Archives. See Mayor, Edward (archival and visual research by Judith Robinson). *The Duncan Grant Murals in Lincoln Cathedral*. Lincoln: Lincoln Cathedral Publications, 2001, p. 42.

77 Patrick Nelson to Duncan Grant, 4 April 1956, Tate Archives.

78 Taylor, Frank Fonda. *To Hell with Paradise: A History of the Jamaican Tourist Industry*. Pittsburgh: University of Pittsburgh Press, 1993, p. 156.

79 Ibid., p. 157.

80 Ibid., pp. 158–9.

81 'Another Jamaica-Canada air link opens', the *Gleaner*, 25 November 1956.

82 Taylor. *To Hell with Paradise*, p. 162.

83 Ibid., p. 163.

84 Ibid., p. 170.

85 Patrick Nelson to Duncan Grant, 7 June 1957, Tate Archives.

86 Patrick Nelson to Duncan Grant, 10 March 1958, Tate Archives.

87 Patrick Nelson to Duncan Grant, 8 March 1959, Tate Archives.

88 Patrick Nelson to Duncan Grant, 7 April 1960, Tate Archives.

89 Susan Lewis, 'From Runaway Bay to Ocho Rios. It's like a world trip', the *Gleaner*, 9 March 1957.

90 'Burton relaxes at Jamaica Inn', the *Gleaner*, 12 June 1956.

91 Susan Lewis, 'From Runaway Bay to Ocho Rios. It's like a world trip', the *Gleaner*, 9 March 1957.

92 Susan Lewis, 'Ocho Rios: "Strictly for Tourists"', the *Gleaner*, 4 September 1956.

93 Ibid.

94 Ibid.

95 Susan Lewis, 'Ocho Rios for middleclass. A prison without bars', 28 August 1956.

96 Ibid.

97 Patrick Nelson to Duncan Grant, 21 June 1956, Tate Archives.

98 Patrick Nelson to Duncan Grant, 7 June 1957, Tate Archives.

Chapter 9

1 Chamberlain, Mary. 'Introduction', in Chamberlain, Mary (ed.). *Caribbean Migration: Globalised Identities*. London: Routledge, 1998, p. 6.

2 Brown, Lawrence. 'Contexts of Migration and Diasporic Identities' in Tracey Skelton (ed.). *In Introduction to the Pan-Caribbean*. Hodder & Stoughton, 2004, p. 128.

3 Carter, Bob, Clive Harris and Shirley Joshi, 'The 1951-55 Conservative Government and the Racialization of Black Immigration' in Winston James and Clive Harris (eds). *Inside Babylon: The Caribbean Diaspora in Britain*. Verso, 1993, p. 56.

4 Chamberlain, 'Introduction', p. 10.

5 Byron, Margaret. 'Migration, work and gender: the case of post-war labour migration from the Caribbean to Britain' in Chamberlain, Mary (ed.). *Caribbean Migration: Globalised Identities*. London: Routledge, 1998, p. 226.

6 'Black Nurses: The Women Who Saved The NHS;' http://www.bbc.co.uk/mediacentre/proginfo/2016/47/black-nurses.

7 A number of studies were produced in 1998, to mark of the fiftieth anniversary of the arrival of the *Empire Windrush*. For example, see Black Cultural Archives, *The Windrush Legacy: Memories of Britain's Post-War Caribbean Immigrants*. London: Black Cultural Archives, 1998 and Phillips, Mike and Trevor Phillips. *Windrush: The Irresistible Rise of Multi-Racial Britain*. London: Harpercollins, 1998.

8 Msiska , Mpalive-Hangson, 'Sam Selvon's *The Lonely Londoners* and the structure of Black metropolitan life', *African and Black Diaspora: An International Journal*, Vol. 2, No. 1 (2009), pp. 5–27, p. 5.

9 Selvon, Samuel. *The Lonely Londoners*. First published 1956. London: Longman, 2004, p. 23.

10 Ellis, Nadia. 'Black Migrants, White Queers and the Archive of Inclusion in Postwar London', *Interventions: International Journal of Postcolonial Studies* (2015), DOI: 10.1080/1369801X.2014.994547, p. 8.

11 Ibid., p. 3.

12 Mai, Nicola and Russell King. 'Love, Sexuality and Migration: Mapping the Issue(s)', *Mobilities*, Vol. 4, No. 3 (2009), pp. 295–307, p. 297.

13 Fortier, Anne-Marie, 'Coming home' Queer migrations and multiple evocations of home, *European Journal of Cultural Studies*, Vol. 4, No. 4 (2001), pp. 405–24.

14 Manalansan, Martin F., 'Queer Intersections: Sexuality and Gender in Migration Studies', *International Migration Review*, Vol. 40, No. 1, Gender and Migration Revisited (Spring, 2006), pp. 224–49, p. 243.

15 Patrick Nelson to Duncan Grant, April 1961, Tate Archives.

16 Patrick Nelson to Duncan Grant, 8 May 1961, Tate Archives.

17 See http://www.qvsr.org.uk/.

18 Patrick Nelson to Duncan Grant, no date, approximately 1960–1, Tate Archives.

19 Ibid.

20 Patrick Nelson to Duncan Grant, 5 May 1962, Tate Archives.

21 Ibid.

22 Patrick Nelson to Duncan Grant, undated, approximately 1962, Tate Archives.

23 Ibid.

24 Patrick Nelson to Duncan Grant, 21 July 1962, Tate Archives.

25 Patrick Nelson to Duncan Grant, 12 November 1962, Tate Archives.

26 Ibid.

27 Jane Hamlett and Rebecca Preston, '"A veritable Palace for the Hard-working Labourer?" Spaces, material culture and inmate experience in London's Rowton Houses, 1892-1918', in Jane Hamlett, Lesley Hoskins and Rebecca Preston (eds). *Residential Institutions in Britain, 1725–1970.* Routledge, 2015, p. 93.

28 Ibid., p. 93.

29 Orwell, George. *Down and Out in Paris and London*. London: Gollancz, 1933.

30 http://www.madness.co.uk/songs/one-better-day/.

31 Various electoral registers for Arlington Road, via ancestry.co.uk.

32 Hamlett and Preston, '"A veritable Palace for the Hard-working Labourer?"', p. 105.

33 London, England, Electoral Registers, 1832–1965, showing Arlington House, 1961, via ancestry.co.uk.

34 Morris, Terence and Pauline Morris, 'The Experience of Imprisonment', *The British Journal of Criminology*, Vol. 2, No. 4 (April 1962), pp. 337–60 pp. 338–9.

35 Pankhurst, Richard. 'An Early Somali Autobiography', *Africa: Rivista trimestrale di studi e documentazione dell'Istituto italiano per l'Africa e l'Oriente*, Vol. 32, No. 3 (1977), pp. 355–84, p. 379.

36 Ibid., p. 380.

37 Kavanagh, Patrick. *The Green Fool. [autobiographical Reminiscences.].* Michael Joseph: London, 1938.

38 'Appointments And Situations-Public: Business: Domestic.' *The Times*, 2 December 1937, p. 3.

39 London, England, Electoral Registers, 1832–1965 for Onnik Vosguerchian; 1911 England Census for Onnik Vosguerchian, and Onnik Vosguerchian in the British Army WWI Service Records, 1914–1920 via ancestry.co.uk.

40 Margaret Eden, 'A Modern Observation Ward and the Psychiatric Social Worker', *British Journal of Psychiatric Social Work*, Vol. 3, No. 1 (1955–1956), pp. 13–18, p. 18.

41 http://hansard.millbanksystems.com/lords/1961/jun/13/criminal-justice-bill#S5LV0232P0_19610613_HOL_177.

42 Spalding, *Grant.*, p. 429.

43 Ibid., pp. 428–9.

44 Ibid., p. 432.

45 Ibid., p. 433.

46 Ibid., p. 434.

47 http://www.christies.com/lotfinder/paintings/duncan-grant-portrait-of-pat-nelson-5569405-details.aspx?from=salesummary&intObjectID=5569405&sid=50c491dd-27b0-4939-9b61-ec58b3f39d48.

48 Patrick Nelson to Duncan Grant, 12 November 1962, Tate Archives.

49 Edkins, Jenny. *Trauma and the Memory of Politics*. Cambridge: Cambridge University Press, 2003, p. 57.

50 Ibid., p. 57.

51 Ibid., p. 60.

52 Ibid., p. 64.

53 Ibid., p. 64.

54 Ibid., p. 71.

55 Ibid., p. 72.

56 Olusoga, David. *The World's War. Forgotten Soldiers of Empire*, p. 401.

57 'War Dead Honored in Europe', *The Hartford Courant*, 12 November 1962, p. 13b

58 Patrick Nelson to Duncan Grant, 4 May 1963, Tate Archives.

59 Letter to the editor from Richie Riley, Seymour Place, *The Stage*, 30 October 1952 and London, England, Electoral Registers, 1832–1965 via ancestry.co.uk.

60 Richie Riley interviewed, Black Cultural Archives, digitized as part of the Moving Here project, Catalogue Reference: AMBH/BCA RROT/BCA. Transcript of interview.

61 Ibid.

62 Ibid.

63 Ibid.

64 Ellis. *Territories of the Soul*, pp. 142–3.

65 Cited in ibid, p. 144.

66 Patrick Nelson to Duncan Grant, 7 June 1963, Tate Archives.

67 Ibid.

68 Richie Riley to Duncan Grant, 17 June 1963, Tate Archives.

69 Copy of 1963 Death Certificate for Patrick Leopold Nelson, General Register Office.

70 Richie Riley to Duncan Grant, 4 August 1963, Tate Archives.

Epilogue

1 http://www.bbc.co.uk/programmes/b01mn4v4 For a discussion on this programme in relation to black history, see Miranda Kaufmann's website http://www.mirandakaufmann.com/blog/presenting-the-black-past-how-history-must-change-the-media.

2 *Queer Black Spaces*, The Equiano Centre http://www.ucl.ac.uk/equianocentre/projects/qbs.

3 Ajamu X, Topher Campbell and Mary Stevens, 'Love and Lubrication in the Archives, or rukus!: A Black Queer Archive for the United Kingdom', *Archivaria, The Journal of the Association of Canadian Archivists*, Vol. 68 (Fall 2009), pp. 271–94, http://journals.sfu.ca/archivar/index.php/archivaria/article/view/13240/14558.

Bibliography

Primary sources

Archival

Tate Archives and Library: Duncan Grant collection, Charleston Trust; Barbara Ker-Seymer collection

National Library of Jamaica: 'Boy Scouts Association of Jamaica, Report of a meeting of the Committee of the Council held on December 13th, 1923', Pamphlet, Pam 369.43; National Library of Jamaica, List of exhibitions, 1939–1944, MST 156b, Vol 1.

The Jamaica Archives: The Rutty Family by Frank Rutty 7/266; *The Handbook of Jamaica*, Constant Spring Hotel, Strike of employees, 1939,1B/5/77/130.

Ministry of Defence Publication Scheme: Army Personnel Records for Patrick Nelson.

The Jamaica Archives: The Handbook of Jamaica, 1910; Prisoners of War (Jamaicans) – List of, IB/5/77/3.

Bangor Archives: Penrhos collection: Penrhos VIII and Penrhos VII; Geoffrey Butterworth, *The Story of Penrhos*, 4 November 1968

Anglesey Archives: Hugh Jones interview transcript; Cyril Parry interview transcript

The National Archives, UK: MEPO, WO and CO records

Friends' House Library, London: Committee Records, Colour Bar Committee, 1929–31

General Register Office: Copy of 1963 Death Certificate for Patrick Leopold Nelson

Black Cultural Archives: Richie Riley interview, digitised as part of the Moving Here project, Catalogue Reference: AMBH/BCA RROT/BCA

British Museum Central Archive: Claude McKay reader registration letters; Ruth Anna Fisher reader registration letters, 1920

Autobiographies and memoirs

Daley, Harry. *This Small Cloud: A Personal Memoir*. London: Weidenfeld and Nicolson, 1986.

Grant, Cy. *A Member of the Royal Air Force of Indeterminate Race: Wartime Memoirs of a Former RAF Navigator & POW*. Bognor Regis: Woodfield, 2006, revised edition 2012.

Hale, Kathleen. *A Slender Reputation: An Autobiography*. London: Frederick Warne, 1994.

Kavanagh, Patrick. *The Green Fool. [autobiographical Reminiscences.]*. London: Michael
     Joseph, 1938.
McKay, Claude. *A Long Way from Home*. First published 1937 (2007 edition: edited and
     introduction by Gene A. Jarrett). New Brunswick, NJ: Rutgers University Press, 2007.
Thompson, Dudley with Margaret C. Thompson. *From Kingston to Kenya: The Making
     of a Pan-Africanist Lawyer*. Dover, MA: Majority Press, 1993.

Contemporary journals and newspapers

The Gleaner
The Sunday Gleaner
Illustrated London News
The Times
The Lancet
The Stage
The Clarion
The Chicago Defender
Public Opinion
Holyhead and Anglesey Mail
Hartlepool Mail
The Evening News (Portsmouth)
Surrey Mirror and County Post
Buckingham Advertiser and North Bucks Free Press
The Western Morning News and Daily Gazette
The Evening Telegraph (Dundee)
Derby Daily Telegraph
The Athenaeum
The Melody Maker
The Crisis: A Record of the Darker Races
The Keys: The Official Organ of the League of Coloured Peoples, 1933–9.
The Manchester Guardian
The Lincolnshire Standard
The Journal of the Royal Institute of Public Health and Hygiene
The Hartford Courant

Contemporary books and reports

Cundall, Frank. *Historic Jamaica*. London: Pub. for the Institute of Jamaica by the West
     India Committee, 1915.
Eden, Margaret, 'A Modern Observation Ward and the Psychiatric Social Worker',
     British Journal of Psychiatric Social Work, vol. 3, no. 1 (1955–6), pp. 13–18.

The Indian Students' Union and Hostel, London – Sixteenth Annual Report, 1935.

Morris, Terence and Pauline Morris. 'The Experience of Imprisonment', *The British Journal of Criminology*, vol. 2, no. 4 (April 1962), pp. 337–60.

Moyne, Walter E. G. *West India Royal Commission Report*. London: H.M.S.O, 1945.

Orwell, George. *Down and Out in Paris and London*. London: Gollancz, 1933.

Waldemar-Leverton, Edith. *Servants and Their Duties: A Helpful Manual for Mistress and Servant*. London: C. Arthur Pearson, 1912.

Databases and online material

Legacies of British Slave-ownership database, https://www.ucl.ac.uk/lbs

Curt Teich Collection, Lake County Discovery Museum http://www.lcfpd.org/museum/teich/collections

Gay Freedom Movement in Jamaica Archives, Digital Library of the Caribbean, dloc.com/icirngfm

Ancestry, http://home.ancestry.co.uk/

Bangor University, Penrhos Manuscripts, Administrative and biographical history, http://www.archiveswales.org.uk/anw/get_collection.php?inst_id=39&coll_id=10886&expand=

'Obituary: Ivor Cummings' by Val Wilmer, *The Independent*, 4 December 1992 http://www.independent.co.uk/news/people/obituary-ivor-cummings-1561396.html

'The Image of the Black in Western Art', http://www.imageoftheblack.com/

Queen Victoria Seamen's Rest, www.qvsr.org.uk/wp/

Caroline Bressey, 'The Politics of Plantations. Laura and Oak Alley Plantation on the Great River Road', The Equiano Centre Black Presence blog, April 2012 https://www.ucl.ac.uk/equianocentre/blackpresenceblog/previous-posts/apr-2012

'Spaces of Black Modernism', http://www.tate.org.uk/whats-on/tate-britain/display/bp-spotlight-spaces-black-modernism-london-1919-39

'Convention relative to the Treatment of Prisoners of War. Geneva, 27 July 1929', https://www.icrc.org/ihl/INTRO/305?OpenDocument

Black Chronicles II, http://autograph-abp.co.uk/exhibitions/black-chronicles-ii

Cy Grant Trust project and website http://cygrant.com/

The Clarion, http://www.lamsdorf.com/the-clarion.html

Berwick Church website http://www.berwickchurch.org.uk

National Gallery of Jamaica, https://nationalgalleryofjamaica.wordpress.com/tag/london-group/

Madness, http://www.madness.co.uk/songs/one-better-day/

Hansard, http://hansard.millbanksystems.com/lords/1961/jun/13/criminal-justice-bill#S5LV0232P0_19610613_HOL_177

Christie's, http://www.christies.com/lotfinder/paintings/duncan-grant-portrait-of-pat-nelson-5569405-details.aspx?from=salesummary&intObjectID=5569405&sid=50c491dd-27b0-4939-9b61-ec58b3f39d48

The Equiano Centre, http://www.ucl.ac.uk/equianocentre/projects/docl

Family Search, www.familysearch.org

Find My Past http://www.findmypast.co.uk/

Presenting the Past – How the Media Changes History, http://www.bbc.co.uk/programmes/b01mn4v4

Miranda Kaufmann, http://www.mirandakaufmann.com/blog/presenting-the-black-past-how-history-must-change-the-media

The Charleston Papers https://janus.lib.cam.ac.uk/db/node.xsp?id=EAD/GBR/0272/PP/CHA

Secondary sources

Ajamu, X., Topher Campbell and Mary Stevens, 'Love and Lubrication in the Archives, or rukus!: A Black Queer Archive for the United Kingdom', *Archivaria, The Journal of the Association of Canadian Archivists*, vol. 68 (Fall 2009), pp. 271–94.

Adi, Hakim. *Pan-africanism and Communism: The Communist International, Africa and the Diaspora, 1919-1939*. Trenton, NJ: Africa World Press, 2013.

Adi, Hakim. 'The Comintern and Black Workers in Britain and France 1919-37'. *Immigrants & Minorities*, vol. 28, no. 2–3 (2010), pp. 224–45.

Adi, Hakim. *West Africans in Britain, 1900-1960: Nationalism, Pan-Africanism, and Communism*. London: Lawrence & Wishart, 1998.

Adler, K. H. 'Indigènes after Indigènes: post-war France and its North African troops', *European Review of History: Revue européenne d'histoire*, vol. 20, no. 3 (2013).

Anand, Mulk R. *Conversations in Bloomsbury*. Second edition, Delhi: Oxford University Press, 1995.

Arts Council, Portraits by Duncan Grant: an Arts Council Exhibition. London: Arts Council, 1969.

Baptiste, Fitzroy A. *War, Cooperation, and Conflict: The European Possessions in the Caribbean, 1939-1945*. New York: Greenwood Press, 1988.

Bean, Dalea. '"This is an Empire War!": Contextualizing Issues of Britishness, Gender, and Jamaican Loyalty during World Wars I and II', in Matthews, Jodie, and Daniel Travers (eds). *Islands and Britishness: A Global Perspective*. Newcastle upon Tyne: Cambridge Scholars Publishing, 2012.

Bell, Amy H. *London Was Ours: Diaries and Memoirs of the London Blitz*. London: I. B. Tauris, 2008.

Bindman, David, Henry L. Gates, and Karen C. C. Dalton (eds). *The Image of the Black in Western Art*. Cambridge, MA: Belknap Press of Harvard University Press, 2010.

Black Cultural Archives, *The Windrush Legacy: Memories of Britain's Post-War Caribbean Immigrants*. London: Black Cultural Archives, 1998.

Bourne, Stephen. *Black Poppies: Britain's Black Community and the Great War*. Stroud: History Press, 2014.

Bourne, Stephen. *The Motherland Calls: Britain's Black Servicemen & Women, 1939-45*. Stroud, Gloucestershire: The History Press, 2012.

Bourne, Stephen. *Elisabeth Welch: Soft Lights and Sweet Music*. Lanham, MD: Scarecrow Press, 2005.

Bressey, Caroline 'Looking for Work: The Black Presence in Britain 1860-1920' in Bressey, Caroline, and Hakim Adi (eds). *Belonging in Europe: The African Diaspora and Work*. London: Routledge, 2011.

Brown, Lawrence. 'Contexts of Migration and Diasporic Identities' in Skelton, Tracey (ed.), *In Introduction to the Pan-Caribbean*. London Hodder & Stoughton, 2004.

Brown, Wayne. *Edna Manley: The Private Years, 1900-1938*. London: Deutsch, 1976.

Brown-Glaude, Winnifred R. *Higglers in Kingston: Women's Informal Work in Jamaica*. Nashville, TN: Vanderbilt Univ. Press, 2011.

Byron, Margaret. 'Migration, Work and Gender: The Case of Post-war Labour Migration from the Caribbean to Britain' in Chamberlain, Mary (ed.), *Caribbean Migration: Globalised Identities*. London: Routledge, 1998.

Campbell, Kofi Omoniyi Sylvanus. *The Queer Caribbean Speaks: Interviews with Writers, Artists, and Activists*. New York, NY: Palgrave Macmillan, 2014.

Chamberlain, Mary. 'Introduction', in Chamberlain, Mary (ed.), *Caribbean Migration: Globalised Identities*. London: Routledge, 1998.

Carter, Bob, Clive Harris and Shirley Joshi. 'The 1951-55 Conservative Government and the Racialization of Black Immigration', in James, Winston, and Clive Harris (eds). *Inside Babylon: The Caribbean Diaspora in Britain*. New York Verso, 1993.

Clarke, Colin and David Howard. 'Colour, Race and Space: Residential Segregation in Kingston, Jamaica, in the Late Colonial Period', Caribbean Geography, vol. 10 (March 1999), p. 1.

Clarke, Colin and David Howard. 'Race and Religious Pluralism in Kingston, Jamaica', *Population, Space and Place*, vol. 11 (2005), pp. 119–36.

Cocks, Catherine. *Tropical Whites: The Rise of the Tourist South in the Americas*. Philadelphia: University of Pennsylvania Press, 2013.

Cook, Matt. *Queer Domesticities: Homosexuality and Home Life in Twentieth-Century London*. Basingstoke and New York: Palgrave Macmillan, 2014.

Cooper, Wayne F. *Claude Mckay: Rebel Sojourner in the Harlem Renaissance: A Biography*. Baton Rouge: Louisiana State University Press, 1987, paperback 1996.

Cresser, Julian. 'Lucas Cricket Club: A Pioneering Jamaican Cricket Club', *Jamaica Journal*, vol. 30, no. 3, (March/April 2007), pp. 24–7.

Cresser, Julian. 'Sport and Integration: Cricket in Jamaica, 1880-1910', *The Jamaica Historical Review*, vol. XXIV (2009).

Dabydeen, David. *Hogarth's Blacks: Images of Blacks in Eighteenth Century English Art*. Athens: University of Georgia Press, 1987.

Damousi, Joy. *Colonial Voices: A Cultural History of English in Australia, 1840-1940.* Cambridge: Cambridge University Press, 2010.

Dann, Graham M. S. and Robert B. Potter. 'Supplanting the Planters: Hawking Heritage in Barbados', in Dann Graham, and A. V. Seaton (eds). *Slavery, Contested Heritage and Thanatourism*, New York: Haworth Hospitality Press, 2001.

Das, Santanu. 'Indian Sepoy Experience in Europe, 1914–18: Archive, Language, and Feeling', *Twentieth Century British History*, vol. 25, no. 3 (2014).

Deghy, Guy, and Keith Waterhouse. *Café Royal. Ninety Years of Bohemia, Etc.* [with Plates.]. London: Hutchinson, 1955.

Delap, Lucy. *Knowing Their Place: Domestic Service in Twentieth-Century Britain.* Oxford [etc.: Oxford University Press, 2011.

Desmarais, Jane, Martin Postle and William Vaughan (eds). *Model and supermodel: the artist's model in British art and culture.* Manchester: Manchester University Press, 2006.

Dodman, David. 'Post-independence Optimism and the Legacy of Waterfront Redevelopment in Kingston, Jamaica', *Cities*, vol. 24, no. 4 (2007), pp. 273–84.

Edkins, Jenny. *Trauma and the Memory of Politics.* Cambridge: Cambridge University Press, 2003.

Egan, Bill. *Florence Mills: Harlem Jazz Queen.* Lanham, MD: Scarecrow Press, 2004.

Ellis, Nadia. *Territories of the Soul: Queered Belonging in the Black Diaspora.* Durham: Duke University Press, 2015.

Ellis, Nadia. 'Black Migrants, White Queers and the Archive of Inclusion in Postwar London', *Interventions: International Journal of Postcolonial Studies* (2015), pp. 1–23.

Elwin, Rosamund (ed.), *Tongues on Fire: Caribbean Lesbian Lives and Stories.* Toronto: Women's Press, 1997.

Emery, Mary L. *Modernism, the Visual, and Caribbean Literature.* Cambridge: Cambridge University Press, 2007.

Faulkner, S. 'Homoexoticism: John Minton in London and Jamaica, 1950-1951', in Tim Barringer, Douglas Fordham, Geoff Quilley (eds). *Art and the British Empire*, Manchester: Manchester University Press, 2006.

Folly, Martin H. *The Palgrave Concise Historical Atlas of the Second World War.* New York: Palgrave Macmillan, 2004.

Fortier, Anne-Marie. '"Coming home" Queer Migrations and Multiple Evocations of Home, *European Journal of Cultural Studies*, vol. 4, no. 4 (2001), pp. 405-24.

Garnett, David. *Never be a Book Seller*, with a postscript by Richard Garnett and engraving by Howard Phipps. Denby Dale: The Fleece Press, 1995.

Gerzina, Gretchen Holbrook. 'Bushmen and Blackface: Bloomsbury and "Race"', *South Carolina Review*, vol. 38, no. 2 (2006), p. 46.

Gibbens, T. C. N. 'The Prisoner's View of Time – By a Former Prisoner of War.' *The Prison Journal*, vol. 41, no. 2 (1961), pp. 46–9.

Gilmore, Lois J. '"But Somebody you wouldn't Forget in a Hurry": Bloomsbury and the Contradictions of African Art', in Derek Ryan and Stella Bolaki (eds). *Contradictory*

Woolf: Selected Papers from the Twenty-First Annual International Conference on Virginia Woolf, Clemson, SC: Clemson University Digital Press, 2012.

Gilroy, Paul and Tate Gallery. *Picturing Blackness in British Art, 1700s-1990s: 28 November 1995-10 March, 1996, Tate Gallery*. London: Tate Pub, 1995.

Glave, Thomas. *Our Caribbean: A Gathering of Lesbian and Gay Writing from the Antilles*. Durham, N.C: Duke University Press, 2008.

Gregg, V. M. "'How with this Rage Shall Beauty Hold a Plea'": The Writings of Miss Amy Beckford Bailey as Moral Education in the Era of Jamaican Nation Building', *Small Axe*, vol. 11, no. 2 (2007), pp. 16–33.

Griffin, Nicholas, ed. *The Selected Letters of Bertrand Russell: Vol.1*. London, Allen Lane: The Penguin Press, 1992.

Hamlett, Jane and Rebecca Preston. "'A Veritable Palace for the Hard-working Labourer?" Spaces, Material Culture and Inmate Experience in London's Rowton Houses, 1892-1918', in Jane Hamlett, Lesley Hoskins and Rebecca Preston (eds). *Residential Institutions in Britain, 1725–1970*. London: Routledge, 2015.

Hickling, Frederick W. *Psychohistoriography: A Post-Colonial Psychoanalytic and Psychotherapeutic Model*. London: Jessica Kingsley Publishers, 2012.

Hill, Robert A., ed. *The Marcus Garvey and Universal Negro Improvement Association Papers: Vol. 1*. Berkeley: University of California Press, 1983.

Holmes, Colin. *Anti-semitism in British Society, 1876-1939*. London: Edward Arnold, 1979, Routledge, 2016.

Houlbrook, Matt and Chris Waters, 'The Heart in Exile: Detachment and Desire in 1950s London', *History Workshop Journal*, vol. 62, Autumn (2006), pp. 142–63.

Houlbrook, Matt. *Queer London: Perils and Pleasures in the Sexual Metropolis, 1918-1957*. Chicago: University of Chicago Press, 2005.

Howard, David. *Kingston: A Cultural and Literary History*. Kingston, Jamaica: Randle Publ; Oxford: Signal Books, 2005, p. 20.

Jackson, Ashley. 'Supplying War: The High Commission Territories' Military-Logistical Contribution in the Second World War', *The Journal of Military History*, vol. 66, no. 3 (July, 2002), pp. 719–60.

Jackson, Paul. *One of the Boys: Homosexuality in the Military During World War II*. Montréal: McGill-Queen's University Press, 2004.

Jay, John. *Facing Fearful Odds: My Father's Story of Captivity, Escape and Resistance 1940-1945*. South Yorkshire: Pen & Sword Books Ltd, 2014.

Jenkinson, Jacqueline. *Black 1919: Riots, Racism and Resistance in Imperial Britain*. Liverpool: Liverpool University Press, 2009.

Joannou, Maroula. 'Nancy Cunard's English Journey', *Feminist Review*, vol. 78 (2004), pp. 141–63.

Johnson, Howard. 'Cuban Immigrants in Jamaica, 1868–1898', *Immigrants & Minorities*, vol. 29, no. 1 (March 2011), pp. 1–32.

Johnson, Mark. *Caribbean Volunteers at War: The Forgotten Story of Britain's Own 'Tuskegee Airmen'*. Barnsley, UK: Pen & Sword Aviation, 2014.

Johnson, Michele A. '"Decent and Fair": Aspects of Domestic Service in Jamaica, 1920-1970', *The Journal of Caribbean History*, vol. 30 (1996), p. 1.

Jones, Alan W. *Lyulph Stanley: A Study in Educational Politics*. Waterloo, ON: Wilfrid Laurier University Press, 1979.

Kempadoo, Kamala. *Sexing the Caribbean: Gender, Race, and Sexual Labor*. New York: Routledge, 2008.

Killingray, David. 'Race and Rank in the British Army in the Twentieth Century', *Ethnic and Racial Studies*, vol. 10, no. 3 (1987), pp. 276–90.

Kochavi, Arieh J. *Confronting Captivity: Britain and the United States and Their POWs in Nazi Germany*. Chapel Hill: University of North Carolina Press, 2005.

Kochavi, Arieh J. 'Why None of Britain's Long-Term POWs in Nazi Germany Were Repatriated During World War II', *Canadian Journal of Hislory/Annales canadiennes d'histoire*, vol. XXXIX, April/avril (2004), pp. 63–85.

Kushner, Tony, and Katharine Knox. *Refugees in an Age of Genocide: Global, National and Local Perspectives During the Twentieth Century*. London: F. Cass, 1999.

Kushner, Tony. '"Without Intending any of the Most Undesirable Features of a Colour Bar": Race, Science, Europeanness and the British Armed Forces During the Twentieth Century', in Schaffer, Gavin (ed.), *Racializing the Soldier*. London: Routledge, 2013.

Kushner, Tony. *Remembering Refugees: Then and Now*. Manchester: Manchester University Press, 2006.

Kushner, Tony. 'An Alien Occupation – Jewish Refugees and Domestic Service in Britain, 1933-1948', in Mosse, Werner E., and Julius Carlebach (eds). *Second Chance: Two Centuries of German-Speaking Jews in the United Kingdom*. Tübingen: Mohr, 1991.

LaCroix, Hal, and Jorg Meyer. *Journey Out of Darkness: The Real Story of American Heroes in Hitler's POW Camps: An Oral History*. Westport, CT:Praeger Security International, 2007.

Lambo, Roger. 'Achtung! The black prince: West Africans in the Royal Air Force, 1939–46', *Immigrants & Minorities*, vol. 12, no. 3 (1993), pp. 145–63.

Laugesen, Amanda. '*Boredom Is the Enemy': The Intellectual and Imaginative Lives of Australian Soldiers in the Great War and Beyond*. Farnham: Ashgate, 2012.

Laughlin, Nicholas. *Letters from London: Seven Essays by C.L.R. James*. Oxford, UK: Signal Books, 2003.

Lethbridge, Lucy. *Servants: A Downstairs View of Twentieth-Century Britain*. London: Bloomsbury, 2013.

Lewis, Brian. *Wolfenden's Witnesses: Homosexuality in Postwar Britain*. Basingstoke, Hampshire: Palgrave Macmillan, 2016.

Llwyd, Alan. *Black Wales: A History of Black Welsh People*. Gwasg Dinefwr Press, 2005.

Longshore, David. *Encyclopedia of Hurricanes, Typhoons, and Cyclones*. New edition. New York: Facts on File, 2008.

Lubbock, Adelaide. *People in Glass Houses: Growing up at Government House*. London, H. Hamilton, 1978.

Lusane, Clarence. *Hitler's Black Victims: The Historical Experiences of Afro-Germans, European Blacks, Africans, and African Americans in the Nazi Era*. New York: Routledge, 2003.

MacDonald, Robert H. *Sons of the Empire: The Frontier and the Boy Scout Movement, 1890-1918*. Toronto: University of Toronto Press, 1993.

MacKenzie, S.P., 'The Treatment of Prisoners of War in World War II', *The Journal of Modern History*, vol. 66, no. 3 (September, 1994), pp. 487–520.

Mai, Nicola and Russell King. 'Love, Sexuality and Migration: Mapping the Issue(s)', *Mobilities*, vol. 4, no. 3 (2009), pp. 295–307.

Makalani, Minkah. *In the Cause of Freedom: Radical Black Internationalism from Harlem to London, 1917-1939*. Chapel Hill: University of North Carolina Press, 2011.

Makepeace, Clare. 'Living beyond the barbed wire: the familial ties of British prisoners of war held in Europe during the Second World War', *Historical Research*, vol. 86, no. 231 (February 2013).

Manalansan, Martin F., 'Queer Intersections: Sexuality and Gender in Migration Studies', *International Migration Review*, vol. 40, no. 1, Gender and Migration Revisited (Spring, 2006), pp. 224–49.

Marsh, Jan. 'Pictured at Work: Employment in Art (1800-1900)', *Immigrants & Minorities*, vol. 28, no. 2 (2010), pp. 154–63.

Marsh, Jan. (ed.), *Black Victorians: Black People in British Art, 1800-1900*. Aldershot, Hampshire: Lund Humphries, 2005.

Matera, Marc. *Black London: The Imperial Metropolis and Decolonization in the Twentieth Century*. University of California Press, 2015.

Matera, Marc. *Black Internationalism and African and Caribbean Intellectuals in London, 1919-1950*. Dissertation submitted in partial fulfilment of the requirements for the degree of Doctor of Philosophy, New Brunswick, New Jersey, 2008.

Mayor, Edward (archival and visual research by Judith Robinson). *The Duncan Grant Murals in Lincoln Cathedral*. Lincoln: Lincoln Cathedral Publications, 2001.

McKenzie, Earl. 'The Cultural Importance of Edna Manley's Art', *Caribbean Quarterly*, vol. 52, no. 4 (December 2006), pp. 49–56.

Mead, Matthew. 'Empire Windrush: The Cultural Memory of an Imaginary Arrival', *Journal of Postcolonial Writing*, vol. 45, no. 2 (2009), pp. 137–49.

Moore, Brian L., and Michele A. Johnson, 'Introduction' in Moore, Brian L, and Michele A. Johnson (eds). *'Squalid Kingston', 1890-1920: How the Poor Lived, Moved and Had Their Being*. Mona: Social History Project, Dept. of History, University of the West Indies, 2000.

Moore, Brian L., and Michele A. Johnson. *'They Do As They Please': The Jamaican Struggle for Cultural Freedom After Morant Bay*. Kingston: University of the West Indies Press, 2011.

Moss, Pamela. 'Shifting from Nervous to Normal Through Love Machines: Battle Exhaustion, Military Psychiatrists and Emotionally Traumatized Soldiers in World War II', *Emotion Space and Society*, vol. 10 (2014), pp. 63–70.

Msiska, Mpalive-Hangson, 'Sam Selvon's The Lonely Londoners and the structure of Black metropolitan life', *African and Black Diaspora: An International Journal*, vol. 2, no. 1 (2009), pp. 5–27.

Munroe, Trevor, and Arnold Bertram. *Adult Suffrage and Political Administrations in Jamaica, 1944-2002: A Compendium and Commentary*. Kingston, Jamaica: Ian Randle, 2006.

Olusoga, David. *The World's War*. Forgotten Soldiers of Empire. Head of Zeus, 2014.

Oram, Alison, '"A Sudden Orgy of Decadence": Writing about Sex between Women in the Interwar Popular Press', in Laura L. Doan and Jane Garrity (eds). *Sapphic Modernities: Sexuality, Women, and National Culture*. New York: Palgrave Macmillan, 2006.

Palmer, Colin A. *Freedom's Children: The 1938 Labor Rebellion and the Birth of Modern Jamaica*. Chapel Hill: University of North Carolina Press, 2014.

Pankhurst, Richard. 'An Early Somali Autobiography', *Africa: Rivista trimestrale di studi e documentazione dell'Istituto italiano per l'Africa e l 'Oriente*, Anno 32, no. 3 (1977), pp. 355–84.

Paton, Diana. *The Cultural Politics of Obeah: Religion, Colonialism and Modernity in the Caribbean World*. Cambridge and New York: Cambridge University Press, 2015.

Parker, Matthew. *Goldeneye: Where Bond Was Born: Ian Fleming's Jamaica*. London: Windmill Books, 2015.

Patsides, Nicholas. 'Marcus Garvey, Race Idealism and His Vision of Jamaican Self-government', *Caribbean Quarterly*, vol. 51, no. 1 (2005), pp. 37–52.

Pattullo, Polly. *Last Resorts: The Cost of Tourism in the Caribbean*. London: Latin America Bureau, 2005.

Pennybacker, Susan D. *From Scottsboro to Munich: Race and Political Culture in 1930s Britain*. Princeton, NJ: Princeton University Press, 2009.

Phillips, Mike, and Trevor Phillips. *Windrush: The Irresistible Rise of Multi-Racial Britain*. London: Harpercollins, 1998.

Phillips, Sarah R. *Modeling Life: Art Models Speak About Nudity, Sexuality, and the Creative Process*. Albany: State University of New York Press, 2006.

Rhodes-Wood, Major E.H. *A War History of the Royal Pioneer Corps, 1939-1945*. Aldershot, Gale & Polden Ltd, 1960.

Rice, Alan J. *Creating Memorials, Building Identities: The Politics of Memory in the Black Atlantic*. Liverpool: Liverpool University Press, 2010, p. 179.

Robertson, Graham, 'Pioneers in Forensic Psychiatry. Professor T. C. N. Gibbens (1912–83): Academic and Teacher', *The Journal of Forensic Psychiatry*, vol. 5, no. 3 (1994), pp. 551–68.

Robertson, James. 'Late Seventeenth-Century Spanish Town, Jamaica: Building an English City on Spanish Foundations', *Early American Studies*, vol. 6, no. 2 (Fall 2008), pp. 346–90.

Romain, Gemma and Caroline Bressey. 'Claude McKay: Queer Interwar London and Spaces of Black Radicalism', in Katherine M. Graham and Simon Avery (eds). *Sex, Time and Place: Queer Histories of London, c.1850 to the Present*. Bloomsbury Academic, 2016.

Rosner, Victoria, 'Introduction', in Rosner, Victoria, ed. *The Cambridge Companion to the Bloomsbury Group*. New York: Cambridge University Press, 2014.

Rush, Anne S. *Bonds of Empire: West Indians and Britishness from Victoria to Decolonization*. Oxford: Oxford University Press, 2011.

Russell, Bertrand. *Contemplation and Action, 1902-14*, edited by Richard A. Rempel, Andrew Brink and Margaret Moran. London and New York: Routledge, 1993. First published 1985.

Rye, Howard. 'Visiting Fireman – Garland Wilson', *Storyville*, vol. 119 (1985).

Sarti, Raffaella, 'Introduction', *Gender & History*, vol.18, no.2 (August 2006), pp. 187–98.

Scheck, Raffael. *French Colonial Soldiers in German Captivity During World War II*. New York, NY: Cambridge University Press, 2014.

Scheck, Raffael. 'The Killing of Black Soldiers from the French Army by the "Wehrmacht" in 1940: The Question of Authorization', *German Studies Review*, vol. 28, no. 3 (October, 2005), pp. 595–606.

Scheck, Raffael. 'French African Soldiers in German POW Camps, 1940 – 1945', in Byfield, Judith A, Carolyn A. Brown, Timothy Parsons, and Ahmad A. Sikainga (eds). *Africa and World War II*. New York: Cambridge University Press, 2015.

Selvon, Samuel. *The Lonely Londoners*. First published 1956. London: Longman, 2004.

Shone, Richard. *Bloomsbury Portraits: Vanessa Bell, Duncan Grant and Their Circle*. London: Phaidon Press, 1993, first published 1976.

Silvera, Makeda. 'Man Royals and Sodomites: Some Thoughts on the Invisibility of Afro-Caribbean Lesbians', in Makeda Silvera (anthologised by). *Piece of My Heart: A Lesbian of Colour Anthology*. Toronto: Sister Vision, 1991.

Smalley, Edward. *The British Expeditionary Force, 1939-40*. New York, NY: Palgrave Macmillan, 2015.

Smith, Richard. *Jamaican Volunteers in the First World War: Race, Masculinity and the Development of National Consciousness*. Manchester: Manchester University. Press, 2004.

Snaith, Anna. 'Conversations in Bloomsbury: Colonial Writers and the Hogarth Press', in Potts, Gina, and Lisa Shahriari (eds). *Virginia Woolf's Bloomsbury: Volume 2*. Basingstoke: Palgrave Macmillan, 2010.

Sotheby's, Catalogue of Valuable Autograph Letters, Literary Manuscripts and Historical Documents: Including the Most Complete Autograph Manuscript of 'in Memoriam' with Other Letters and Poetical Manuscripts by Alfred Lord Tennyson [auction, London, Sotheby's, 21–22 July 1980]. Illustrated Catalogue 9341. London: Sotheby Parke Bernet, 1980.

Spalding, Frances. *Duncan Grant*. London: Pimlico, 1998 (first published 1997).

Stanley, Liz. 'The Epistolarium: On Theorizing Letters and Correspondences', *Auto/Biography*, vol. 12 (2004), pp. 201–35.

Stanley, Peter E. *The House of Stanley: The History of an English Family from the 12th Century*. Edinburgh: Pentland Press, 1998.

Stanley, Thomas H. O. *The Stanleys of Alderley: 1927-2001*. S.l.: AMCD, 2004.

Steedman, Carolyn. *Labours Lost: Domestic Service and the Making of Modern England*. Cambridge, UK: Cambridge University Press, 2009.

Stevenson, Jane. *Edward Burra: Twentieth-century Eye*. London: Jonathan Cape, 2007.

Stolberg, Claus F., 'Introduction', in Stolberg, Claus F., ed. Jamaica 1938: *The Living Conditions of the Urban and Rural Poor: Two Social Surveys*, The Social History Project, Department of History, University of the West Indies, Mona, 1990.

Stoler, Ann Laura. 'Colonial Archives and the Arts of Governance', *Archival Science*, vol. 2 (2002), pp. 87–109.

Taylor, Frank F. *To Hell with Paradise: A History of the Jamaican Tourist Industry*. Pittsburgh, PA: University of Pittsburgh Press, 1993

Taylor, Frank F. 'The Tourist Industry in Jamaica, 1919 to 1939', *Social and Economic Studies*, vol. 22, no. 2 (June 1973), pp. 205–28.

Taylor, John R. *Edward Wolfe*. London: Trefoil Books for Odette Gilbert Gallery, 1986.

Thompson, Krista A. *An Eye for the Tropics: Tourism, Photography, and Framing the Caribbean Picturesque*. Durham: Duke University Press, 2006.

Tobin, Beth Fowkes. *Colonizing Nature: The Tropics in British Arts and Letters, 1760-1820*. Philadelphia: University of Pennsylvania Press, 2011.

Tobin, Beth Fowkes. *Picturing Imperial Power: Colonial Subjects in Eighteenth-Century British Painting*. Durham, N.C: Duke University Press, 1999.

Vickers, Emma. 'Queer Sex in the Metropolis? Place, Subjectivity and the Second World War'. *Feminist Review*, vol. 96, urban spaces (2010), pp. 58–73.

Walkowitz, Judith R. *Nights Out: Life in Cosmopolitan London*. New Haven: Yale University Press, 2012.

Walrond, Eric. 'The Negro in London', *The Black Man*, 1936, reprinted in Louis J. Parascandola (ed.). *Winds Can Wake Up the Dead: An Eric Walrond Reader*. Detroit, MI: Wayne State University Press, 1998.

Watson, Roxanne. 'Marcus Garvey's Trial for Seditious Libel in Jamaica', *Journalism History*, vol. 33 (Fall 2007), p. 3.

Watson, Roxanne. 'Freedom of the Press under Attack during the 1938 Labor Uprisings in Jamaica: The Prosecution of the Publishers of the Jamaica Labour Weekly', *American Journalism*, vol. 29, no. 3 (2012), pp. 84–112.

Whitham, Charlie. 'The Thin End of the Wedge: The British Foreign Office, the West Indies and Avoiding the Destroyers-Bases Deal, 1938-1940', *Journal of Transatlantic Studies*, vol. 11, no. 3 (2013), pp. 234–48.

Whittall, Daniel. 'Creating Black Places in Imperial London: The League of Coloured Peoples and Aggrey House, 1931–1943', *The London Journal*, vol. 36, no. 3 (November, 2011), pp. 225–46.

Wu, Jialin Christina, 'A Life of Make-Belief: Being Boy Scouts and 'Playing Indian' in British Malaya (1910-42)', in Miescher, Stephan, Michele Mitchell, and Naoko Shibusawa (eds). *Gender, Imperialism and Global Exchanges*. Chichester: Wiley Blackwell, 2015.

Wylie, Neville. *Barbed Wire Diplomacy: Britain, Germany, and the Politics of Prisoners of War, 1939-1945*. Oxford: Oxford University Press, 2010.

Index